SO-BJG-159

THE ROLE OF THE MESSENGER
AND MESSAGE
IN THE ANCIENT NEAR EAST

Program in Judaic Studies
Brown University
BROWN JUDAIC STUDIES
Edited by
Jacob Neusner,
Wendell S. Dietrich, Ernest S. Frerichs, William Scott Green,
Calvin Goldscheider, David Hirsch, Alan Zuckerman

Project Editors (Project)

David Blumenthal, Emory University (Approaches to Medieval Judaism)
William Brinner (Approaches to Judaism and Islam)
Ernest S. Frerichs, Brown University (Dissertations and Monographs)
Lenn Evan Goodman, University of Hawaii (Studies in Medieval Judaism)
William Scott Green, University of Rochester (Approaches to Ancient Judaism)
Norbert Samuelson, Temple University (Jewish Philosophy)
Jonathan Z. Smith, University of Chicago (Studia Philonica)

Number 169
THE ROLE OF THE MESSENGER AND MESSAGE IN THE ANCIENT NEAR E.
by
John T. Greene

THE ROLE OF THE MESSENGER
AND MESSAGE
IN THE ANCIENT NEAR EAST
Oral and Written Communication in the Ancient Near East
and in the Hebrew Scriptures:
Communicators and Communiques in Context

G. Allen Fleece Library
Columbia International University
Columbia, SC 29203

by
John T. Greene

Scholars Press
Atlanta, Georgia

THE ROLE OF THE MESSENGER
AND MESSAGE
IN THE ANCIENT NEAR EAST

© 1989
Brown University

A. Allen Freece Library
Columbia International University
Columbia, SC 29203

Library of Congress Cataloging in Publication Data

Greene, John T.
  The role of the messenger and message in the ancient Near East /
by John T. Greene.
     p.   cm. -- (Brown Judaic studies : no. 169)
  Bibliography: p.
  ISBN 1-55540-324-7 (alk. paper)
  1. Bible. O.T.--Criticism, interpretation, etc. 2. Prophecy-
-Comparative studies. 3. Messengers in literature. 4. Divine
messengers in literature. 5. Assyro-Babylonian literature--Relation
to the Old Testament. 6. Ugaritic literature--Relation to the Old
Testament. 7. Egyptian literature--Relation to the Old Testament.
I. Title. II. Series
BS1198.073 1989
291.6'3'09394--dc19   89-30232
                                             CIP

Printed in the United States of America
on acid-free paper

For

Jamie Julia Johnson Greene
my mother and first reading teacher

Professor James D. Purvis
for suggesting the subject

Professors Jacob Neusner and Ernest Frerichs
incomparable mentors who believed in me

Professor Robert Michael Berchman
who threw down the gauntlet

Frau Studienrätin Andrea-Renee Gabriele Misler
for unstinting and unselfish technical and moral
support during a hectic period of final production

In Memory Of

Nolan Bartlett Greene, Sr.
my late father and abiding *Vorbild*

Professor Shlomo Marenof
who inculcated in me a love for the Hebrew Language

Professor H. Neil Richardson
my late doctor father

CONTENTS

ABBREVIATIONS

Ac Or	Acta Orientalia
AJSLL	The American Journal of Semitic Languages and Literatures
ANE	Ancient Near East(ern)
ANET	The Ancient Near East: Texts and Pictures Relating to the Old Testament
ANES	Ancient Near East Supplement
B	Biblica
BA	Biblical Archaeologist
BASOR	Bulletin American Schools of Oriental Research
BK	Biblischer Kommentar
BZAW	Beihefte zur Zeitschrift für die Alttestamentliche Wissenschaft
CBQ	Catholic Biblical Quarterly
Ev. Th.	Evangelische Theologie
FAT	Forschung am Alten Testament
GIP	Great individual Prophet
HS	Hebrew Scriptures (Scriptural)
HUCA	Hebrew Union College Annual
HTR	Harvard Theological Review
IDBSV	Interpreter's Dictionary of the Bible, Supplementary Volume
IEJ	Israel Exploration Journal
JCS	Journal of Cuneiform Studies
JBL	Journal of Biblical Literature
KAT	Kommentar zum Alten Testament
NThT	Niewe Theologische Tijdschrift
ThStKr	Theologische Studien und Kritiken
VT	Vetus Testamentum
VTS	Vetus Testamentum Supplement

PREFACE

There is no unanimity of learned opinion among scholars of ancient Near Eastern studies as to what a messenger was or did. As a result, misunderstanding this term has led many of these scholars to false conclusions in other areas of their ANE oriented work. The reasons for this I will unpack below.

The issues of this book, for the problem at hand, are to first define what a messenger was and did, and what a messenger would have been understood by that contemporaneous ANE society to have been and to have done. This is the scholar on the ANE's first unresolved problem. I will resolve this problem by examining the literary evidence from ANE literature which reflects views concerning messengers from ca. 3000 to ca. 30 BCE. Only then will I offer a solid and irrefutable definition from the ANE point of view.

The second issue is to apply the same rigorous standards to the unresolved problem of defining what a message would been and what the contemporaneous ANE societies would have understood a message to have been, and then to offer a solid and irrefutable definition of that term as well.

Whether the messenger and message as reflected in the Hebrew Scriptures were understood in the same way in ancient Israel as they were understood by members of the greater ANE societies, constitutes the third issue. It is an issue because many scholars argue uncritically that this body of ANE literature is somehow unusual, and therefore that the messengers and messages mentioned therein are also somehow unusual. That is to say, the messengers and messages contained within the HS do not share in all of the characteristics of ANE messengers and messages. This stance has led many scholars into error. Rather than take the same approach to this issue as that which will be taken in resolving the first two issues, I shall use that evidence to identify messengers and messages in the HS and then provide a taxonomy of both from the HS evidence. The results will provide the necessary corrective to the stated view of this body of ANE literature.

To my knowledge, and as a result of my research, such a taxonomy has never been undertaken before.

The results of the study of the ANE literature data base as pursued within the framework of these first three issues, and the problems the results resolve, will contribute clarity, a more thorough understanding of ANE communication techniques and praxis, which in turn will enable scholars of ANE studies to speak with definition and precision about messengers and messages in the ANE. Resolving the problems addressed by the above three issues is the **sole** purpose of PART I of this work.

Messenger as employed herein refers to one who has been charged with the delivery of a specific message (whether the specific message is to be delivered all at once, or over an extended period of time depends on the specific type of messenger), or one who has been charged with the execution of a specific task. The messenger may be human, or may be cast (by the literature) as a divine or superhuman being. The messenger (as that messenger appears in literature) may be male or female. The individual who has charged the messenger is understood to be a person (or divinity) of authority (dictated by the immediate situation). Further, it is understood that the messenger delivers a verbatim message, either orally or in writing--or both!--to the party for whom the message was intended, or performs an assigned task if that is the reason for dispatch in the first place. Of course, circumstances must allow in either case. Moreover, the execution of the message or task does not preclude automatically additional elaboration or gestures by the messengers through their own commentary and/or deeds.

The results of this research distinguish five major types of messengers: 1) the **ambassador**, 2) the **emissary-courrier**, 3) the **envoy**, 4) the **herald** and 5) the **harbinger**. The following definitions have also been drawn from the results of the research on the messsenger types throughout this work. The references at the end of each definition serve as ready reference among somewhat familiar material. However, the foundation on which these definitions rest is much more broad.

The **ambassador** is a high-ranking diplomatic agent sent by one sovereign or state to another. An ambasssador may be sent either as a resident representative, or on a temporary period of service. An ambassador is always an authorized representative and messenger (2 Samuel 10:1-5).

The **emissary-courrier** is an agent sent on a specific errand or mission, open or secret, which would involve the delivery of an oral or written message. As an example, note David's emissary-courriers who were sent to Hanun, king of Ammon (2 Samuel 10:1-5), and Joshua's messenger/spies (Joshua 2:17ff.).

The **envoy** is a messenger representative who is sent by a ruler or state to transact diplomatic business with another. Envoy as a rank is usually second to that of ambassador. Envoys are sent by Merodach-baladan, king of Babylonia, to King Hezekiah to enlist his aid against Assyria (2 Kings 20:12-19; Isaiah 39).

The **harbinger** is one who goes before to make known the approach of another. As those who are sent in advance of troops to provide secure lodgings, or perform specific functions, harbingers are specifically identified as messengers in Joshua 2:17ff. where they perform the same function.

The **herald** either carries state messages from one capital or headquarters to another, or proclaims and announces significant news or tidings. Heralds are known in Hebrew by at least two names, *mebasser* (from the Semitic *bs/sr*, bringer of tidings), and *mazkir*, one of several titles of main officials at the courts of David and Solomon (2 Samuel 8:15-18).

Throughout this work a messenger is not a mouthpiece of deities, demons, or spirits, but is one who speaks clearly, in the language of those to whom the message is to be communicated, without aid of interpreters, and never in a state of ecstatic frenzy. This, then, is what I mean when I employ the term messenger herein.

The **message** is essentially the main errand of the messenger. Here no more need be said.

"Geography," wrote Norman Gottwald, "is the womb within which history and culture grow."[1] Accordingly, the geographical area of the cultural sphere in which the messenger activity took place must be demarkated.

The Near or Middle East is a large area of land which is the point of confluence of the continents of Africa, Asia and Europe.

Numerous present-day states occupy its territory: Iran, Iraq, Syria, Lebanon, Jordan, Turkey, Israel, Saudi-Arabia and neighboring peninsula states, and Egypt. Many geographers and political scientists would argue as well for the inclusion of North Africa in general. The ancient Near East (hereafter cited as ANE) is essentially coterminous with most of this area. Note, however, that ancient borders, which were determined by military hegemony, trade, and cultural contacts, were far more fluid than today's borders. Thus, no exact limits can be fully known for the political units of the past.

As a result of the research, the following are axiomatic, and the portions in parentheses become integral parts of the chain of communication in the ANE.

1. The messenger has been commissioned to deliver a message or perform a specific function. (**authorization**)

2. The one who commissions the messenger is usually of higher rank than the messenger who is sent. (**stratification**)

3. The messenger, in most cases, and unless otherwise stated, memorizes the message and gestures of the sender. (**mnemonization**)

4. Some distance separates the sender of a message from its intended recipient. (**sectionalization**)

5. Before delivering the message, the messenger precedes the actual delivery by a recognizeable legitimizing formula such as "Thus says (said) XX," which is intended to authenticate the message. (**legitimation/authentication**)

6. Oftentimes the message is unwelcome from the point of view of the intended recipient(s). (**rejection**)

7. Oftentimes the messenger is identified
with the contents of the message
delivered, and is sometimes maltreated
or killed. (**identification**)
8. There are numerous types of
messengers who deliver numerous
types of messages, or who perform
numerous tasks and services.
(**specialization/diversification**)

The fourth issue involves the great individual prophets of the
Hebrew Scriptures (HS) who are frequently termed messengers.
References to these prophets' 'messages' or 'message' by modern
scholars in a general way, and by form-critical scholars in a specific
way have been widely accepted. To substantiate their views, scholars
have pointed to the use by messengers of the ANE of a legitimizing
formula such as "Hear the word of XX," or "Thus (So) says XX." They
argue that these formulae are the same as those used by the prophets
of the HS. It is well known that the prophets have been depicted as
employing language similar to that employed by an officer of an
ancient Israelite court as well. Does employing forensic rhetoric make
one an officer of the court? Similarly, one must ask whether
employing, or better, being depicted as employing, a formula similar to
that known to have been employed by legitimate, unquestioned
messengers makes one a messenger. PART II of the present work
examines the popular view which holds that the great individual
prophets of the Hebrew Scriptures were indeed messengers, and that
they were so understood by their contemporaries. This popular view's
validity is examined against the backdrop of the phenomena of the
messenger and message in the ANE from approximately 3000 BCE to
approximately the third decade of the first century of that same era.

PART II's chief purpose is to respond to the challenge
presented by PART I's evidence and conclusions, i.e., how they may be
found indispensable in testing the varacity of numerous claims that the
great individual prophets were messengers. Moreover, it responds to
those claims as they are made by form-critics (on the basis of their
Gattungsforschungen), by historians (who mostly assume

uncritically that prophets were messengers, but have no real vested interest in whether prophets were or not), and by theologians (for whom it appears to be terribly important that the prophets be considered as having been messengers, and in addition, who assume that the prophets understood themselves, and were considered by their hearers, as having been messengers). All three groups inform other scholars about the great individual prophets. They are also read by the general reading public.

East Lansing, Michigan
January 9, 1989

PART I

**BEING IN TWO PLACES AT ONCE:
THE EVIDENCE OF THE MESSENGER
IN THE ANCIENT NEAR EAST**

PART I
INTRODUCTORY
The Unfolding of an Ancient
Near Eastern Phenomenon

PART I studies the messenger of the ANE. Moreover, it studies the messenger as a link in the chain of human communication, and focuses on the human messenger link of the communication chain of the ANE--although sometimes literary figures such as deities or birds are employed in the literature being examined to show the human messenger's influence on contemporaneous literature. This human messenger delivered either verbatim or written messages (or both!), and/or performed certain tasks.

Although knowledge of the history of the ANE continues to expand, still very little is known about messengers and the roles they played collectively in helping to shape that history. It may be stated reasonably that most moderns take the mass media and communications techniques of today for granted. They have only a recipient-user understanding of them and how they work--especially television, radio, modems, computers and the like--moderns have almost no idea of the communication techniques employed in the ANE. This would include many modern scholars who specialize in ANE studies.

Modern works on communication such as Wilbur Schramm, **Men, Messages, and Media: A Look At Human Communication**, (New York: Harper & Row, 1973), and its expanded edition **Men, Women, Messages and Media: Understanding Human Communication** written with William C. Porter 2d. ed., (New York: Harper & Row, 1982); Harold Laswell et al., **Propaganda and Communication In World History**, (Published for the East-West Center by the University Press of Hawaii, c 1979 c 1980); Colin Cherry, **On Human Communication: A Review, A Survey, And A Criticism** 3rd ed., (Cambridge, MA: MIT Press, 1978); David C.

Mortensen, **Communication: The Study of Human Interaction**, (New York: McGraw-Hill, 1972); and Raymond Williams, Ed. **Contact--Human Communication And Its History** (London: Thames and Hudson, 1981), although the titles imply it, do not include the ANE messenger's important role in the chain of communication history to any appreciable degree. But were we also to judge from Robert Harper, Assyrian And Babylonian Literature: Selected Translations, (New York: D. Appleton and Company, 1904); Cyrus Gordon, Ugaritic Literature: A Comprehensive Translation Of The Poetic And Prose Texts, (Roma: Pontificium Institutum Biblicum, 1949); or even James Baikie, Egyptian Papyri And Papyrus-Hunting, (London: The Religious Tract Society, 1925)--to select works which cover a large portion of the ANE real estate literarily--we would still have no true picture of the messenger's role and importance throughout that region. Moreover, the extant texts offer no reliable picture of the pervasiveness of messengers and/or the types of messages they delivered, or the errands they performed, or even the services they provided, as well as what impact all three had on ANE society as a whole, as these texts exist separately.

How were the various stories containing the pre-flood and post-flood motif (Noah, Gilgamesh and Atrahasis epics) distributed over most of the ANE? The "Jobian motif," as it has been called, appears in Mesopotamian, Canaanite, and Egyptian literature. How did this motif come to be so widely distributed? Many so-called "wisdom motifs" are equally identifiable in examples of literature from all parts of the ANE. The Solomonic Court had a "physical plant" which was modeled on the contemporaneous Egyptian Court, while the person and role of the king were borrowed from the Mesopotamian shepherd-king model as well as the Jebusite priest-king model. How was information on making this possible obtained by and relayed to the Jerusalem Court? Only the Jebusite influence is apparent. What happened in the event of a news blackout in some country, or city or private residence of the ANE due to natural catastrophes or devastating wars? How were vast empires acquired and controlled, or squandered and lost, and how were the mighty ANE rulers whose stories we follow fascinated brought low? Once one begins to think about it, the questions become legion, but answers do not immediately follow. It becomes increasingly clear that the extant documents of the ANE, which preserve only isolated fragments of information about messengers, as well as about ANE life and civilization (and then painted with the broadest of strokes) when combined can produce a picture of ancient human communication techniques and contemporaneous praxis heretofore unacknowledged. PART I provides this picture.

The divisions of this part are based upon the available information and the major types of messengers and messages which clearly emerge from an examination of numerous sources. There are three major foci of PART I.

The first raises the question of the appearance and activity of the messenger. I began the study with an overview of the messenger in ancient Sumer, then continued along the trajectory of the Fertile Crescent, i.e., to Babylonia, Assyria, Hatti, Ugarit and finally to Egypt. I then divided the extant literature into genres such as historical texts, fiction, and funerary and tomb texts to get a better feel for how various types of literature employed the messenger motif, or employed messengers in their narrative portions. A working definition of 'messenger' and how that term was understood by inhabitants of the ANE over a period of several millennia was the result. An analytical summary of the evidence followed.

The second focus is concerned with the message itself which had been delivered by various messengers. Again I followed the Fertile Crescent trajectory, this time focusing on both countries and specific city-state locales within these countries, noting even the type of writing surface on which the message was written (which spoke to the developing technology of producing records of the spoken word). Again a working definition of 'message' was derived, and numerous examples thereof were collected and examined as to their content and action or inaction taken as a result of receipt of such messages. The evidence was summarized and analyzed.

The third focus centers on the messengers as they appear in the historical narrative material of selected literature from the HS as well as the messages contained therein. Having treated messengers and messages separately in the first two chapters, I reasoned that for purposes of study and analysis no further separation was necessary. I reasoned further that the evidence presented in this chapter would be better served by first demonstrating that the messengers as they appeared in the HS were no different from messengers as they appeared in the literature from the greater ANE, by examining just how the messenger was seen to have been of importance to the writers of the HS. To that end I approached the study thematically,and focused instead on the Hebrew technical terms for messenger. In this way the texts yielded the *mal'ak*, the *'ebed*, the *rakab*, *rakab sus*, and allied terms, the *magid*, the *miraglim*, as well as some obscure and/or debated terms which signalled the presence of even more messengers. Among them were *mal'akiy*, *mada'*, *nassar*, *mazkir*, and miscellaneous envoys. Again, the evidence was summarized and analyzed.

It is hoped that the reader will appreciate this effort to help close a lacuna in the understanding of the socio-political life of the ANE and its communication techniques involving messengers, including those mirrored in the HS.

CHAPTER I

The Messenger in the Ancient Near East

A. PURPOSE

Enuma Elish, the Babylonian Creation Story, is dated to the period when the first Babylonian Dynasty (1894-1594 BCE) enjoyed political hegemony and supremacy over its neighbors. The story is written in the form of a poem. An excerpt therefrom reads: "He commanded with his mouth, and the garment was destroyed. He commanded again, and the garment was restored. When the gods, his fathers, beheld the power of his word they were glad (and) did homage (saying:) 'Marduk is king.'"[1] This passage reflects the power which the spoken word enjoyed in the ANE; people stood or trembled in awe of it. A closer reading of the passage shows that the command--spoken, not written--was central in importance. The Semitic conquerors of Mesopotamia adopted the Sumerian-invented form of writing, but long before this the oral form of communication was the predominant medium. Even after writing had established itself as a medium of communication, it was mainly used to record business transactions or to write down the oral message(s). These written messages were not intended to replace oral messages; they served rather as a record of the messages which had been delivered, or to ensure the flawless delivery of an oral message by having its text in written form. Thus, one speaks of the power of both the spoken word as well as the necessity of accurate delivery of that spoken word.[2] The role and purpose of the messenger, then, was primarily that of extending temporally and geographically the existing power of one person's spoken words or will; allowing that person to be in two places at once.

A major complaint registered by students of history is that most of what is known about the past (i.e., the written historical period), generally tends to reflect the view of the upper classes. They clamor more for the *Weltanschauung* of the 'common folk' to balance this historical equation. They prefer more bio- and autobiographical works produced within a given period whenever possible. Of this work they would initially ask: "Would not the study of the messenger and message of the ANE turn out to be another one-sided, one-class approach to history?" "Are not messengers usually sent by kings or other such rulers to other rulers, or from rulers to officials, all of whom enjoyed high social status?" In face of these questions it is well to keep in mind the advances which have been made in oral traditions of the ANE, especially of the HS. Although we cannot always supply biographies or autobiographies of each messenger we encounter in this study, the oral literature does expose a more popular level which is at least closer to the 'marketplace *Weltanschauung*' of ANE human experience and existence. Messengers delivered messages from members of all social classes, so the study is not restricted to, nor does it reflect the views of any one particular social class.

I purpose to study representative literature produced by the inhabitants of the ANE which contains references to messengers and/or messages. Much of this literature has already been translated and commented upon by modern scholars. I shall examine a great quantity of this literature in an attempt to yield a variety of types of messengers. Here I shall determine whether all of the messengers I find have anything in common, how and why they functioned, and how they were regarded by those who sent them as well as by those to whom they were sent. I further purpose to address their function and place in the societies of the ANE, and to paint a portrait of the ANE messenger in both a general and specific way. Thus, a study of the messenger will allow the reader insights into the ordinary life of the periods covered; insights which for us moderns could come in no other way.

B. THE MESSENGER

How does one begin to find messengers of any kind in the literature of the ANE? The Semitic languages, along with ancient

Sumerian, Hurrian, Hittite, Egyptian, Persian, and Greek provide the most expeditious route. These languages are full of synonyms or parasynonyms. For instance, Hebrew provides such synonyms as 'ama/shipha,' 'bondmaid/handmaid.' One may compare these synonyms, writes K.A. Kitchen, with the Egyptian "use of five different words for boats on the historical stela of King Kamose, ca. 1560 BCE."[3] Important also is the free use of the practically synonymous terms *rakbu* and *mar-shipri*, 'envoy' and 'messenger' in a prism inscription of King Ashurbanipal about Gyges of Lydia.[4] Even the antiquity of the biblical Aramaic term for herald is well established:

> The words *krz*, 'make proclamation,'
> and *krzw*, 'herald' in Biblical Aramaic
> have been assigned a Greek origin and
> more recently an Old Persian origin.
> But a study of Hurrian *kirenzi* (from a
> **kirezzi*), 'proclamation,' indicates
> that forms from *krz* had begun to enter
> Semitic at least a millennium earlier
> than any of us had hitherto suspected.[5]

1. Sumer

The expeditious route of language produced the following Sumerian texts containing either direct references to messengers, or whose presence is understood from the context. The words messenger and message occur in Sumerian literature as

a-ag-(ga)	message
a-ag	to send, give command to
agriz	one sent or appointed, minister
kin	to send, order
lu kin-gi-a	messenger
mar shipri	messenger
shaparu	an order, and so a task to be done
sukkal	messenger, servant[6]

Five Sumerian reading passages provide information on messenger activity there. Passage VII, line 58ff. reads: "The messenger of Utu-hegal Tirigan and his wife (and) son in Dubrum captured."[7] That is to say, the messenger of Utu-hegal captured Tirigan, his wife and son in Dubrum. The text is from the Inscription of Utu-hegal, king of Erech. No further information is given concerning this messenger. The word 'captured' suggests that the messenger had a military function. His mission, as seen from the text, is that of accomplishing a certain task, not the delivery of any specific verbal message. When we discuss the Egyptian material below, we will see that the term 'messenger' was indeed the court title of a ranking military officer, specifically the king's messenger; even when the king is a female.

Passage XIII comes from the Inscriptions of the Gudea Cylinder where two examples of messengers are found, although no messengers are directly mentioned. Line 7ff. reads: "Unto Ninzagga was sent word; copper like great loads of grain that are brought, to Gudea, who was building the temple, was (continually) being delivered."[8] And beginning with line 10 of the same passage: "To Ninsikila was word sent; great willows(?), ebony, and abba-wood, for the governor as he built Eninnu they hewed."[9] A note to lines 7 and 10 states that orders were being sent to the craftsmen who were working under the patronage of the god Ningirsu. We the readers are not enlightened further, however, as to whether the messenger was human or superhuman (i.e., strictly a literary character).

Part of a Sumerian hymn to the weather-god is found in Passage XX, and reads beginning with line 20: "... let the lightning, thy messenger, go before thee, storm, & c. (thou) who art my son, go, go; who is like thee(?) in his assault?"[10] Lightning here, although a natural element, goes before the storm to signal its approach. It therefore functions as a harbinger to the storm. The imagery here is taken from the harbinger function in ancient Sumerian society.

The subject matter of Passage XXI is a hymn of praise to the sun-deity:

Sun-god, when to the midst of heaven
thou enterest, may the bright barrier of
heaven speak peace unto thee, may the
door of heaven speak salutation unto
thee, may the divine justice, thy
beloved messenger, make straight (the
way) for thee, unto Ebarra, the abode
of thy royalty, let thy majesty
proceed.[11]

Passage XXVII is the text of a record of a legal decision in
favor of one Hala-Bau, wife of Ur-Bau. Beginning with line 12 it ends:
"The house to Hala-Bau was confirmed. Eagadada the royal messenger
and Ur-Lamma, son of Kalla, were presidents."[12]

A work entitled "Sumerian Sacred Marriage Texts" provides a
messenger in a narrative poem with the title "Love in the Gipar."[13]

The maid, singing, sent a messenger to
her father, Inanna, dancing, sent a
messenger to her father: "My house,
my house, let him make it 'long' for me,
I the queen--my house let him make it
long for me, ...[14]

Kramer summarizes this poem by stating:

The second stanza tells of the meeting
between the bejeweled Inanna and
Dumuzi in the Eanna of Erech, a
meeting which so fills Inanna with
desire and passion that she sends a
special messenger to her father (no
doubt the god Sin) with the request

> that he (that is, perhaps, her father)
> make her house 'long' so that she and
> her lover can have their pleasure in
> it.[15]

Summarizing the Sumerian material, the texts yielded two human messengers (Passages VII and XXVII); one unspecified messenger (Passage XIII); and three superhuman messengers (Passages XX, XXI, and the "Love in the Gipar" poem). As to their function, the two human messengers had specific, missions; to capture the enemy of King Utu-hegal of Erech (VII), and to function as co-presiding officers at a property settlement (perhaps convened by the monarch who was represented by his royal messenger, XXVII). The unspecified messenger (XIII) brought specific words in the form of directions for a building project. Two of the superhuman messengers (XX and XXI) had missions as harbingers to the weather-deity and sun-deity respectively. The remaining super-human messenger delivered a message of request that a 'long' house be provided for two divine lovers (Love in the Gipar).

In addition, we know the names of two messengers who were active at Sumer. Royal records from Ur of the Chaldees, for example, mention two Eblaites by name--Ili-Dagan and Gura. 'Surim, the messenger, the man from Ebla,' even made votive offerings to the local god."[16] And Gelb states: "A unique piece of information is found in an unpublished tablet from Drehem . . .'*dDa-gan-a-bu lu kin gi -a Ia-si-li-im ensi Tu-tu-la ki*,' that is 'Dagan-abu, the messenger of Ia-si-li-im, the ensi of Tuttul."[17]

2. Babylonia

Oftentimes a messenger did not execute a commission as instructed. Sometimes extenuating and mitigating circumstances prevented it. At other times matters of the heart superceded duty--which likewise meant derelection of duty. In the Gilgamesh Epic (18th century BCE) Enkidu is depicted as a warrior/messenger.[18] He was sent by the gods in response to the people's cry for a liberator and deliverer from the oppressive rule of King Gilgamesh. Instead of conflict, however, friendship grew between Enkidu and Gilgamesh to whom he had been sent as an adversary. The major theme of the epic is death and dying, and after the death of Enkidu, one man's search for the secret of immortality--coupled with the finding and then loss of it.

A letter found at Tell el-Amarna in Egypt, but originating in Babylonia, and sent by the Babylonian King Burnaburi-iash, mentions messengers several times. Early in the correspondence the Babylonian king assumes an apologetical stance. "Since the letter-carrier (messenger) of my brother arrived at my court I have not been well so that the letter-carrier of my brother has had no chance to dine with me. When you see your letter-carrier again, ask and you will find out that my health is very bad . . ."[19]

King Burnaburi-iash was vexed at the Egyptian king for not having condoled with him. The letter-carrier attempted to explain to the ailing king that Egypt lay at a considerable distance from Babylon and that the Egyptian king had no way of knowing about his illness. When the ailing king asked the letter-carrier whether it was true that such a great distance separated their two realms, the letter-carrier replied: "Summon thy messengers and ask them."[20] This was all a ruse on the part of the Babylonian king to get the sympathy of the Egyptian king, for the former knew quite well how far Egypt was from Babylonia.

On other matters Burnaburi-iash wrote to the king of Egypt: "Thou art retaining one of my letter-carriers, whereas I have given injunctions to yours and sent him back to you. Do likewise to my letter-carrier at once."[21] He went on to explain that due to hazardous road conditions, scorching heat, and lack of water, he was sending very few gifts by the returning letter-carrier, but promised: "If the weather be fair, the next messenger will bring more presents."[22] The Babylonian, no longer apologetic, finished his letter with a blunt reminder that: "As to Zalmu, my letter-carrier, he has been robbed twice en route. Biriamaza plundered his caravan the first time and Pamahu the second time. Since this happened in your land, see to it that my letter-carier is paid for his losses."[23]

This revealing letter shows that the letter-carrier had more responsibility than just carrying letters; he carried presents--among them gold and horses--explained certain matters on behalf of the king, was of sufficiently high social station as to be able to dine with the king, travelled by caravan, and was subject to the dangers of highwaymen. This letter-carrier/messenger functioned as an envoy. This envoy was named Zalmu.

3. Assyria

King Sennacherib's victory prism offers an interesting function of a royal messenger. Sennacherib, king of Assyria (704-681 BCE) campaigned in the west in the year 701 BCE. These campaigns were recorded on clay cylinders called prisms. The final edition of these annals is recorded on the Taylor Prisms of the British Museum, with an even better copy housed at the Oriental Institute of the University of Chicago.[24] Sennacherib names such cities as Sidon, Beth-Dagon and Joppa as having fallen before his army. He also mentions having laid siege to Jerusalem, ruled at that time by King Hezekiah. Sennacherib boasted:

> Hezekiah himself, whom the terror-inspiring splendor of my lordship had overwhelmed and whose irregular and elite troops which he had brought into Jerusalem, his royal residence, in order to strengthen it, had deserted him, did send me, later, to Nineveh . . . all kinds of valuable treasures, his own daughters, concubines, male and female musicians. In order to deliver the tribute and to do obeisance as a slave he sent his personal messenger.[25]

It is not clear just who this 'personal messenger' was. It is highly possible that it was the *mazkir* or royal herald (to be discussed in greater detail below) though this is pure conjecture. What is not left to conjecture is the mission of this messenger; he delivered the heavy tribute which Hezekiah was forced to pay. He also did obeisance in the king's stead as a slave to King Sennacherib. Put differently, the role of this messenger was to suffer the humiliation (public and private) of a conquered king who had been reduced to the status of vassal. Since we get no indication that this was a unique case of a king being reduced to the status of vassal, it would appear that this practice was *de rigeur* for the conquering Assyrians. As such, numerous messengers must have functioned in this capacity. That is, their social function was to extend the humiliation and public embarassment of the conquered by making it appear that he (the vassal) was there in the conquerer's homeland and capital constantly groveling.This messenger was also of a very high social station.

The example of Hezekiah's messenger, although found on an Assyrian prism, and as such justified to be included herein, does not give an example of specifically Assyrian messenger activity. The inscription of Tiglath-pileser III (745-727 BCE) contains the following reference to a messenger. "With the understanding, skill and far-reaching thought which the messenger of the gods, the prince Nugimmut had given me, a palace of cedar and a porch, like a palace in the land of the Hittites, I built for my enjoyment more than that of the former places of my fathers from the middle of the Tigris."[26] Evidently in Assyrian mythological thought Nugimmut brought the advantageous commodities of understanding, skill, and far-reaching thought to worthy mortals from the gods.

The cylinder inscription of Sargon II (722-705 BCE) tells of his having conquered: "The subjects of the four quarters (of the world, speaking) strange languages and varied dialects, . . . whom I carried into captivity in the name of Ashur, my lord, with powerful staff, I made one speech and settled them therein (i.e., the city of Bel)."[27] Sargon boasted how he made one language universal among those whom he settled, for he added: "I sent to them Assyrians, men of knowledge and insight, learned men and scribes, to teach them the fear of god and king."[28] These learned, insightful Assyrian scribes were sent as messengers with the specific task of teaching Assyrian state religion and reverence for the king. As official royal pedagogues, these messengers performed the task of propagandizing with the specific aim of converting the captured and inculcating in them the official world-view of their captors.

The annals of Ashurbanipal (668-626 BCE) from the Rassam Cylinder contains this account:

> In my first campaign I marched to Makkan and Meluhha. Tirhaka, King of Egypt and Ethiopia, whose defeat Esarhaddon, my father, had brought about, and whose land he had possession of--he, Tirhaka, forgot the power of Ashur, Ishtar, and the great gods, my lords, and trusted in his own forces. He marched against the kings, the prefects, whom my father had appointed in Egypt; in order to slay and plunder and to take Egypt; against them he went in and settled in Memphis; a city which my father had conquered and added to the territory of Assyria. A swift messenger came to Nineveh and brought me the tidings.[29]

Here the one who brings tidings is identified by the king as a messenger.

Ashurbanipal went to Egypt, vanquished the forces of Tirhaka, restored order, strengthened his garrisons there, and returned to Nineveh. Shortly after his return many of those whom he had appointed to stations in Egypt ". . . sent their messengers to Tirhaka, King of Ethiopia, to make a compact and league, saying: 'Let a league be established between us and let us be a help to each other. If we divide the country among ourselves, then there shall not be another lord between us.'"[30] Ashurbanipal became privy to their plot. "My military governors heard of these things. They intercepted their (the rebels') messengers together with their dispatches (written messages),

and learned their rebellious deeds."[31] That the dispatches were in written form does not preclude their having been intended for oral delivery. In fact, it points to the oral and written traditions side by side.
Ashurbanipal also reported that:

> Ashur, the god, my creator, revealed my name in a dream to Gyges, King of Lydia, . . . saying: 'Lay hold of the feet of Ashurbanipal, King of Assyria, and through the influence of his name conquer thy enemies.' On the very day on which he saw this vision he sent his messenger to ask of my welfare. This vision which he had seen he sent by his messenger and repeated it to me.[32]

Success followed success after Gyges became the vassal of Ashurbanipal. But as usual, when too much success had been enjoyed too swiftly, ". . . he discontinued his messenger whom he had continually sent to ask after my welfare."[33] Discontinuing to send a messenger to the lord or suzerain was the first sign of a revolt or intended revolt by a vassal. As such, the messenger served as a political barometer. The Cimmerians, a people whom Gyges had defeated earlier, turned the tables of fate and defeated him in battle, and proved to be his undoing. It resulted in his death. The annal continued: "After him his son took his seat upon his throne. Through his messenger he sent me tidings of the disasterous calamity . . ."[34]

4. Hatti

Unlike other ANE nations, the Hittites created their own literary style and forms for the purpose of government and statescraft. Many Hittite state documents opened with the terse formula: 'Thus speaks King NN, great king, king of Hatti, the hero, son of MM, great king, king of Hatti, the hero.'[35] There are variations in this title which either cause it to be expanded or contracted somewhat. This title is affixed to many types of documents; the royal decree, military campaign annals, treaties, or any kind of correspondence deemed worthy and official. "Formally," writes Gurney referring to the titles, "these are all branches of a single stem, the root of which may be traced back to the earliest times."[36] 'Thus speaks' is in and of itself not enough to designate a certain form of speech as messenger speech as scholars cited in PART II below will maintain. In addition, this traditional form is found in a document dating from the reign of Hattusilis III. It tells of his attempt to justify his action of driving Uhri-Teshub, his nephew, from the throne. This document which has been called his autobiography opens as follows:

> Thus speaks Tabarna Hattusilis, the great king, King of Hatti, son of Mursilis, the great king of Hatti, grandson of Suppiluliumus, the great king, king of Hatti, descendant of Hattusilis, king of Kussara.[37]

Westerners have been conditioned to expect a message to follow such an opening formula. What is discovered instead is ". . . a piece of reasoned argument, amounting almost to legal pleading, of a type which occurs elsewhere in Hittite literature, but has few parallels in that of the other peoples of pre-classical antiquity."[38] 'Thus says . . .' may be used as an introductory formula for many different kinds of speech (written or oral), and need not introduce a message. It remains to be observed, however, whether the presence of the imperfect tense in the Hittite formula--as compared with the usual perfect tense of the so-called (by form-critics) messenger formula--is of prime importance in arguing for a distinction.[39]

A text important because it depicts messenger activity is a Hittite legend which employs the expression 'evil tidings'(brought by a herald). The story is summarized in the following manner. "It will be seen that the story consists of a series of incidents which provoked the wrath of the king at the incompetence of his (military) officers (who

keep sending him unwelcome messages about the battle's progress)."[40]
Read for example: "They broke the battering-ram. The king waxed
wroth and his face was grim: 'They constantly bring me evil tidings;
may the weather-god carry you away in a flood!'[41] Although the
receipt of 'evil tidings' occupies our attention, it should be noted that
behind all this lies an anonymous messenger responsible for heralding
such tidings. Since the text is legendary, the anonymous messenger is a
literary and not a historical figure.

Hittite mythology also provides an example of a messenger.
The source, called "The Myth of the Missing God,' describes the
absence and return of fertility to earth as a result of the corresponding
disappearance and reappearance of the fertility god.[42] An important
excerpt states:

> Then the weather-god remembered his
> son Telipinu (saying): "Telipinu is not
> in the land; he was angry and has gone
> away and taken all good things with
> him. The gods great and small set out
> to search for Telipinu. The Sun-god
> sent the eagle as his messenger saying:
> "Go, search the dark-blue waters. The
> eagle went forth; but he found him not,
> and reported to the Sun-god, saying: 'I
> have not found him, Telipinu, the
> mighty god.'[43]

This excerpt, though mythological, provides a great deal of
information concerning human messengers. Firstly, the messenger has
been commissioned to perform a specific task. The task dictated the
type of messenger chosen. Secondly, upon receiving the commission,
the messenger departed to discharge the responsibility. Thirdly, having
attempted to discharge that responsibility, the messenger returns to
the source of the commissioning and reports whether or not the
mission was successful. Thus even mythological texts are quite helpful

because they reflect real-life praxis. Furthermore, with the exception of the legitimizing formula, Thus says XX," being absent from the text, this myth exemplifies complete messenger activity, or the complete communication chain.

5. Ugarit

At some point among the Canaanites, the messenger must have captured a special place in the hearts and minds of the people.[44] The Kirtu (Keret) legend, for instance, depicts Canaanite society's marriage convention of the royal wooing "as a military expedition to besiege the stronghold of the prospective bride's father."[45] This legend reflects actual historical practice. The wooing of the prospective bride was accomplished in two phases; (1) the suitor employed a messenger to take messages of suit to his beloved as well as to her father or guardian, then, (2) after polite refusal of his overtures, the suitor pressed the suit in person. An example of how he would have employed a messenger is seen in the following.

> The moon, the Luminary of Heaven, sends to *Hrhb*, The Summer's King; Give Nikkal; the Moon will pay the bridepiece, . . . A thousand pieces of gold; I will send gems of lapis lazuli; I will make her fallow field into a vineyard . . .[46]

When King Kirtu attempted to woo a bride he employed two messengers. After a sufficient mourning period following the loss of his entire family, and after Kirtu had made his first offer, "The bride's father, thus beset, makes an overture to *Krt* through two messengers."[47] As with the first example, this offer is rejected and Kirtu personally states his demand: "Give me the damsel Hry, the fair, thy first-begotten, . . ."[48]

More messenger activity depicted in Canaanite literature relates to the god Ba'al's struggle with Mot, the god of death, drought and sterility. Anticipating the inevitable battle with Mot, Ba'al exclaims: "I shall indeed send a guide for the god Mot; a herald for the Hero, the favorite of El. to call Mot to his grave . . . I alone am he that shall be king over the gods, ruling over gods and men, . . ."[49] Ba'al then sent his messenger(s) Gepen wa-Ugar with a defiant message to Mot in the underworld.[50] Later, Ba'al descended to the underworld to combat Mot, who defeated and killed him. Thereupon, messengers brought the announcement of his death to the surface of the earth. Messengers are here used to announce sad or evil tidings to the chief god, El, who mourned his death.[51]

Messenger activity is also evident at the situation attending the death of Aqhat, the Hero, son of King Dan'el, who being at first childless, was granted a son by the god El. This son, upon maturing, was given a composite bow made by the divine craftsman Kothar (Koshar) wa-Hasis. The goddess Anat coveted this bow and made several offers to Aqat, who refused. With permission from El--gained through subterfuge--Anat had Aqat killed. After his death, two messengers announce the tragic news to his father, King Dan'el.[52]

6. Egypt

With the possible exception of the HS, the number of examples of messengers found in Egyptian texts far outnumber those found in texts from her ANE neighbors. Because of their nature and contents the Egyptian texts are separated into the categories of a. historical texts, b. historico-romantic, c. fiction, d. wisdom, e. love-song, f. funerary and tomb texts for purposes of analysis.

a. Historical Texts

The Harris Papyrus records an account of the exploiting of copper mines in Punt. A pharaoh stated: "I sent my messengers to the land of Atika to the great copper workings which are there. Their sea-going boats were laden with them, and the great rode on asses . . . The copper workings were found, and the ore was loaded by thousands into the sea-going boats."[53] These were obviously messengers with a specific task to perform which did not involve apparently the delivery of a message.

Messengers were involved in just about every human activity; even in the midst of court intrigue one finds them active. When Ramses III's reign was drawing to a close, the wives of the harem began to plot to have placed upon the throne the son of the favorite among themselves. The favorite was generally never the royal wife. Many court officials were enlisted to help bring the plot to fruition. Among them were the Chief of the Chamber and the Royal Butler. They also won over the chief of the palace guard "so that messages freely passed out and in between the two sets of conspirators."[54] The contents of one such message reads: "Excite the people, goad on the enemies to begin hostilities against their lord."[55] It is clear what the function of the messengers was. It is equally obvious that both males and females functioned as messengers in this conspiratorial situation.

The M.W.Golenischeff Papyrus contains the story of the envoy-courier Wenamon. In it one follows an envoy/messenger on his mission. In its essential outline, Ramses XII's High Priest at Thebes, Herhor, resolved that a new ceremonial barge for the deity Amen of Thebes was needed. The barge was used for the customary sacred festival during which the deity is believed to have ridden in it. Cedar was needed for such a vessel, and Wenamon was commissioned with the task of going to the Prince of Byblos, Zakar-Ba'al, in Lebanon to arrange for its acquisition. Along the way Wenamon encountered numerous difficulties and survived many vicissitudes. "He wept: but he persisted, and he got his timber in the end, though we do not know how it got to Thebes."[56]

When Wenamon's mission had gotten as far as Sidon, the money with which he was to purchase the cedar was stolen. He appealed to the Prince of Sidon who, instead of passing him so that he could regain his money, became his antagonist. At one period Egypt had held political and military hegemony over Lebanon. Now with Egypt in a politically weak period of her history, her former vassals wasted no time in humiliating the officials of Egypt every chance they received. Wenamon represented Egypt, and as its representative was being made to suffer its humiliation as if all Egypt was there in person. News of this theft reached Byblos long before Wenamon and his party did. Upon arriving at Byblos, a message from Zakar-Ba'al was waiting for him: "Get out of my harbor!" The messenger was the royal harbor-master. Wenamon, in return, and due to his impecunious state, sent a message to the prince requesting permission to wait for the first ship sailing for Egypt. This message was answered by another message from the palace: "Get out of my harbor!" Again, the messenger was the royal harbor-master. Somehow--the reader is not told how--Wenamon's financial situation changes for the better. One evening just as he was about to board a ship bound for Egypt, on which he had booked passage, a message arrived from the palace: "Remain near the prince till morning." This new and rather surprising message had been brought about by the utterances of a royal page during the prince's offering of the evening sacrifice. This page had fallen into an ecstatic frenzy and had shouted continually: "Bring the god hither. Bring the messenger of Amen who hath him. Send him, and let him go."[57] Wenamon remained as requested. During his conversation with the prince the following day he asked:

> Let my scribe be brought to me that I
> may send him to Nesubanebded and
> Tentamen, the rulers whom Amen hath
> given to the North of his land, and they
> will send all of that which I shall write
> to them, saying, 'Let it be brought,'
> until I return to the South, and send
> thee all, all thy trifles again.'[58]

Taking up the task of interpreting this situation, James Baikie writes:

> Wenamon dispatched his secretary to
> Egypt by the first ship, and pending his
> return, Zakar-Baal allowed the most

important timbers of the barge of
Amen, the keel, the forefoot, the
sternpost, and four other great beams,
to be sent with him. In forty-eight days
the messenger returned with gold and
silver, 500 rolls of papyrus, linen
cordade, dried fish, and oxhides, while
Tentamen sent a special present for
Wenamon himself.[59]

At another time Wenamon reminded Zakar-Ba'al of how in
earlier times Egyptian envoys were treated with great respect, to which
the prince retorted:

After all, you are better off than the envoys
whom Ramses IX sent here, for they were detained
for seventeen years, and died here . . . Indeed
I have not done to thee that which they did to
the messengers of Ramses IX, when they died in
this place.[60]

To which the dauntless Wenamon retorted:

No! . . .mere people were the
messengers whom Ramses IX sent;
there was no god among his
messengers . . . Don't I know that thou
wilt say, 'Amen-Ra, king of gods, sent
to me his divine messenger, Amen-of-
the-way, and Wenamon his human
messenger, after the timber for the
great and august barge of Amen-Ra,
king of the gods . . . Then in future days

> when any messenger comes from the
> land of Egypt who is able to write, and
> reads thy name upon the stele, thou
> shalt receive water in the west, like the
> gods who are there.[61]

Wenamon, now feeling that all was in order, and having the prince's permission, prepared once more to leave for Egypt with the remainder of the logs of cedar. Again, his departure was blocked, this time by his enemy from Sidon, who, arriving with a small fleet, instructed the harbor-master to place him under arrest. This whole affair proved a bit embarassing for Zakar-Ba'al who sent a messenger to the chafed Wenamon in the person of a charming woman named Tetnut. She was a professional musician living in Byblos and had been sent to Wenamon by Zakar-Ba'al to calm his troubled nerves with sweet-sounding, soothing songs, as well as to deliver a message: "Eat, drink, and let not thy heart feel apprehension. Thou shalt hear all that I have to say in the morning."[62]

Eventually Wenamon accomplished his mission and returned home to write about it. His account is full of references to messengers and messages; all the more interesting since the account was written by a messenger! Tetnut was a female messenger who performed a specific task, and who delivered a verbatim message. Wenamon's scribe in his role as messenger delivered valuable portions of the barge-to-be back to Egypt, visited two allies of Wenamon, and delivered a verbatim message to them in writing. The harbor-master functioned as a messenger for both Zakar-Ba'al and the prince of Sidon. Earlier messengers were mentioned as having been sent once on the same mission as Wenamon, but without his success. Wenamon most importantly referred to himself as the human messenger of the divine-human messenger pair sent, he said, by the god Amen-Ra on this mission. This last point is extremely important because it has been claimed for several Israelite prophets that they were messengers from their god Yahweh. While PART II will explore this claim thoroughly, one should note here that those prophets may have one predecessor to this claim in Wenamon (i.e., that he was a deity's messenger, not that he was a prophet).

Wenamon belonged to the Egypt of the Twenty-First Dynasty (11th century BCE). From an earlier period, the Middle Kingdom (ca. 2400-1580 BCE), messenger activity in Egypt is noted in the story involving Sinuhe.

> Amenemhet I died while his son, Senusert (or Sesostris) I, was campaigning in the western Delta against the Libyans. Word of the king's death was dispatched to the son who upon receiving it kept the news secret until he could get back to the palace and establish himself firmly as king before any pretender could precede him. With Sesostris I in the field was a noble of high rank named Sinuhe. Accidentally overhearing the message about Amenemhet's death, he fled the country immediately for political reasons and returned only in his old age and upon the pardon of Senusert.[63]

Many are familiar with the travels of Sinuhe through Syria-Palestine, and of his desire to die on his native soil. Note, however, that within this already familiar story is one more example of the kind of message or tiding brought by messengers.

Messengers are likewise alluded to in the famous Israel Stela, or Hymn of the Victory of Merneptah (ca. 1224-1211 BCE). After telling of his victories in all lands, his victories against the Libyans was cause for great joy and celebration. Since the dreaded Libyans had been vanquished, the Egyptians could resume their normal lifestyle without fear or apprehension. In fact, "The battlements of the walls are restful, and it is the sun (not the enemy) that shall awaken their watchmen . . ."[64] His victory was so complete that "Strongholds are left to themselves; the wells are open and accessible to messengers."[65] I interpret this to mean--in light of the picture shaping up here--that messengers, whose freedom to come and go in the land giving it effective communication, were so important to the country that when this form of communication was restored it had the same effect as a present-day settlement of a large newspaper strike involving a nationally syndicated newspaper chain; it was cause for great relief and rejoicing.

During the time of Ahmose I (ca. 1570-1545 BCE), famous for expelling the dreaded Hyksos from Egypt (according to one historical school), and Thutmose I (ca. 1525-1495 BCE) who (according to the same school) pursued them into Syria-Palestine, one Ahmose, son of Eben, made a testimony of his participation in, and valor during these campaigns. "Then there was fighting on the water in the canal Pa-Djedku of Avaris. Thereupon I made a capture, and I carried away a hand. It was reported to the king's herald. Then the Gold of Valor was given to me."[66] Ahmose was given a second award for capturing a living prisoner. Note, however, who received the reports of valiant actions in the field; the king's herald. Either the herald made these reports to the pharaoh who then had the awards made, or the herald was empowered or commissioned to make such necessary field citations by his lord. The king's herald appears to have been a military *attache* assigned to the front lines during campaigns who acted on behalf of the king during warfare as if the king were personally there, especially rewarding his valiant troops and boosting morale.

On the walls of the temple of Karnak are carved the "Annals of Thut-mose III's military campaigns. In reference to the Battle of Megiddo a strategy session was taking place when ". . . messages were brought in about that wretched enemy, and discussion was continued of that problem on which they had previously spoken."[67] It is not stated, but from the context, the 'messages' were most probably field reconnaissance reports of the enemy's movements, and preparation for the battle.

The Hammamat Inscription of Henu, minister to Mentuhotep (last of the Eleventh Dynasty) tells how Henu was sent by his lord to the land of Punt in charge of an expedition to bring myrrh. Henu, basking in his glorious position, boasted: "Every official body of his majesty was placed under my authority . They reported messengers to me, as one alone commanding, to whom many hearken."[68] When a person had messengers their person, will, and power were extended great distances. Thus, to have messengers report to oneself was a definite outward manifestation of one's personal power.

The vizier or prime minister under Thutmose III was a man who enjoyed much personal power. He was a most important man in the pharaoh's court. He relied heavily upon messengers to maintain law, order, and effective communication between himself and his officers in the far-flung provinces of the empire or kingdom. The vizier's messengers were also special; so special that regulations were drawn up as to the duties and treatment of these select persons.

As for every messenger whom the vizier sends with a message for an official, from the first official to the last, let him not be swerved and let him not be conducted; the official shall repeat his vizierial message while he (the messenger) stands before the official, repeating his message and going forth to wait for him. His messenger shall seize the mayors and village sheiks for the judgment hall; his messenger shall give the regulation _____ his messenger gives answer saying: "I have been sent with a message for the official so and so; he caused that I be conducted, and he caused that something be entrusted to me. Hear the affair of this official _____ expiate those things, about which there has been litigation by the vizier in his hall, in every crime, with greater punishment than by cutting off a limb.[69]

The vizier's messengers had numerous duties. When a petitioner was summoned: "Now, as for every messenger whom the vizier sends on account of any petitioner, he shall cause that he go to him."[70] Or in reference to real estate cases: "Now, as for every petitioner to the vizier concerning lands, he shall dispatch him (the messenger) to him, in addition to a hearing of the land-overseer and local council of the district."[71] Concerning the daily opening of the king's-house one is told "Now, after each has reported to the other, of the two officials, then the vizier shall send to open every gate of the king's-house, to cause to go in all that goes in, (and) to go out all that goes out likewise, by his messenger, who shall cause it to be put into writing."[72] When the vizier sat in his hall arrayed in splendor and was surrounded by the trappings of his office, hearing petitions and complaints "One shall be heard after another, without allowing one who is behind to be heard before who is in front. If one in front says: "There is none at my hand,' then he shall be taken by the messenger to the vizier."[73] In the daily order of business between the palace and the outside world "Now, as for everything going in (and) everything going out on the floor of the court, they shall go out (and) they shall go in through his messenger, who shall cause them to go in (and) go out."[74] It is thus the vizier "who exacts the ships for every requisition made upon him. It is he who dispatches every messenger of the king's-house to_____ . . . It is he who seals the edicts_____ of the keeper of_____who is dispatched with a message of the king's-house."[75] From the context one is also forced to conclude that the vizier himself was the number one messenger of the pharaoh.

Shortly before Queen Hatshepsut's ninth year as queen, she made an expedition to the land of Punt. A relief illustrating this expedition was carved on the walls of her Deir el-Bahri temple. One of the members of this expedition was the "King's-Messenger," of whom it is written: "The arrival of the king's-messenger in God's Land, together with the army which is behind him, before the chiefs of Punt; dispatched with every good thing from the court, L.P.H., for Hathor, mistress of Punt; for the sake of life, prosperity, and health of her majesty."[76] Further references to this king's-messenger state that "Pitching the tent of the king's-messenger and his army, in the myrrh-terraces of Punt on the side of the sea, in order to receive the chiefs of the country."[77] And, "The coming of the chief of Punt bearing tribute at the side of the sea before the king's-mesenger _____ "[78]

Similarly, a rock inscription in the Wadi Maghara, belonging to the time of Thutmose III, contains only three somewhat mutilated lines:

> Came the king's-messenger at the head
> of his army, to traverse the inaccessible
> valleys, to please Horus who is in the
> palace, by bringing that which exists to
> his majesty_____, living again,
> revered.[79]

Notice in the preceding excerpts that the title "king's-messenger" applies obviously to a commanding officer of troops, since he regularly appears at the head of an army. It may be that at the time of Thutmose III this was the commander's official title, for although Hatshepsut ruled as a bearded queen, the title "king's-messenger" was still used for this commander's position. Likewise, we have the title "king's-son" which refers to the position of viceroy, vizier, or prime minister.[80]

The Assuan Inscription dating from the time of Thutmose II, among other subjects, narrates "The arrival of a messenger who announces to his majesty a rebellion in Kush, and mentions a frontier fortress of the king's father, Thutmose I."[81] Within the inscription and concerning Thutmose I's domain we read: "His southern boundary is as far as the Horns of the Earth, (his) northern as far as the ends; the marshes of Asia are the domain of his majesty, the arm of his messenger is not repulsed among the lands of the Fenkhu."[82] The king's-messenger indubitably extended the (military) power and will of the one who had sent him.

The study of historical texts is rounded out by considering a stela erected at the direction of Sheshonk (Shishak), the Libyan first

king of the Twenty-Second Dynasty. The stela contains the following
passage which pertains to a statue of Namlot, which was sent to
Abydos.

> His majesty sent the statue of Osiris,
> the great chief to me, great chief of
> chiefs, Namlot, triumphant, northward
> to Abydos. There were_____ _____
> _____ a great army, in order to protect
> it, having numerous ships _____ _____
> without number, and the messengers of
> the great chief of me, in order to
> deposit it in the august palace, . . .[83]

It is impossible to escape the conclusion that in Egypt especially, the
title 'messenger' was an official title which oftentimes referred to a
person of high military rank. For Egypt 'messenger' was both a rank
and a situation in which persons of many ranks could and did find
themselves.

b. Historico-Romantic Texts

A papyrus which has woven history and romance together is
called the First Sallier Papyrus. It contains the story of:

> an embassy sent by the Hyksos king
> Apepy to Seqenen-Ra, the Theban
> prince who led the Egyptians in their
> great struggle which ended in the
> expulsion of the Hyksos; an embassy
> whose object was manifestly that of
> picking a quarrel with the Theban, and
> giving an excuse for making war upon
> him.[84]

One reads therein: "And the King Apepy sought words to send a message to the King Seqenen-Ra, the prince of the Southern City."[85] After consulting his advisors a device was hit upon.

> Now many days after this, King Apepy sent to the prince of the Southern City the report which his scribes and wise men had spoken to him. Now when the messenger whom King Apepy had sent reached the Southern City, he was taken to the prince of the city. Then said one to the mesenger of King Apepy, "What brings thee to the Southern City, and wherefore hast thou travelled hither?" The messenger said to him, "King Apepy sends to thee saying, 'My messenger has come to thee, concerning the splashing of the hippopotami, which are in the pool in the city (Thebes). For they allow me no sleep, day and night the sound of them is in my ear."[86]

Being five hundred miles apart it was a puzzle to the prince as to how he should answer the messenger. Methods of conciliation were tried, but to no purpose. Here one gets a glimpse of the messenger having bargaining power and going well beyond the simple delivery of the message. Later he returned to King Apepy and delivered the reply. Then the Prince Seqenen-Ra called his generals and made them aware of Apepy's scheme and machinations. They, too, were perplexed as to how to answer. Just then the papyrus continues: "Then the King Apepy sent to . . ."[87] At this point, however, the fragment breaks off, so we will probably never know what message followed.

Before leaving this papyrus, attention must be called to the following. The phrases "Then said one to the messenger," and "The messenger said to him," after which the message is delivered seem to suggest that a message intended for Prince Seqenen-Ra was not delivered directly to the prince. The problem revolves around the prince being named throughout the document on the one hand, while the nebulous 'one' seems to suggest another individual. If this is indeed the case, I have chronicled the first exception to the rule that messages were delivered directly to the person for whom they were intended.

c. Fiction

A famous piece of Egyptian fiction is known as the Tale of the Two Brothers. The story involves Anpu and his younger brother Bata-- who in many ways reminds the reader of Joseph in Egypt. Due to the infidelity of Anpu's wife, she involved Bata in a scheme which resulted in Anpu attempting to kill his brother. The reader knows that Bata has been falsely accused, and sympathizes with him. This much of the story is generally well-known. There is, however, much more to the story of Bata, especially after he left his brother's home to find his own fortune. Bata eventually married a beautiful woman who one day took a walk along a river and rested under an Acacia tree--against the expressed wishes of her husband before he had departed for a rather long journey. Being such a beauty, the river chased her and the Acacia tree snatched a lock of her hair, and threw it into the river. The river took the lock of hair to Egypt where it was eventually mingled with the pharaoh's linen which was being washed by the royal laundryman. The lock of hair caused all of the pharaoh's linen to smell of the sweet odor of ointment. The pharaoh, annoyed beyond measure, questioned why this was so, and was told why by the laundryman. The lock was taken to the pharaoh who summoned his wise men and magicians to find out from whom the lock had come. He was told that the lock belonged to the daughter of the Ra-Harakhte, who had in her the essence of all the gods; the lock had come to him as a tribute from a foreign land. They told him to " . . . send forth messengers to all foreign lands to seek for this girl: and let the messenger whom thou dost send to the valley of the Acacia be accompanied by many men that they may bring her back."[88] The messengers who had been sent to far-away lands returned and reported a negative finding to the pharaoh. Those who had been sent to the valley of the Acacia did not return--save one--for they had all been killed by Bata. Bata allowed one to live to return and report to the pharaoh. More messengers were sent; this time accompanied by heavily-armed troops. All were accompanied by a special female messsenger who was armed with only trinkets and ornaments. These were the 'weapons' which eventually succeeded in bringing Bata's wife back to Egypt by this messenger.

d. Wisdom

In its international form, wisdom literature is characterized by its attempt to promote a lifestyle in which one lives well and wisely. The hero of such literature is the tranquil sage and ethicist, as opposed to the brash, 'hot'(headed) person. In its simplest form, wisdom literature takes the form of the learned treatise. The form which falls between these two levels is the instruction of the wise men. Two famous Egyptian wise men were Ptah-hotep, a vizier (i.e., viceroy) to Pharaoh Izezi of the Fifth Dynasty (ca. 2450 BCE), and Ipu-wer of the Early Intermediate Period. To envoys Ptah-hotep recommended the following conduct.

If thou art a confidant whom prince sendeth to prince, be strictly exact when he sendeth thee. Do his errand for him as he telleth it. Beware of embittering with words that may incense(?) prince against prince. Hold fast to truth and transgress her not. Verily the satisfaction of a grudge is not told to a man's credit. Quarrel with no man great or small, for that is an abomination.[89]

This advised the correct delivery of a message which was considered of the utmost importance. Forgetfulness or improvisation on the part of the messenger could incite prince against prince by a mere 'slip of the lip,' and was to be avoided by being thoughtful and prudent.

Ipu-wer, contemplating the disasters which had befallen Egypt--especially the anarchy of the Intermediate Period-- complained: "The possessor of property is now one who has naught. Behold, servants have become masters of butler; He who was a messenger now sends another."[90] One may gather that Ipu-wer was not against messengers as such, nor did this imply that messengers occupied a low station in Egyptian life of even this period. He was merely attempting to paint a clear picture of exactly how upside down Egyptian society had become; messengers were an integral and important part of that anarchistic society as well.

e. Love-songs

The Chester Beatty Papyrus Number One contains a love-song. Over a week without his lover, a heartsick male moans: "It is seven days yesterday since I saw the sister, And sickness encroaches upon me, . . . The coming and going of her messengers is that which revives my heart. Better for me is the sister than any , medicine . . ."[91] Messengers kept two lovers in communication although circumstances deemed it necessary that they be apart.

A song which portrays the impatience of a maid for the arrival of her lover states:

> O that you mayest come to the sister
> quickly like a royal messenger whose
> lord is impatient for his message, and
> his heart is fain to hear it; even a
> messenger for whom all the stables
> have been harnessed, and he has horses
> at the halting places, and the chariot is

ready yoked in its place, and there is no
rest for him upon the road. He reaches
the house of the sister, and his heart
rejoices.[92]

This love-song affords a glimpse into the real world of some
messengers' importance. Gleaned is the fact that messengers were
supported by an elaborate transportation system of 'way stations'
along a certain route. The mode of transportation was the chariot; but
one would think horseback to have been the most common mode.
Moreover, one learns that the messenger delivered the message with
dispatch, and wasted little time at these way stations; the chariot was
ready when the messenger arrived.

f. Funerary and Tomb Texts

The pyramid texts of the Fifth and Sixth Dynasties, and the
mortuary temples and tombs of the Eighteenth Dynasty shed light on
the presence and duties of the messenger. Concerning one of the
former texts, the major subject is the victory of the living over death.
In the tomb of king Unas he is reported as enjoying a cannibalistic
feast in the other world, and is describedd as the one who ". . . eats men
and lives on gods, Lord of messengers, who dispatches his messengers;
. . ."[93] Some of these messengers are the Seizers of Horns; the Erect of
Head; He who is upon the Willows; the Wanderer who slaughters
Lords; and He of the Winepress. They perform such duties as lassoing,
guarding and holding, binding, strangling, and drawing forth the
entrails of the king's victims. These messengers are sent forth to
punish, and all of this is done in an effort to have the power and magic
of those devoured enter into the king's body.
From the time of Amenhotep III (Eighteenth Dynasty) a
mortuary temple edict concerning the blessings on preservers of the
ka-chapel reads:

Amen-Re, king of the gods, shall
reward them with prosperous life. The
king of your day, shall reward you as he
rewards _____. There shall be
doubled for you office upon office, ye
shall receive from son to son, and heir
to heir. They shall be sent on as
messengers, and the king of their day
will reward them. Their bodies shall
rest in the west after (a life of) 110
years, doubled to you shall be the
mortuary obligations likewise.[94]

An inscription on the wall of the tomb of Rekhmire, a prime
minister, or vizier during the latter half of the reign of Thutmose III,
contains an account of the instructions apparently given to each vizier.

Behold, as for an official, when he has
reported water and wind of all his
doings, behold, his deeds shall not be
unknown ___ ___ ___ ___; he is not
brought in because of the speech of the
responsible officer, (but) it is known by
the speech of his messenger as the one
stating it; he is by the side of the
responsible officer as the speaker; he is
not the one lifting up the voice, a
messenger petitioning ___ ___ ___ ___
or an official.[95]

The text is very fragmentary and is at points obscure. In essence,
however: " . . . the vizier is exhorted: to legal, just and impartial
decisions; not to be excessively forbidding, but still to keep himself
aloof from the people; finally that his office is really to be

administered according to the instructions given."[96] Messengers served here in the capacity of advocates who spoke for, on behalf of, a client official who had been brought before the vizier for disciplinary action. The messenger-advocate accompanied the charged officer and spoke on his behalf. From the texts one learns that these messenger-advocates were highly skilled in speech, and knew how to ascertain the mood and frame of mind of the vizier by observing his body movements, especially the unconscious nodding of the head while listening to a plea. Line seventeen states: "Lo, they will say (of the vizier), the petitioner loves him who nods the head . . ."[97] It is not difficult to understand how messengers here could be advocates with a legal function. As advocates they 'spoke for someone else' in the tone that best relayed how the ones spoken for would have needed to have spoken had they been skilled enough in the jurisprudence of the day themselves. Advocacy then appears here to have developed as a natural outgrowth of one of the basic understandings of what a messenger's primary function was.

A text containing a story of the old age of the sun-god became part of a book of spells, portions of which were inscribed in the tombs of Seti I (Ninteenth Dynasty) and Ramses III (Twentieth Dynasty).

> . . . when Re, the sun-god, grew old mankind plotted to overthrow him. Thereupon he sent the goddess Hathor, who is identified in myth with his eye, to destroy mankind. After the work of destruction had begun, however, he repented and devised a scheme to save the remainder from the fury of the goddess.[98]

Concerning messengers one reads

And the majesty of Re said, . . .Send
forth thine Eye that it may slay them
for thee when she ascends as Hathor.
So this goddess returned, when she had
slain mankind in the desert. Said the
majesty of this god, welcome, welcome,
Hathor, thou hast done that for which I
sent thee.[99]

But now repenting

. . . Re said, Come, call unto me swift-
speeding messengers, that they may
run like the shadow of a body. And
these   messengers   were   brought
forthwith. And the majesty of this god
said, Hasten ye to Elephantine and
bring me much red ochre. And this
ochre was brought to him.[100]

This ochre was mixed with a barley beer which turned the brew blood-
red. The goddess, thinking it was human blood, drank her fill, and
under the influence of this brew forgot about her mission to destroy
mankind.

A short quotation from Pindar's *Paeans*, found among the
manuscripts of Bacchylides, yielded the following.

And when they had placed in the sore-
lamented tomb the mighty corpse of
the son of Peleus, went messengers
over the sea waves, and came again
bringing from Scyros Neoptolemus,

great in strength, who sacked the city
of Ilion.[101]

Messengers went abroad and returned with the apparent replacement
for a deceased mighty hero.

7. Analytical Summary

When that which is considered obvious and simple is placed
under the light of rigid scrutiny one notices that the whole is
constituted of numerous parts. If the whole is to be comprehended, the
several parts must be examined. It is not enough to examine two or
three parts and then compare them, because one always runs the risk
of getting exactly what one seeks in the way of results, and of calling
those results valid. It is most unscientific. The messenger phenomenon
of the ANE as a topic of serious, sustained study has--like the
considered obvious and simple--received little attention. The
preceding has produced a plethora of messengers which were mined
from literatures produced from the Persian Gulf to the southern part
of Cush following the Fertile Crescent trajectory. One important fact
demonstrated was that messengers were ubiquitous throughout this
area; they were an integtral part of its warp and woof. They were there
in all aspects of its social, political and religious life. They were there
in all types of literature as active heroic and villainous characters.
They were in the literature which speculated on the lives of those who
were beyond the grave or beyond the heavens. Messengers--if one
takes this literature seriously--were important in the ANE societies
von der Wiege bis zur Bahre! But to say this is the beginning, not
the end. The messenger phenomenon must be described, ways of
identifying and categorizing messengers must be developed, and
relationships between messengers and their audiences (or those with
whom they interact) must be raised in relief and assigned a value for
those interested in the ANE. This then establishes the validity of the
study.

At this stage I need only demonstrate the messenger
phenomenon and establish the fact that for an extended period of time
messenger, as understood by the inhabitants of the ANE, was constant;

as a concept it did not change from year to year, decade to decade, century to century, or even millennium to millennium. Messengers-- and what that term meant to the ANE--was not a fly-by-night operation or phenomenon. Since the preceding pages have demonstrated this by a mass of evidence, what remains is to summarize the evidence to this point.

It has been demonstrated thus far that the messenger existed in the ANE primarily for the purpose of extending temporally and geographically the existing power of another's spoken/written words or will. The analysis of texts from Sumer to Egypt/Cush verified that fact. The representative literature supplied evidence of numerous types of messengers. Among them were military men (Sumer and Egypt--especially the King's-Messenger) who performed the specific task of extending a monarch's power and will militarily moreso than who delivered verbatim messages (although this can in no wise ever be ruled out). There were also men of social position (the royal messenger of Sumer and the vizier's messenger(s) of Egypt, where the vizier himself was understood as the chief royal messenger.

Not all messengers were male. Tetnut, the Egyptian minstrel-lady, whose mission was to Wenamon; the woman who was sent to lure Bata's wife back to Egypt for the disgruntled pharaoh with the sweet-smelling clothes; the goddess Hathor, Eye of the sun-god; as well as the women of Ramses' harem who were engaged in court intrigue, are also counted among messengers

From the Canaanite and Egyptian texts one learned that messengers played very active and essential roles in courtships; in Canaan preceding the actual pressing of the suit of marriage by the suitor in person, and in Egypt, by keeping the channels of communication open between two lovers who had been kept apart by circumstances.

The humanness of the messengers impressed the reader when one was able to identify certain messengers by name. One knows, therefore, that historical personages bearing the names Surin (Ebla), Dagan-abu and Zalmu (Mesopotamia), Eagadada (Sumeria), Wenamon (Egypt), and Tetnut (Egyptian, living in Lebanon) all served as messengers in history.

Messengers were not only active historically, they were active as literary characters as well. ANE literature--and this will be demonstrated to be true for biblical literature as well--found it difficult to be interesting without them, for that literature mirrored everyday life in many of its aspects. An Enkidu in the Babylonian Genesis is necessary to the overall plot. By failing to accomplish his primary commission, he allows Gilgamesh to live and to go on his quest for the secret of immortality--only to also fail in the end. Likewise, the dispatching of a special messenger by the goddess Inanna to her father, the god Sin, to have a 'long' house provided for her lover Dumuzi and for herself, added a bit of romanticism to a Sumerian tale. The weather-god in Hittite mythology was depicted as 'almost human' when he dispatched an eagle on a desperate mission as a messenger to find his son, Telipinu, who had disappeared. This act on the part of the weather-god solicited pity and compassion for him from the reader who readily identified with the anguished parent. Thus, real-life situations were made to stand in relief by the author's use of the messenger at strategic points in the tales.

In all of the above, however, we did not go beyond that which all messengers had in common; extension of another's power, will, and spoken/written word temporally and geographically. In addition to extending one's power, messengers sometimes bore one's shame and humiliation. A case in point was the personal messenger of the Judahite King Hezekiah, who did obeisance as a slave in the king's stead to Sennacherib, conquering king of Assyria. What remains intact, however, is the understanding of the extension of the person of Hezekiah temporally and geographically as if he were in two places at once. This was especially true of the Egyptian vizier's messenger with his 'book of rules for conduct,' and also for the King's-Messenger. These positions were so important that a sage such as Ptah-hotep wrote a special code of conduct for the envoy of his day.

There was no ANE historical civilization without its messengers. In some cases (Ebla, Mesopotamia, and Egypt) 'messenger' appeared as an official title of members of a given court, leading to the belief that each court was in most respects a carbon copy of many others. We now know that communication between allies, and even between potentially hostile neighbors (Egyptian Historico-

Romantic Text) was impossible without the messenger. For this reason messengers were hand-picked, reliable persons whose fidelity was rarely, if ever, questioned. From the Merneptah stele one learned that when the messenger was allowed the freedom to complete a mission--it having been curtailed due to hostilities between two or more countries--it was cause for great jubilation on the part of both kings and general population.

Noteworthy was the claim of the Egyptian envoy Wenamon that he was a messenger of, and that he was sent by, the god Amen-Ra. To my knowledge this is the first recorded claim by a secular person that a god had sent him as a messenger to other humans.

If one can imagine living in a country which has no radio, television, computers, postmen, newspapers, or libraries, and where films are of the 'wholesome family type' only, or where people are forbidden to congregate to gossip and exchange bits of news and information, then one can imagine what cultural isolation is like; it is a dark age as long as these conditions exist and prevail. Such an age prevailed at times in the ANE whenever messengers for one reason or another were hampered from their missions. Such was their impact and importance in the ANE.

CHAPTER II

The Message in the Ancient Near East

The message is essentially one of the errands and functions of the messenger. While it is difficult to separate oral and written products with precision, written messages themselves offer some assistance. Oral tradition can modify written works. The reverse is also true, for oftentimes written works are but crystallizations of messages which were intended to be read aloud. Written literature was thus in many cases 'oral' even when it was read. However, differences between oral and written did exist; a fact which should be kept in mind.[1]

It will be noticed at times that the message, although preserved in letter form, dictated that it be delivered orally. For this information one generally relys upon the opening formula, but as has already been illustrated with Hittite literature, this formula does not introduce the message exclusively.

Here relevant ANE literature will be examined, the most important of which is the letter.[2] The evidence of this oral/written literature is examined to ascertain the nature, content and impact of one of the main errands of the messenger; the message.

1. Mari

Mari produced a text which referred to the "killing of an ass" (i.e., the making or cutting of a covenant). It reads in part: "To my lord say: Thus Ibal-il, thy servant. The tablet of Ibal-Adad from Aslakka reached me and I went to Aslakka to 'kill an ass' between the Hanu and Idamaras . . ."[3] Here the message is obviously written, but it is to be said, i.e., orally delivered. This then is an example of oral and written traditions side by side; many more follow below.

The use of two other forms of communication in the ANE, the signal fire and the trumpet, is mentioned in a passage in Jeremiah 6:1ff: "Blow the trumpet in Tekoa, and raise the signal (fire) on *Beth-hacheren*." A parallel text from Mari reads:

> To my lord say: Thus Bannum, thy servant. Yesterday I departed from Mari; and spent the night at Zuruban. All the Benjaminites raised fire-signals. . . all the cities of the Benjaminites of the Terqa district raised fire-signals in response; and so far I have not ascertained the meaning of those signals.[4]

Again, this is a written message, but the presence of 'say' shows that it was intended for oral delivery by the messenger. The message also demonstrates that all communication techniques in the ANE were not automatically understood by everyone else. The fire-signals of these Benjaminites had their own set of meanings, evidently understood only by members of the Terqa district.

Another oral/written message from Mari contains an optimistic, nationalistic prophecy.

> Speak to my lord: Thus (says/said) Mukannisum your servant: I had offered the sacrifices to Dagan of Tutul for the life of my lord.The "answerer" of Dagan of Tutul arose, thus he spoke, namely: Babylon what are you still up to? I will drive (assemble) you into the snare (/) . . .the houses/families of the seven partners and whatever their

possessions (are) I shall put into the
hand of Zimri-Lim.[5]

The messengers who delivered these messages must, alas, remain
anonymous. It is known in each case, however, who commissioned
each; Ibal-Il, Bannum and Mukannisum respectively.

William Moran translated several letters from the Mari
archives. In addition to their serving as written messages, they
designate the status of those receiving them. These include ecstatics,
private persons, and a prophetess. These written messages are also
important because they reflect a stage of message delivery wherein the
message was (again) both delivered orally while at the same time
having been written down. The most telling evidence for this is the
"Speak to my lord: Thus XX your servant."

Moran studied these messages according to their subject
matter. Mari messages were concerned with (1) a royal decree of
equity; (2) a substitute king; (3) a happy reign; (4) divine revelations;
(5) a letter to a deity; (6) punishment by fire; (7) treaties and
coalitions; (8) the god of my father; (9) a loan between gentlemen; and
(10) a boy to his mother.[6] Moran also included a message from one
Mar-Ishtar, the bishop of Esagila, to Esarhaddon, king of Assyria.
Moran believed that this man "served as a kind of ambassador at
large."[7] Thus, his presence provided a reason to suspect a very special
category of messenger/ambassador. As an example of one of these
messages, and because of its unusually-intended recipient, I quote the
following.

Speak to Ida (the river god) my lord:
Thus Zimri-Lim your servant. I
herewith send a gold cup to my lord. At
an earlier date I wrote my report to my
lord; my lord revealed a sign. May my
lord make the sign which he revealed
come true for me. Moreover, may my
lord not turn his face elsewhere,

besides me may my lord have need of
no one else.[8]

What we have here is a letter/message written to a deity by Zimri-Lim,
king of Mari. The reader is not told who the messenger was who was to
speak this message before the god Ida. Ida being a river-deity and not a
transcendant sky-deity, however, no superhuman messenger appears
to have been necessary. A priest was probably the ritual messenger for
the king in this case. What is most important to notice in this example
is that the king chose not to exercise the practice of son-of-god(s) and
deliver the message himself, but chose the method of being in two
places at once by employing a messenger to do this in his stead. Sacral
kingship in the ANE would not de facto make the messenger
necessary!

2. Mesopotamia

Babylonian and Assyrian Laws, Contracts and Letters devotes
a chapter to a discussion of Babylonian and Assyrian letter-messages.[9]
These messages are devoted to a number of subjects. Among them are
(1) the letters of Hammurabi; (2) the letters of Samu-iluna and his
immediate successors; (3) private letters of the first dynasty of
Babylon; (4) Sennacherib's letters to his father, Sargon; (5) letters
from the last year of Shamash-shum-ukin; (6) letters regarding affairs
in Southern Babylonia; (7) letters about Elam and Southern
Babylonia; (8) miscellaneous Assyrian Letters; and (9) letters of the
Second Babylonian Empire. One of the major differences to be noted
between the Babylonian and Assyrian letters is their opening
formulae. The Babylonian messages usually began, "To A say: Thus
saith B," while the Assyrian messages began, "To A thus B" with B
adding "thy servant" if B is subordinate to A. The "say" is also omitted
from the Assyrian messages. Both formulae, however, served the same
purpose; to legitimize what followed.

a. Babylonian

From the messages sent by King Hammurabi to his subjects, one concerning the canals of the country reads:

> To Sin-iddinam say, thus saith
> Hammurabi: Summon the people who
> hold fields on the side of the Damanu
> canal, that they may scour the Damanu
> canal. Within the present month let
> them finish scouring the Damanu
> canal.[10]

Concerning a message of an annual sheep-shearing at Babylon:

> To Ibni-Sin, son of Marduk-nasir, say,
> thus saith Ammi-zaduga: A sheep-
> shearing will take place in the house of
> the New Year's Festival. On receipt of
> this note, take the sheep . . . and the
> sheep which are sealed, which thou
> shall set in motion, and come to
> Babylon. Delay not, reach Babylon on
> the first of Adar.[11]

According to the scholars Budge and King:

> The earliest mention of the actual
> name of the country of Assyria in the
> cuneiform inscriptions is found in a
> letter addressed by Hammurabi to his
> viceroy, Sin-idinnam, whom he
> instructs to dispatch to him two

> hundred and forty men of a regiment
> called the "king's company," under the
> command of Nannar-iddina, who the
> king goes on to say, "have left the
> country of *Ashur* and the district of
> Shitullum."[12]

A letter, surviving as a fragment of a late Assyrian copy, contains the names of two Assyrian kings, Ashur-narara and Nabu-dani (both ca. 1250 BCE). The letter was sent by Adad-shum-nasir, king of Babylonia.[13]

b. Assyrian[14]

Part of an important message sent by King Ashurbanipal reads:

> Message of the king to Sin-tabni-usur:
> It is well with me. May thy heart be
> cheered. Concerning Sin-shar-usar,
> what thou didst send. How could he say
> evil words of thee and I hear anything
> of them? Shamash perverted his heart
> and Ummanigash slandered thee
> before me and would give thee to
> death. Ashur, my god, withholds me.[15]

What proves invaluable for this study is the fact that the king specifically terms his letter a message. This provides evidence that letters were indeed intended as messages.

A letter from Kudur, a faithful servant of Ashurbanipal, who thanks the king for special favors, contains the following information:

The benefits of the king, my lord,
toward me are manifold. I will come to
see the king, my lord. I say to myself, I
will go and I will see the face of the
king, my lord; then I will return and
live. The chief baker made me return
to Erech from the journey, saying, "A
special messenger has brought a sealed
dispatch to thee from the palace, and
thou must return with me to Erech."
He sent me this order and made me
return to Erech. The king, my lord,
must know this.[16]

Ashur-ubalit, king of Assyria (ca. 1362-1327), a contemporary
of Amenhotep IV of Egypt, and Suppiluliumas of Hatti, corresponded
with Amenhotep IV. This, too, is a spoken/written message example.

To the king of Egypt, say: Thus saith
Ashur-ubalit, king of Assyria: With
thee, thy home, thy wives, thy chariots
and thy chief men may it be well![17]

The annals of King Ashur-nasir-pal relate how he crossed the
Tigris and encamped in the land of Kummukhi. Column 1, line 74ff.
has the king stating:

. . . and I received tribute from the
lands of Kummukhi and Mushki,
vessels of bronze and cattle, sheep and
wine.[18]

But of greater importance is the following account of lines 75-76.

> While yet I remained in the land of
> Kummukhi, *one brought me tidings*,
> saying: "The city of Suru which is in
> Bit-Khalupe hath revolted, and they
> have slain Khamatai, their governor,
> and Akhiababa, the son of a nobody,
> whom they have brought from Bit-
> Adini, have they set up as king over
> them."[19]

In line 101 Ashur-nasir-pal states that:

> In the same eponymy (see line 99's "In
> the eponymy, the year called by my
> name, . . .") while yet I remained in
> Nineveh, they brought me tidings,
> saying that the Assyrians and Khulai,
> their governor, whom Shalmaneser, the
> king of Assyria, the former prince who
> preceded me, had settled in the city of
> Khalzidipkha, had revolted and had
> marched against Damdamusa, my royal
> city to take it.[20]

And in column II line 23:

> In the eponymy of Ashur-idin they
> brought me tidings, saying "Nur-Adad,
> the prince of the land of Dagara, hath

revolted, and the men throughout the
whole of the land of Zamua have
banded themselves together, and they
have built a wall in the pass of Babite";
(and they added) that they were
coming to wage battle and war against
me.[21]

Moreover, column II line 49 reads:

In the eponymy of Limutti-aku while
yet I remained in Nineveh, men
brought me tidings, saying that Ameka
and Arashtu had discontinued the
tribute and forced labor . . .[22]

Finally, in column III line 26 one reads:

While I was in the city of Calah they
brought me tidings, saying: "The men
of the land of Lake, and the city of
Khinadanu, and the land of Sukhi have
all revolted, and have crossed over the
Euphrates."[23]

All of the preceding excerpts have in common the phrase *ti-e-mu ut-
te-ru-ni ma-a*, "they brought me tidings, saying:" which is another
reliable indication of messenger activity in the ANE literature. In each
of the above instances a message--either verbatim or recounted--
followed the phrase. What the reader is left to ponder, however, is who
commissioned these messengers.[24]

3. Hatti

Early Hittite kings warred with, and conquered their foes and neighbors, and made no excuses for their aggressiveness. By the fourteenth century, however, Hittite kings of the Empire sought desperately to justify any declaration of war. The justification of hostilities involved the dispatching of a letter demanding the extradition of Hittite subjects who had taken refuge in the enemy's territory. If the demand was refused, a second letter would follow charging the enemy with having committed the first act of aggression. After this the matter would be subject to the judgment of heaven, to be settled--obviously--by ordeal of war.[25] Correspondence which preceded the attack on Hayasa in the seventh year of Mursilis II declares:

> After I had conquered the land of Tipiya, I sent a letter to Anniyas, the king of Azzi, and wrote to him: "My subjects who went over to . . . give them back to me." But the king of the land of Azzi wrote back to me . . . "I will not give them back," . . . But I wrote back thus: "I have come and encamped before the frontier of your country . . . Therefore the gods shall take their stand on my side, and shall decide the case in my favor.[26]

That these were specifically letters does not detract from messenger activity. A messenger delivering these letters had to deliver them orally. In fact, an earlier challenge made by Mursilis to the king of Arzawa is so succinct and terse that it almost begs verbal delivery.

> My subjects who went over to you,
> when I demanded them back from you,
> you did not restore them to me; and
> you called me a child and made light of
> me. Up then! Let us fight, and let the
> Storm-god, my Lord, decide our
> case![27]

Messengers, then, were intimately involved in ancient Hittite Empire warfare; warfare which was preceded by a special kind of taunting message designed to justify aggression.

Not all demands for surrender by Hittite kings resulted in warfare, however. One king tells of such a capitulation.

> As soon as Manapa-Dattas, the son of
> Muwa-the-lion, heard about me "His
> majesty   is   coming."   he   sent   a
> messenger to meet me and wrote to me
> . . . "My lord, slay me not, but take me
> into allegiance . . ."[28]

It appears, however, that Manapa-Dattas had been the recipient of earlier acts of kindness from the Hittite king, and had not shown the proper attitude of gratefulness. Finding that the king was proceeding to destroy him, Manapa-Dattas sent a verbal message by his mother who fell before the king and spoke: "Our lord, do not destroy us, but take us, our lord, into allegiance."[29] The king was thus persuaded not to attack.

Discussing the military fame of King Suppiluliumas before he attacked the city of Carchemish, O. Gurney states:

There arrived a messenger from Egypt
bearing a letter from his queen in the
following words: "My husband has died
and I have no son, but of you it is said
that you have many sons. If you would
send me one of your sons, he would
become my husband. I will on no
account take one of my subjects; to
make him my husband would be
abhorrent me."[30]

The surprised and suspicious Suppiluliumas sent an envoy to Egypt to
verify this message. He returned with a second message from the
queen:

Why do you say "They wish to deceive
me?" If I had a son, would I write to a
foreigner to publish my distress and
that of my country? You have insulted
me in *speaking* thus. He who was my
husband is dead and I have no son.
Must I then take one of my subjects
and marry him? I have written to no
one but you. Everyone says you have
many sons; give me one of them that he
may become my husband.[31]

Suppiluliumas also corresponded with Amenhotep IV whom he
called Huria. One of his letters contains the following:

Thus hath Suppiluliumas, the great
king, king of Hatti-land, to Huria, king
of Egypt, my brother, *spoken*: I am

well. With thee may it be well. With thy
wives, thy sons, thy house, thy
warriors, thy chariots, and in thy land,
may it be very well. Now, thou, my
brother, hast ascended the throne of
thy father and, just as thy father and I
mutually requested presents, so wilt
also thou and I now be mutually good
friends.[32]

This is another fine example of the orally-delivered, written message
which is preceded by a somewhat extended messenger formula.

4. Ugarit

That Canaanite messages were delivered simultaneously in
oral and written form may be demonstrated by a letter sent by the king
of Beirut: "I have <u>hearkened</u> to the words of the tablets of the king, my
lord, my god . . ."[33]

Ugaritic letters began "To NN, say: Message of NN," which is
similar to the familiar "Say to NN, Thus says NN" of Hebrew
literature. The same formula for Ugaritic letters is also found at the
beginning of messenger narratives in mythological texts. James Ross
indicates that this formula was generally not taken lightly. Using a
mythological text he argues:

A broken passage in Ras Shamra 137
(IIIAB): 38-42 may be relevant here.
El has granted the request of Yamm,
brought by his messengers, that Baal
be surrendered to him; Baal is angry
and seizes weapons, but is restrained
by Ashtoreth (and Anath or Ashera?).
They apparently ask how he can
presume to strike a messenger, for "a

messenger has upon his shoulders the
word of his lord."[34]

The message which so angered Baal is as follows.

> They told the bull El his father: "The
> message of Yamm your lord, (of) your
> sire judge Nahar (is this): "Give up,
> gods, him whom you protect, on whom
> the multitudes wait, give up Baal and
> his lackeys, (even) Dagon's son, (that)
> I may inherit his portion."[35]

Note that Ugaritic *ml'ak*, 'messenger,' and *t'dt*, 'embassy,' are used in
synonymous parallelism in the following account.

> Afterwards the messengers of Yamm,/
> the embassy of judge Nahar, arrived;/
> they verily fell down at the feet of El,/
> verily bowed down (in) full
> convocation; / (then) rising they . . .
> and repeated their report.[36]

A message in the mythological text *Krt* (KRT A): 124-137
reads:

> Then he will send two messengers unto
> thee, Unto Keret, to the camp:
> "Message of King Pabel:--Take silver
> and yellow-glittering gold; Friendship
> by covenant and vassalage forever;

One-third of the chariot-steeds In the
stable of a handmaid's son. Take it,
Keret, in peace, in peace. And flee, O
king from my house; withdraw, O
Keret, from my court. Vex not Udum
the Great, Even Udum the Grand.
Udum is a gift of El, Even a present of
the Father of Man."[37]

King Keret (Kirtu) had arrived at the realm of King Pabel in order to
personally press the suit of marriage for Princess *Hry*. Pabel had sent
the above message in order to persuade Kirtu into accepting his peace
offerings and to depart. He answered Pabel's with a message of
refusal.

Several Ugaritic letter-messages have been preserved.
Numbers 85 and 95 are well-preserved, while number 54 contains
numerous gaps. Text 95 reads:

To my mother, our lady, speak. "The
message of Tlmyn and 'Ahatmalk, thy
slaves: "At the feet of our lady, from
afar, we bow down. May the gods guard
(and) preserve thee. Lo with us all is
very well; even I am at ease. (As to)
whatever the welfare there with our
lady, mayest thou send back word to
thy slaves."[38]

It is not farfetched to assume that the messenger who delivered this
message actually bowed down while delivering it.

5. Palestine

Several well-preserved messages in letter form have come to
light by way of archaeological excavations.

a. Arad

Three of the ostraca discovered at Arad contain messages.
Two of these messages were sent to one Eliashib, while a Nahum
received the third. The first was "Perhaps written," says Pritchard, "by
the secretary of a high official in Jerusalem to the military commander
of the southern mountain district."[39] The first message to Eliashib
reads:

> To my lord Eliashib: May Yahweh
> grant thy welfare! And (as) of now,
> give Shemariah half an aroura (of
> ground) and to Kerosi give a quarter
> aroura and to the sanctuary give what
> thou didst recommend to me. As for
> Shallum, he shall stay at the temple of
> Yahweh.[40]

Of the second message Pritchard says that it: "is an official
memorandum, so that the salutations is missing. The apparent
occasion for it is that the local mercenaries had been complaining
about the food and drink supplied to them."[41] Thus one reads:

> To Eliashib--and (as) of now: Give the
> Kittiyim three baths of wine and write
> the exact date. And from what is left of
> the old wheat grind up one (kor) of
> wheat to make bread for them. Serve
> the wine in punch bowls.[42]

The third message is also a memorandum.

> To Nahum, and (as) of now: Go to the
> house of Eliashib, son of Oshiyau, and
> get from him one (bath) of oil, and
> send it to me in haste, sealing it with
> my seal. On the 24th of the month
> Nahum delivered the oil into the hand
> of the Kitti.[43]

b. Lachish

The Lachish Letters are a group of twenty-one ostraca
discovered in 1935 and 1938. Many of them date from ca. 589/8 BCE.
One is dated exactly in the ninth year of the reign of King Zedekiah of
Jerusalem. Concerning the important Lachish ostraca, the scribe
began to write the message on the smooth outerside of the sherd.
When more space was needed, however, the writer resorted to using
the rough inner surface also.[44]

The Lachish Letters are also to be treated as messages. These
messages tell of events during the final days of Judah under the
onslaught of Nebuchadnezzar II. In addition, the third Lachish Letter
contains both the words 'sent' and 'cause my lord to hear tidings of
peace,' i.e., specific messenger vocabulary. It is this letter which will
serve as the example of the Lachish message.

> Thy servant Hoshaiah hath sent to
> inform my lord Yoash: May Yahweh
> cause my lord to hear tidings of peace.
> And now thou hast sent a letter, but my
> lord did not enlighten thy servant
> concerning the letter which thou didst

send to thy servant yesterday evening, though the heart of thy servant hath been sick since thou didst write to thy servant. And as for what my lord said, "Dost thou not understand?--call a scribe.", as Yahweh liveth no one hath ever undertaken to call a scribe for me; and as for any scribe who might have come to me, truly I did not call him nor would I give anything at all for him. And it hath been reported to thy servant, saying, "The commander of the host, Coniah son of Elnathan, hath come in order to go into Egypt; and unto Hodoviah son of Abijah and his men hath he sent to obtain . . . from him." And as for the letter of Tobiah, servant of the king, which came to Shallum, son of Jaddua through the prophet, saying, "Beware." thy servant hath sent it to my lord.[45]

c. *Mesad Hashavyahu*

An ostracon containing fourteen lines of Hebrew written in ink and dating from the seventh century BCE was discovered one mile south of *Minet Rubin* at *Mesad Hashavyahu*. It is commonly referred to as the Letter of *Yavney-Yam*.[46] J. Naveh's line for line translation reads:

1. Let my lord the governor
   hear
2. the word of his servant.
   Thy servant

3. (behold) thy servant was
   reaping in *Ra*
4. *sar-asam*, and thy servant
   reaped
5. and finished; and I
   gathered in about a
   ynm before my
6. rest. When thy [se]rvant
   had fin[ished] his
   reaping, he gath-
7. ered in about a *ynm*, and
   there came Hashabaihu
   the son of Shoa-
8. i, and took thy servant's
   garment. After I had
   finished
9. my reaping, that is a *ynm*,
   did he take thy
   servant's garment.
10. And all my brethren will
    witness on my behalf,
    they who reap with me
    in the heat
11. [of the sun], my brethren
    will witness on my
    behalf 'verily', I am
    free of gu-
12. [ilt. Restore] my garment.
    And I will pay the
    governor in full to rest-
13. [ore my garment] ------(?)
14. ------thy [se]rvant, and be
    not helpless to save.
15. ------------------------47

d. Samaria

From the third quarter of the eighth century BCE comes an ostracon from Samaria. It is an order for barley from Samaria and is known as the Barley Letter. The translation is tentative.

> Baruch (son of) Shallum . . . O Baruch
> pay attention and give (?) to . . . son of
> Yimnah (Imnah) barley (to the amount
> of) two (or three?) measures.[48]

6. Egypt

Evidence of Egyptian messages is as plentiful as was the evidence of Egyptian messengers.

a. Tell el-Amarna

The Tell el-Amarna Letters provide another view of the ANE message. Messengers were particularly active during this period (ca. 1417-1362 BCE); a period already known for the great literary output of both Egypt and her neighbors. From these messages one also gains access to the known political situation that existed in Canaan in the fourteenth century--Egypt was on the decline--as well as a glimpse of what life was like in the independent city-states of the western Levant. What is generally overlooked is the oral nature of these famous documents. In the Letter from Lab'ayu one reads: "To the king my lord, say: Thus Lab'ayu, thy servant . . ."[49] This is an example of what is commonly referred to as the commissioning of a messenger, followed by a form of the messenger formula. These are followed by the text to be delivered orally, for the message is to be said. The example provides evidence of the oral and written traditions side by side.

Likewise, the Letter from 'Abdu-Heba (Abdi-Heba) begins the exact same way. This letter contains one of the first-known references outside the Hebrew Scriptures to Jerusalem. This letter/message in particular contains the first recorded reference outside of the Hebrew Scriptures to Bethlehem (but it does not specify whether this reference is to Bethlehem of Galilee or Bethlehem of Judah) in the name *Bit-Lahmi*; spoken for the first time by messengers.[50]

A Tell el-Amarna letter sent to Amenhotep IV by Ashur-uballit--Number 28,179 in the National Egyptian Museum at Cairo-- tells how Ashur-nadin-akhe, the father of Ashur-uballit, established favorable diplomatic relations with the king of Egypt, from whom he had once received a gift of gold.[51] In the same letter Ashur-nadin-akhe:

> excuses himself for not having dismissed the Egyptian envoys sooner, by saying that had he done so they would probably have been slain by some nomad tribe. This passage shows that the kings of Assyria and Egypt at this period were in the habit of sending envoys to each other's court.[52]

An urgent message from Birdiya, prince of Megiddo reads:

> To the king, my lord, and my sun-god, say: Thus Birdiya, the faithful servant of the king. At the two feet of the king, my lord, and my sun-god, seven and seven times I fall. Let the king know that ever since the archers returned (to Egypt?), Lab'ayu has carried on hostilities against me, and we are not able to go outside the gate in the presence of Lab'ayu, since he learned that thou hast not given archers; and

now his face is set to take Megiddo, but
let the king protect his city, lest
Lab'ayu seize it. Verily, the city is
destroyed by death from pestilence and
disease. Let the king give one hundred
garrison troops to guard the city lest
Lab'ayu seize it. Verily, there is no
other purpose in Lab'ayu. He seeks to
destroy Megiddo.[53]

The fact that this letter was discovered in Egypt indicates that the
messenger was successful in delivering it. If Birdiya is not inflating this
message when he writes that " . . . *we are not able to go outside the
gate* . . .", then it shows the danger to the messenger involved, for he
apparently had to run a blockade which existed as a result of the city
being under siege.

b. Aramaic Papyri

The historian John Bright intimates that there was quite a bit
of messenger activity during the period of Persian rule of the ANE.
Writing on the enlightened rule of Cyrus the Great he writes:

Though he and his successors kept firm
control   through   a   complex
bureaucracy--most of the high officials
of which were Persians or Medes--
through their army, and through an
efficient system of communications
their rule was not harsh.[54]

Adding validity to Bright's statement about the communication
system and its efficiency is the following observation.

Tattenai, satrap of Abar-nahara (the
Trans-Euphrates satrapy, which
included Syria-Palestine) received
reports that possible seditious activity
was transpiring at Jerusalem attending
the rebuilding of the temple and the
messianic role of Zerubbabel was
supposed to play. He questioned the
matters for himself, was told that
Cyrus' edict had given them permission
to begin work and wrote to Darius for
confirmation. This he received.[55]

Among the messages of the Persian period which include the
Elephantine papyri of the fifth century is a letter from one Arsames,
Persian satrap of Egypt and probably of Babylonia and Trans-
Euphrates. It was sent to the officer Nakt-Hor the Comptroller and his
colleagues the accountants in Egypt, and reads:

Now, Petosiri (as he is called), a
forester, a servant of mine, has written
to me as follows: "In the matter of my
father Pamun (as he[was called). when]
(2) the rebellion occurred in Egypt, in
the course of it my father the said
Pamun (as he was called) pe[rished]
and the farm occupied by him,
measuring a seed requirement of 30
ardabs, was abandoned; for our staff
perished to a man. [Therefore, let them
assign] (3) the farm of my father
Pamun to me. Take thought on my
behalf: let me occupy."[56]

Arsames commanded that Petosiri be awarded the land.

c. Egyptian Papyri

A papyrus entitled How Tahuti took the Town of Joppa dates from the time of the Twentieth Dynasty. The events recounted therein, however, belong to the time of Thutmosis (Thotmes) III. Tahuti was one of Thutmosis III's honored knights; a veteran of over fifteen campaigns in Syria. He was given the assignment of capturing the sheikh of the town of Joppa who had rebelled against the Egyptian king. Troops accompanied him on this assignment. He desired, however, no fighting to accomplish his mission. Moreover, he let the word be spread that he wanted to become a part of the rebel's staff. To make his claim more appealing, word was spread that he had taken the leading-staff of Thutmosis III; the staff was reputed to have had magical powers. After effecting his plan to capture the rebel:

> Then he went out and spake to the charioteer of the foe of Joppa: 'Thy master is fallen! Now, therefore, go, call to his wife and say, 'Rejoice, for Sutekh has delivered into our hands Tahuti, with his wife and his children."[57]

The charioteer--now a commissioned messenger--went to Joppa, to the rebel's wife, and delivered the message. Believing that the contents of the message were true, Tahuti's forces were allowed to enter the gates of Joppa, after which they promptly took possession of the city. The papyrus continues:

> When the army of Pharaoh (life! health! strength!) had taken possession

of the town, Tahuti took his ease, and
sent a message to Egypt, to the king
Menkheperra (life! health! strength!),
his master to say, 'Rejoice! Amen, thy
father, hath given thee the foe in
Joppa, with all his subjects, and also his
town. Let troops come to take them
into captivity, that thou mayest fill the
house of thy father, Amen, king of the
gods, with slaves and servants who may
be under thy two feet for ever and
ever![58]

A later papyrus (ca. 119 BCE) contains a message to a superior
concerning an assault on a minor official.

To Horus, greeting, On the first of the
current month at about the eleventh
hour a disturbance occurred in the
village, and on running out we found a
crowd of the villagers who had come to
the assistance of Polemon, who is
performing the duties of overseer of
the village. When we inquired into the
matter they informed us that
Apollodorus and his son Maron had
assaulted Polemon; that Apollodorus
had escaped, but Maron had appeared
before Ptolemaeus the king's cousin
and Strategos on the 1st. We thought it
well to notify the matter for your
information. Good-bye. The 3rd year,
Mesore 2.[59]

A letter to the viceroy of Kush by Ramses XII dispatches the viceroy to ensure the completion of the building of a shrine; a completion long overdue:

> "Go forth [--after] the major-domo, the butler of the Pharaoh, L.P.H., and cause him to proceed with the business of Pharaoh, L.P.H., his lord, which he was sent to do, in the southern region. When the *writing* of Pharaoh, thy lord, reaches thee, thou shalt join thyself to him, to cause that he do the business of Pharaoh, L.P.H., his lord, whereon he was sent."[60]

d. Inscriptions

A message from the time of Thutmosis II found on the Assuan Inscription announces a rebellion.

> One came to inform his majesty as follows: Kush has begun to rebel, those who are under the dominion of the Lord of the Two Lands purpose hostility, beginning to smite him. The inhabitants of Egypt are about to bring away the cattle behind this fortress which thy father built in his campaigns, the King of Upper and Lower Egypt, Okheperkere (Thutmose I), living forever, in order to repulse the rebellious barbarians, the Nubian Troglodytes of Khenthennofer, for those who are there on the north of the

wretched Kush ___ ___ ___ with the
two Nubian Troglodytes among the
children of the chief of the wretched
Kush who ___ before the Lord of the
Two Lands ___ ___. "His majesty was
furious thereat like a panther, when he
heard it. Said his majesty, "I swear, as
He loves me, as my father, lord of
gods, Amon, lord of Thebes, favors me,
I will not let live anyone among their
males ___ among them."[61]

A royal message from King Amenhotep III (Eighteenth
Dynasty) promoted one Nebnefer. The message is recorded on the
back of a statue which was probably brought back by Nebnefer.[62]

On this day, behold [his majesty was in
the temple] of Ptah-South-of-His-Wall,
lord   of   Life-of-the-Two-Lands.
Message, concerning which the king's-
scribe, the steward, Khampet, came to
the chief treasurer, the High Priest of
Amon, [Meriptah] --------from the
Pharaoh, L.P.H., (saying): "Let the
chief measurer of the storehouse of the
divine offerings be brought--before his
fathers; ------------Hui being put into
his place in the storehouse of divine
offerings of Amon."[63]

From the Piankhi (Twenty-Third Dynasty) Stela one reads:

<u>One came to say to his majesty</u>: "A chief of the West, the great prince in Neter, Tefnakhte is in the nome of ----- , in the nome of Xois, in Hapi, in --- in Ayan, in Pernub, and in Memphis. He has seized the whole West from the backlands to Ithtowe, coming southward with a numerous army, while the Two Lands are united behind him, and the princes and rulers of walled towns are as dogs at his heels. No stronghold has closed [its door in] the nomes of the South . . . He turned to the East, they opened to him likewise . . . Behold, [he] besieges Heracleopolis, he has completely invested it, not letting the goers-in go in, fighting every day. He measured it off in its whole circuit, every prince knows his wall; he stations every man of the princes and rulers of walled towns over his (respective) portion."[64]

The Tell el-Amarna messages are here recalled and how they were received by the pharaohs Amenhotep III and IV when one reads:

Then [his majesty] <u>heard</u> [the message] with courageous heart, laughing, and joyous of heart . . . These princes and commanders of the army who were in their cities sent to his majesty daily, saying: "Wilt thou be silent, even to forgetting the Southland, the nomes of the [court]? While Tefnakhte advances

his conquest and finds none to repel his
arm."[65]

But unlike the pharaohs of the Amarna Period, Piankhi eventually
responds to the situation, for

> Then his majesty <u>sent</u> to the princes
> and commanders of the army who were
> in Egypt: . . . every commander of his
> majesty who was in Egypt (saying):
> "Hasten into battle line, engage in
> battle, surround _____ capture its
> people, its cattle, its ships upon the
> river. Let not the peasants go forth to
> the field, let not not the plowmen plow,
> beset the frontier of the Hare nome,
> fight against it daily." Then they did
> so.[66]

Once Piankhi began returning the battle to his old foe,
Tefnakhte, he repeatedly won back his territory. After Piankhi's
victory at Mesed, Tefnakhte decided to capitulate. The following
serves as the final example of my message evidence.

> Then the chief of Me, Tefnakhte, <u>heard</u>
> of it and <u>caused a messenger to come</u>
> <u>to the place</u> where his majesty was,
> with flattery, <u>saying</u>: "Be thou
> appeased! I have not beheld thy face
> for shame; I cannot stand before thy
> flame, I tremble at thy might. . .For
> verily I am a wretched man. Thou
> shouldst not smite me according to the

measure of the crime; weighing with the balances, knowing with the kidet-weights . . . Cleanse (thy) servant of his fault, let my possessions be received into the Treasury, of gold and every costly stone, and the best of the horses, even payment for everything. Send to me a <u>messenger</u> quickly, that he may expel fear from my heart. Let me go forth before him to the temple, that I may cleanse myself with a divine oath."[67]

7. Analytical Summary

My purpose was to examine the ANE message evidence as it had been preserved in letter form, as well as those forms which occurred in literary texts--mythological and historical--and preserved on stone, papyrus, sherds, and clay tablets. Many of these letter/messages had been preserved in various archives, but one could not fail to notice that they still bore the stamp of having been delivered orally. The opening formula was the most important clue in determining whether a given message had been--or had been intended to be--delivered orally.

Many of the messages began with a legitimizing formula, with the actual message following thereupon. Thus, one reads, "To my Lord say: Thus XX, thy servant" (Mari); "Speak to my Lord" (Mari); "Message of the king to XX" (Assyria): "Thus hath XX spoken" (Hatti); "To my lord XX: and as of now" (Palestine). Such messages were fairly easy to locate because of these recognizeable formulae. Requiring greater scrutiny to be detected were messages which had been couched in various narratives, and which were not preceded by the above-mentioned formulae. Note for example "While yet I remained in . . ., one brought me tidings, saying:" (Assyria); "But the king of the land of Azzi wrote back to me . . ." (Hatti); "I sent a letter to Anniyas, and wrote to him . . ." (Hatti); "May Yahweh cause my lord to hear tidings of peace" (Lachish); "Now, therefore, go, call to his wife and say . . ." (Egyptian Papyri); "To Horus, greeting" (Egyptian Papyri); "One came to inform his majesty as follows:" (Egyptian Inscriptions); and "One came to say to his majesty:" (Egyptian Inscriptions).

Rarely was the study blessed with the indisputable markers "Message of the king to Sin-tabni-usur: (Assyria); "Tahuti took his ease and sent a message to Egypt," (Egyptian Papyri); or "Then his majesty heard the message . . ." (Egyptian Inscriptions).

The contents of these messages reflected numerous concerns. A Mari subordinate reported to his lord that he had presided over a covenant-making ceremony, while another informed his lord about suspicious signal-fires used by a group of Benjaminites in the district of Terqa. The most unusual was a message sent by King Zimri-Lim of Mari to a deity! The Babylonian King Hammurabi sent a message to one of his local administrators instructing him to have the canal in his area scoured, while Ashurbanipal, king of Assyria assured a loyal subject that his life was in no danger from him, although he (the subject) had been slandered before him. An Egyptian queen, recently widowed, sent a message to the powerful Hittite King Suppiluliumas requesting that one of his many sons be sent to replace her deceased husband. Hittite kings also used the message to goad their enemies into open hostilities. And when a foe of Pharaoh Piankhi was nearing total defeat, he sent a message which was carefully worded and intended to flatter the pharaoh to the point that when defeat came his life would be spared.

All of these messages have in common the fact that they extended the sender's power and will temporally and geographically. In the sender's name someone was moved to take action which either maintained or added to their power. Receipt of a message was the catalyst which was added to the critical mass of that immediate existential situation, and which caused the status quo to become altered as if the sender was there actually bringing it about, or at least attempting to do so.

These messages lent to the historical senders and recipients a sort of humanness (i.e., they appear as credible humans to us the readers), a quality generally lacking when one reads normally of historical personages. When one attempts to recreate the immediate history of the situation contained in the letters, the senders and recipients challenge us as three-dimensional persons, not literary-historical characters. Many of the letter/messages were intended to be private communiques. Thus, the conscious editing process which takes place when a letter is subject to public scrutiny is noticeably absent from the evidence, and lends greater credibility to it.

Taken as a whole, these messages fill in numerous *lacunae* in the knowledge of the chronology of the ANE by providing a most personal vantage point from which to observe some of the more intimate aspects and details of history and history-causing/making events. In addition, access was gained into the personal lives of many people who held the same concerns as we moderns. The message as the evidence has depicted it demonstrated that humankind has not changed drastically in its essential concerns in almost five thousand years. The written messages, mainly in the form of letters, still have the power to bring before the reader the loves and hates, the fears and hopes of humans who though now only dust and ashes, once were animated by the blood which flowed passionately through their veins.

CHAPTER III

The Messenger and Message in the Hebrew Scriptures
A Taxonomic Study of the Biblical Evidence

A. PURPOSE

The purpose of this chapter is to examine the messenger and message as they appear in selected narrative material of the Hebrew Scriptures. These narratives will be subjected to the same type of analysis as that in the preceding chapters in order to ascertain whether the messengers of the Hebrew Scriptures truly share all of the characteristics of their overall ANE counterparts. The evidence will contribute much to a discussion of whether these narratives are reasonably reliable (and to what extent!) as ANE literature which can be mined to shed light on ANE history. Likewise, it is desirable to ascertain whether the messages of the HS messenger share all of the characteristics of the ANE counterpart as laid out by the evidence contained in the preceding chapters. Separate sections in the present chapter devoted to first the study of the messenger and then the message are deemed unnecessary. The preceding chapters have established their distinction and respective characteristics quite clearly. The present purpose, therefore, is much better served by a study of the messenger and message taxonomically, for then one sees more clearly how ubiquitous and active they were in the life of "Israel."

I purpose herein to study only the human messengers, and the messages delivered by them. Further, I shall investigate the messengers of the so-called Hexateuch, Judges, the Samuel books, Kings, Chronicles, and Nehemiah only. That is, those books other than the prophetic *corpus* and the Writings which could be said loosely to contain historical accounts since they are imbedded in historical narrative. Again, this study makes no claim to being exhaustive. It does provide more than adequate study of the messenger and messages produced by (and held to be important to) the framers of the Hebrew Scriptures.

B. THE MESSENGER AND MESSAGE

The evidence for messenger activity in the Hebrew Scriptures is prodigious. The word messenger within the context of scriptural passages is enumerated by R. Young in <u>Analytical Concordance to the Bible</u>,[1] and Nelson's <u>Complete Concordance of the Revised Standard Version</u>.[2] Other occurrences of the word are found through merely a random reading of the Hebrew Scriptures themselves. Expressions such as 'tidings,' 'sent,' 'dispatch,' 'cause to go before,' 'tell,' and 'announce' are reliable indicators of the presence of messenger activity in a given text which has not been cited by either of the above-mentioned concordances.

What one naturally misses by employing either of the concordances is the <u>Hebrew</u> expression which English-language concordances translate as messenger, for it is not always the same word. Therefore, the most reliable source for assistance is the <u>Veteris Testamenti Concordantiae: Hebraicae Atque Chaldaicae</u> by Solomon Mandelkern.[3] Thus, where 'messenger' appears in Young or Nelson, Mandelkern correctly lists such words as *ml'ak* (messenger); *'bd* (servant); *rkb ssym/rkb hss* (horseman); *hmgd* (the informer/informant); and *mrglym* (spies). This does not exhaust the possible Hebrew words which could be rendered 'messenger,' but these are the Hebrew words which occur in the following texts.

There is a third group of expressions which has given rise to some heated and often lively comparative philological debate. The expressions are all Hebrew and are believed by some scholars to also be rendered into English as 'messenger,' 'envoy,' or 'herald.' They will be discussed along with the above Hebrew expressions. Thus, numerous types of messenger activity, signalled by numerous Hebrew and English expressions--some obvious and some not so obvious--are present within the Hebrew Scriptures. This chapter brings them together for analysis and explication.

Preliminary study indicates that from an editorial point of view, an absence of messengers in all of their various forms and roles would have made the Hebrew Scriptures a most difficult anthology to construct. "Is it possible to omit messengers wherever they appear therein and still have Hebrew Scriptures which are intelligible?" is a question which should be kept in mind.

1. *ml'k*

The Hebrew word *ml'k* (pronounced mal-ach [as in German Bach]) is the most common one to be rendered by English 'messenger.' When the occurrences of *ml'k*, gleaned from a study of the historical narrative material, are closely scrutinized, a taxonomic, as opposed to a chronological, exposition of these occurrences enables their appearance to be exploited to maximum benefit.

Characteristics of the Messenger and Message

1) Complete and Incomplete Messenger Activity: The Broken and Full Messages

Genesis 32:3-6 contains an account of Jacob sending messengers to Esau to make contact. The entire episode (32:1-21) is located at the end of the Jacob cycle of texts. An encounter with Esau after many years of separation is imminent; the reader is drawn to share Jacob's anxiety. From a literary-critical viewpoint it is possible that the messages are used here as a literary "bridge" the purpose of which is to connect two separate stories about Jacob. The text reads:

> And Jacob sent messengers before him
> to Esau his brother in the land of Seir,
> the country of Edom, instructing them,
> "Thus you shall say to my lord Esau:
> Thus says your servant Jacob, 'I have
> sojourned with Laban and stayed until
> now: and I have oxen, asses, flocks,
> menservants and maidservants; and I
> have sent to tell my lord, in order that I

> may find favor in your sight.' "And the
> messengers returned to Jacob, saying,
> "We came to your brother Esau, and he
> is coming to meet you, and four
> hundred men are with him." (Gen.
> 32:3-6)

The above literary-critical observation having been made, in light of
the ANE messengers and messages both Jacob's sending forth of
messengers (specifically harbingers) to announce his approach after a
long period of time, and the contents of the message, are quite
credible. One notices, too, that Jacob commissioned his messengers in
the same manner that ANE messengers were commissioned. The
messengers completed their assigned task(s) and returned to the
sender (Jacob), and reported. Here the messengers carried a simple
message, but brought no reply. This is an example of incomplete
messenger activity. By complete messenger activity is meant a
situation wherein all of the steps of the communication chain are
present, that is (1) the commissioning, (2) the sending forth, (3) the
messenger formula, (4) the delivery, (5) the return, and (6) the reply.
Likewise, a broken message has the messenger formula, or legitimizing
device missing from the example, while a full message contains the
legitimizing device also. Examples of full messages are seen in 2 Kings
9:17-19 and in 2 Kings 18:13-18. An example of full messenger activity
is contained in 1 Samuel 25:1-13.

2) 1 Samuel 25:1-13: An Example of Complete Messenger Activity

1 Samuel 25:1-13 is a fine example of the commissioning of a
messenger, the stating of a message, how some distance separates the
sender from the intended recipient, the waiting for the reply, the
delivery of the reply to the one who had originally commissioned the
messenger, and finally, the action which was taken upon the
messenger's return. The example involves David's attempted extortion
of Nabal of Carmel. Several messengers carry a message from David to
Nabal. Although they are not specifically called messengers in the

account of their being commissioned, one finds that in what follows they are understood to have been messengers. Naboth's reply was not welcomed by David:

> But one of the young men told Abigail, Nabal's wife, "Behold, David sent messengers out of the wilderness to salute our master; and he railed against them. (1 Sam. 25:14)

The young man's statement is basically a summary of the longer message and reply contained in the preceding verses.

3) The Message To One Of Equal Standing

There is a type of messenger speech which operates with more than the legitimizing formula "Thus says NN." It is important for an understanding of a similar form of prophetic speech. It is a message to one of equal standing. At Numbers 22 "Israel" is encamped in the plains of Moab. Moab was in great dread after seeing what Israel had done to the Amorites.

> So Balak the son of Sippur, who was king of Moab at that time, sent messengers to Balaam the son of Beor at Pethor, which is near the River, in the land of Amaw to call him,,saying, "Behold, a people has come out of Egypt: They cover the face of the earth, and they are dwelling opposite me. Come, curse this people for me, since they are too mighty for me; perhaps I shall be able to defeat them and drive them from the land; for I

know that he whom you bless is blessed
and he whom you curse is cursed."
                                        (Num. 22:4c-6)

The messengers were high-ranking men; elders of Moab and elders of Midian who even carried with them money for the payment of Balaam's divination services. According to Klaus Koch, this message has the following characteristics.

> 1. It is highly formal in that it calls for *parallelismus membrorum.*

> 2. It contains two imperatives which are understood to authorize the message.[4]

> 3. There is a long section which preceded the message's core (vs. 6) and indicates the present situation which needs to be remedied immediately. And finally:

> 4. After the message has been delivered there is a concluding characterization wherein the abilities of the recipient of the message are extolled or disparaged.[5]

Other examples of this type of message are seen in Genesis 45:9ff.; 1 Kings 20:5ff.; and 2 Kings 14:9ff.

Numbers 22:15ff. continues the above account. This time messengers are not specifically stated, but it is obvious from the context that messengers are involved. Again, as in Numbers 22:5ff., the messengers are high-ranking men.

> Once again Balak <u>sent</u> princes, more in
> number and more honorable than they.
> And they came to Balaam and said to
> him, "Thus says Balak the son of
> Sippor: 'Let nothing hinder you from
> coming to me; for I will surely do you
> great honor, and whatever you say to
> me I will do; come, curse this people
> for me."
>
> (Num. 22:15-17)

4)   Official Speech Between Superior and Subordinate: The
Commissioning of a Messenger

2 Kings 1ff. affords an opportunity to discuss the official
speech between those of different standing, and the messenger
formula. Ahaziah the son of King Ahab of Judah:

> Fell through the lattice in his upper
> chamber in Samaria, and lay sick; so he
> sent messengers telling them, "<u>Go,
> inquire</u> of Baalzebub, the god of
> Ekron, whether I shall recover from
> this sickness."
>
> (2 Kg. 1: 1-2)

The messenger would have received far greater instructions which
might have included even the taking of gifts (as Balak's messengers
had done) to the priests and/or cult prophets at Ekron.[6]
    Form-critically, the commissioning of a messenger began with
an imperative, 'Go,' which was followed by a second, instructing
imperative, 'inquire.' Added to these two imperatives were the
indication of a place to go and the party with whom they should speak

there. Says Koch, these "are the characteristics of many speeches by a man of high station to a servant whom he is entrusting with a duty."[7] This is one of several forms in which a messenger was commissioned (cf. Gen. 45:9; 2 Kg. 18:19) especially if he was of lower rank. Other examples of commissionings which began with two imperatives are found at 2 Kg. 5:10 ("And Elisha sent a messenger to him, saying, "Go and wash in the Jordan seven times . . ."); 1 Kg. 17:13 ("Yet the Lord warned Israel and Judah by every prophet and every seer saying, "Turn from your evil ways and keep my commandments and statutes, . . ."); 2 Kg. 4:3 ("Then he said, "Go outside and borrow vessels of all your neighbors, . . ."); and 2 Kg. 9:17 ("And Joram said, "Take a horseman (messenger), and send to meet them, . . .").[8]

5) A Prophet's Messenger And A Message Which Overthrows A Dynasty: The Use Of The Imperative

The Israelite King Joram was wounded in a pitched battle with the Syrians over Ramoth-gilead. Ahaziah, king of Judah, came to visit Joram in Jezreel where the Israelite was convalescing (2 Kg. 8:28-29).

> Then Elisha the prophet called one of the sons of the prophets and said to him, "Gird up your loins, and take this flask of oil in your hand, and go to Ramoth-gilead. And when you arrive, look there for Jehu the son of Jehoshaphat, son of Nimshi; and go in and bid him rise from among his fellows, and lead him to an inner chamber. Then take the flask of oil, and pour it on his head, and say, "Thus says the Lord, I anoint you king over Israel." And when he came, behold, the commanders of the army were in

council; and he said,"I have an *errand*
to you, O commander."

(2 Kg. 9:1-5)

The prophet's message is slightly longer than the one Elisha
commissioned him to deliver. To this longer version is added a literary
elaboration which extends to verse 10. Nevertheless, here are 1) a good
example of a prophet commissioning a subordinate prophet as a
messenger, as evidenced by the multiple use of the (underlined)
imperatives; 2) the message preceded by the messenger formula; 3) the
recipient; and 4) the delivery. This messenger also performed the
function of anointing the king-designate. "I have an errand to you" may
also be viewed as part of a messenger's announcement, especially in
cases where there was no message to be delivered *verbatim*.

Now the watchman was standing on the
tower in Jezreel; and he spied the
company of Jehu as he came, and said,
"I see a company." And Joram said,
"<u>Take</u> a horseman (messenger) and
<u>send</u> to meet them, and <u>let him say</u>, "Is
it peace?" So a man on horseback went
to meet him, (as a messenger and
errand-person) and said, "Thus says
the king, "Is it peace?" And Jehu said,
"What have you got to do with peace?
Turn around and ride behind me." And
the watchman reported, saying, "The
<u>messenger</u> reached them, but he is not
coming back." Then he <u>sent</u> out a
second horseman, who came to them
and said, "Thus the king has said, "Is it
peace?"

(2 Kg. 9:17-19)

This messenger also remained with Jehu. Thus messengers were present at a crucial point in Israel's political history. The retention of the king's messengers by Jehu, and his refusal to return a reply by them was (as we have seen before) an obvious affront to the king's person. The prophet's message rang loudly in Jehu's ears; he was resolute, on a course of action from which there would be no turning back. He killed Joram and had Ahaziah killed also. Upon entering Jezreel he had the queen mother, Jezebel, thrown from an upper floor to her death.

6) The Messenger Formula

A messenger usually began the delivery of a message with "Thus says," followed by the sender's name, e.g. "Thus says XX:". As seen in Chapter II, the purpose of this formula was to legitimize the speaker and to compel the hearer to accept the message which followed as indeed coming from the sender of the message.[9] This messenger formula has been replaced by the official stamp on written correspondence nowadays, or by the official seal of times past (e.g. 1 Kg. 21:8). In ancient times, however, this formula was found still on written documents, for although written, they were still being delivered orally.

7) The Purpose Of The Message

a. The Message To A Subordinate

If the message was intended for those in a subordinate position to the sender, it was punctuated with imperatives. Judges 11:12 and 2 Kings 18:19 contain examples wherein the message consists of a question in reproach or scorn. A subordinate standing before the king, for instance, would have been addressed in this manner, thus the message extended the person and word of the sender. This, I maintain, was the main purpose of the ANE messenger and message. "The sender of a message," Koch summarizes, "is brought as near to the recipient of it, and speaks to him in just the same tone, as if the two were face to face."[10] It was a form of being in two places at once. The messenger must have also attempted to emulate this original tone (probably accompanied also by emulated gesticulations) when he or she delivered the oral message.

b. Passages Through Territories: The Message To Affect Passage

Shortly following the incident at the waters of Meriba (Num. 20:14), Moses desired to pass through Edom with his host.

> Moses sent messengers from Kadesh to the king of Edom, "Thus says your brother Israel: you know all the adversity that has befallen us . . . and when we cried to the Lord, he heard our voice, and sent a messenger and brought us forth out of Egypt; and here we are in Kadesh, a city on the edge of your territory. Now let us pass through your land . . ."
>
> (Num. 20:14-17)

The king of Edom refused to allow the Moses host to pass through his country; he threatened to confront them with military force if they attempted to do so. Perhaps this account contains a reliable example of a typical message from one group who desired to cross the territorial boundaries of another. I call it, therefore, the <u>message to affect passage</u>.

Israel was also refused entry into Arad; they destroyed it. They wandered subsequently to Mount Hor, to the Red Sea, to Oboth, to Iyeabarim, to Zered, to Arnon, to Beer, to Matanah, to Nahaliel, to Bamoth, to the valley region of Moab by the top of Pisgah which looked down upon the desert (Num. 21:1-20).

Then Israel sent messengers to Sihon,
king of the Amorites, saying, "Let me
pass through your land: we will not
turn aside into field or vineyard; we
will not drink the water of a well; we
will go the King's Highway (same as
Num. 20:14) until we have passed
through your territory."

(Num. 21:21-22)

Here, too, Israel was refused entry, defeated Sihon's forces, and
occupied the land of the Amorites. This message is much shorter than
the one of Numbers 20:14ff. Thus, this was probably a standard
message, while that of Numbers 20:14ff. was most probably an
elaboration. Both, however, are examples of the message to affect
passage.

Deuteronomy 2:26ff. is a parallel text to the text of Numbers
21:1-20. Only minimal changes are to be seen. Here I call attention to
the differences in detail.

Numbers 21:21-22   Deuteronomy 2:26-29

Then Israel sent
messengers to Sihon, king
of the Amorites, saying,
"Let me pass through the
land;

we will not turn aside
into field or vineyards;

we will not drink water
of a well;

So I sent messengers from the
wilderness of Kedemoth to Sihon the king of Heshbon, with
words of peace, saying, "Let
me pass through your land; I
will go only by the road, I
will turn aside neither to
the right nor to the left.
You shall sell me food for
money, that I may eat, and
give me water for money, that
I may drink; only let me pass
through on foot, as the sons
of Esau who live in Seir and

we will go the King's
Highway until we have
passed through your
territory."

the Moabites who live in Ar
did for me, until I go over
the Jordan into the land
which the Lord our God gives
us."

c. Spies And Spy Activity

1) The Messenger As Spy

At Jericho Israel marched around the walls in order to cause
them to fall. When Joshua deliberated the fate of the inhabitants of the
city after Israel gained entry, he stated:

> And the city and all that is within it
> shall be devoted to the Lord for
> destruction; only Rahab the harlot and
> all who are with her in her house shall
> live, because she hid the messengers
> that we sent.
>
> (Josh. 6:17)

Joshua 6:22 and 6:25 indicate that these messengers were spies. They
performed the specific function of harbingers; preparing the way for
the invasion of Jericho with inside help. Joshua 7:2ff. gives an example
of the commissioning of spy-messengers. David also commissioned a
spy-messenger to send or bring him messages concerning Absalom (2
Sam. 15:35-37).

2) The Commissioning Of A Spy: Establishing A Messenger Network

David and his supporters fled Jerusalem when Absalom's
revolt gathered strength. 2 Samuel 15:32-35 tells of David
commissioning a spy-messenger at Jerusalem after he had been forced
to flee. He told Hushai the Archite his spy-messenger:

> Are not Zadok and Abiathar the
> priests with you there? So whatever
> you hear from the king's house, tell it
> to Abiathar and Zadok the priests.
> Behold their two sons are with them
> there, Ahimaaz, Zadok's son, and
> Jonathan, Abiathar's son; and by them
> you shall send to me everything you
> hear."
>
> (2 Sam. 15:35-36)

Thus, through Hushai a spy-messenger network was set up which kept David informed of Absalom's moves.[11]

3) David's Envoys To Ammon

David consolidated his kingdom and set his house in order. He extended royal favor to Mephibosheth (Meribaal) son of Jonathan, son of Saul, thus paying in some way a debt to his erstwhile friend and companion, Jonathan. Then one reads:

> After this the king of the Ammonites
> died, and Hanun his son reigned in his
> stead. And David said, "I will deal
> loyally with Hanun the son of Nahash,
> as his father dealt loyally with me." So
> David sent by his servants to console
> him concerning his father. And David's
> servants came into the land of the
> Ammonites. But the princes of the
> Ammonites said to Hanun their lord,
> "Do you think, because David has sent
> comforters to you that he is honoring

your father? Has not David sent his
servants to you to <u>search the city</u> and to
<u>spy it out</u>, and to <u>overthrow</u> it?" So
Hanun took David's servants, and
shaved off half the beard of each, and
cut off their garments in the middle, at
their hips, and sent them away. When <u>it
was told</u> David, <u>he sent messengers</u> to
meet them, for the men were greatly
ashamed. And the king said, "Remain
at Jericho until your beards have
grown, and then return."

(2 Sam. 10:1-5)

This account yields much valuable information concerning the role of
the messenger. The mission of David's servants was to relay his
condolances to the heir of the throne of Ammon. From the way
Hanun's princes reacted, it can be inferred that the royal messengers
as envoys sometimes served as spies and usurpers. Such measures were
not beyond David's ambitions. That their suspicions were not the fruit
of overfertile imaginations, attention may be called to Joshua's spies at
Jericho.

Since the messenger-envoys were an extension of David's
person and power, the shaving off of half their beards and the cutting
off "their garments in the middle at the hips" represented a personal
affront and insult to David. One understands further that not only
were the envoys ashamed, David was also ashamed! Redress was
imperative. In an indirect way, therefore, the way that David's
messengers fared is the starting-point of the building of his petty
empire.

If one compares the results of what happened to David's
messengers with the account of the Egyptian Wenamon (*infra*
Chapter I), one immediately understands the weak position of Egypt
politically and militarily during his time. Wenamon had no powerful
lord to redress his having been insulted and abused. How an envoy-
messenger was treated by those to whom he was sent was usually a

reliable indicator of the view of the political and military status of that sending country by the host country. Hanun and his princes were bereft of accurate information before performing their deed. They paid for their mistake.

4) Reconnaissance-Messengers

Several lepers who usually sat at the entrance to the city of Samaria went to the camp of the Syrians who had besieged Samaria. They found the camp abandoned and proceeded to help themselves to food, drink, and various objects of wealth. Afterwards, they decided to inform someone in a position of authority. When the king was informed he became suspicious and decided to check out the matter:

> So they took the two mounted men, and the king sent them after the army of the Syrians, saying "Go and see." So they went after them as far as the Jordan; and lo; all the way was littered with garments and equipment which the Syrians had thrown away in their haste. And the messengers returned and told the king.
>
> (2 Kg. 7:14-15)

Here messengers were spies and reconnaissance persons as in Joshua 2:17. Note, too, the double imperative in the commissioning statement.

d. Military Matters

1) The Message To Goad Another Into Battle

Ben-hadad of Syria and his thirty-two king coalition besieged Samaria:

And he sent messengers into the city to Ahab King of Israel, and he said to him, "Thus says Ben-Hadad: 'Your silver and your gold are mine; your fairest children and wives are also mine.'" And the king of Israel answered, "As you say, my lord O king, I am yours, and all that I have." The messengers came again and said, "Thus says Ben-Hadad: 'I sent to you saying, "Deliver to me your silver and your gold, your wives and your children," nevertheless I will send my servants to you tomorrow about this time, and they shall search your house and the house of your servants, and lay hands on whatever pleases them, and take it away.' "So he said to the messengers of Benhadad, "Tell my lord the king, "All that you first demanded of your servant I will do; but this thing I cannot do.' "And the messengers departed and brought him word again. Ben-hadad sent to him and said, "The gods do so to me, and more also, if the dust of Samaria shall suffice for the handfuls for all the people who follow me." And the king of Israel answered, "Tell him, 'Let not him that girds on his armor boast himself as he that puts it off.' When Ben-hadad <u>heard</u> this message as he was drinking with the kings in the booths, he said to his men, "Take your positions." And they took their positions against the city.

(1 Kg. 20:2-12)

In this example messengers and errand-persons were again combined in the same person. Note that the messengers' duty was to carry threats back and forth until the decision was made to besiege the city. This, another example of the message of threat, is reminiscent of the messages sent by the Hittite kings (*infra* Chapter II) to goad their enemies into warfare.

2) The Message Of Threat

After Elijah's feats, performed on Mount Carmel, Ahab was both astounded and frightened.

> Ahab told Jezebel all that Elijah had done, and how he had slain all the prophets with the sword. Then Jezebel sent a messenger to Elijah, saying, "So may the gods do to me, and more also, if I do not make your life as the life of one of them by this time tomorrow."
>
> (1 Kg. 19:1-2)

This message frightened Elijah; he fled pragmatically to the Negev.

3) The Message Of Muster

Shortly after Gideon had received his new name, Jerubaal, (i.e., let Baal contend against him) for pulling down the altar of Baal in his town, the Midianites and Amalekites, and the peoples of the East came together, crossed the Jordan and encamped in the Jezreel valley. Gideon

> . . . sounded the trumpet, and the
> Abiezrites were called out to follow
> him. And he sent messengers
> throughout all Manasseh; and they too
> were called out to follow him. And he
> sent messengers to Asher, Zebulun,
> and Naphtali; and they went up to meet
> them.
>
> (Jud. 6:34b-35)

These messengers were used to call the participating tribes to engage in Yahweh War with the Midianite League.[12] Gideon and his army conducted psychological warfare against the Midianites. The figure 'one hundred men' of Judges 7:19 is intentionally played down (although the reader is told that Zebulun, Naphtali, and Asher were participating) in order to play up the belief that Yahweh was fighting the war. The Midianites fled.

> And Gideon sent messengers
> throughout all the hill country of
> Ephriam, saying, "Come down against
> them, as far as Beth-barach, and also
> the Jordan."
>
> (Jud. 7:24)

Messengers were employed to call out the participating groups of Israelites. This and the preceding example I designate the message of muster.

4) A Combined Message Of Threat And Muster

Messengers oftentimes played an important role in finding a judge or *nagid* for Israel. In the case of Saul son of Kish, Nahash the Gileadite besieged Jabesh-gilead, which attempted to negotiate a treaty with him to no avail. Moreover, Nahash made a condition so strong that the leaders of Jabesh had to see if from their people a champion would come forth and save them.

> The elders of Jabesh said to him (i.e., Nahash), "Give us seven days respite that we may send messengers through all the territory of Israel. Then, if there is no one to save us, we will give ourselves up to you." When the messengers came to Gibeah of Saul, they reported the matter in the ears of the people and all the people wept aloud. Now Saul was coming from the field behind the oxen, and Saul said, "What ails the people, that they are weeping?' So they told him the tidings of the men of Jabesh.
>
> (1 Sam. 11:3-5)

When Saul found out what had happened he became angry and took

> . . . a yoke of oxen, and cut them into pieces (sometimes messengers took objects as one reads here) and sent them throughout all the territory of Israel by the hand of messengers, saying, "Whoever does not come out after Saul and Samuel, so shall it be done to his oxen!"
>
> (1 Sam. 11:72)

They came mostly out of fear and dread at Saul's threat.

> And they said to the messengers who
> had come, "Thus shall you say to the
> men of Jabesh-gilead: 'Tomorrow, by
> the time the sun is hot, you shall have
> deliverance.' When the messengers
> came and told the men of Jabesh, they
> were glad.
>
> (1 Sam. 11:9)

Saul formed three companies of troops and defeated the Ammonites.

This passage is important for this study because it contains several elements of the ANE communication chain: 1) the sender (or the one who commissions the messenger); 2) the message; 3) the messenger, and 4) the recipients. The passage has also shown that messengers sometimes carried objects (here a symbolic object) with them which were designed to make more poignant the point of a message. Finally, note that 'message' and 'tidings' are used synonymously, thus clarifying communication terminology and signalling evidence for detecting messenger activity where no messengers are specifically mentioned.

5) The Message Of Military Strategy

Abimelech, son of Gideon, was made *nagid* by the Shechemites. One Ga'al the son of Ebed rose to oppose his leadership. Zebul the ruler of Shechem heard of this.

> And he sent messengers to Abimelech
> at Arumah, saying, "Behold, Ga'al the
> son of Ebed and his kinsmen have
> come to Shechem, and they are stirring
> up the city against you. Now, therefore,
> go by night, you and the men that are

> with you, and lie in wait in the fields.
> Then in the morning, as soon as the sun
> is up, rise early and rush upon the city;
> and when he and the men that are with
> him come out against you, you may do
> to them as occasion offers."
>
> (Jud. 9:31-33)

Receipt of this message led not only to the defeat of Ga'al's forces, but eventually to the destruction of Shechem as well (Jud. 9:45). The messengers carried a <u>message of military strategy</u> to Abimelech. As a result, Abimelech attempted "the Shechem experiment," an ill-fated and short-lived attempt at kingship during the period of the judges (i.e., the *shofetim* or chieftains).

6) The First Message Of Battle Progress

    Concerning David's plot against Uriah the Hittite and his campaign against Hanun,

> . . . Joab <u>sent</u> and told David all the
> <u>news</u> about the fighting; and he
> instructed the <u>messenger</u> . . .
>
> (2 Sam. 11:18ff.)

to wait and see in what mood this news (message) placed the king. If it displeased him, the messenger was to spring on David the good news that Uriah was also dead. Not only was there a message, there were also special instructions to the messsenger as to exactly how to deliver it for the desired effect. It was a <u>message of battle progress</u> with a special accompanying message. Then

> David said to the messenger, "Thus
> shall you say to Joab, 'Do not let this
> matter trouble you, for the sword
> devours now one now another;
> strengthen your attack upon the city,
> and overthrow it.' And encourage him."
> (2 Sam. 11:26)

In addition to delivering the message of battle progress, the same messenger was charged with the responsibility of delivering a return message as well as encouraging him. Messenger and errand-person were combined in one person here.

7) A Second Message Of Battle Progress

After Joab had pressed his attack on Rabbah he

> . . . sent messengers to David, and said,
> "I have fought against Rabbah;
> moreover, I have taken the city of
> waters. Now, then, gather the rest of
> the people together, and encamp
> against the city, and take it; lest I take
> the city, and it be called by my name."
> (2 Sam. 12:27-28)

David complied and the victory was recorded in his name.

8) A Parable-Message To The King Of Judah

After killing ten thousand Edomites in the Valley of Salt, as well as taking Sela, Amaziah the king of Judah entered into battle with Joash the king of Israel.

> Then Amaziah sent messengers to
> Joash the son of Jehoahaz, son of Jehu,
> king of Israel, saying, "Come let us look
> one another in the face." And Joash
> king of Israel sent word to Amaziah
> king of Judah, "A thistle of Lebanon
> sent to a cedar on Lebanon, saying,
> "Give your daughter to my son for a
> wife; and a wild beast of Lebanon
> passed by and trampled down the
> thistle. You have indeed smitten
> Edom, and your heart has lifted you
> up. Be content with your glory, and
> stay at home; for why should you
> provoke trouble so that you fall, and
> Judah with you?"
>
> (2 Kg. 14:8-10)

The result was that Judah was defeated by Israel, and Amaziah was taken prisoner. In addition, the wall of Jerusalem was breached for a considerable distance, and the temple treasure was taken. The message is unique in that a portion of it was comprised of a parable. This is the first such parable-message this study has been able to document.

9) The Message Requesting To Be Rescued

During the reign of Ahaz, king of Judah, Pekah, king of Israel, and Rezin, king of Syria besieged Ahaz at Jerusalem during what became known as the Syro-Ephriamitic War against Judah. They could not defeat Ahaz. Judah was also threatened from the South, for the king of Edom had wrenched Elath from Judah.

> So Ahaz sent messengers to Tiglath-
> pileser king of Assyria, saying, "I am

> your servant and your son. Come up
> and rescue me from the hand of the
> king of Syria and from the hand of the
> king of Israel, who are attacking me."
>
> (2 Kg. 16:7)

Ahaz also sent silver and gold to Tiglath-pileser. In return the
Assyrians marched on Damascus, took it, and executed Rezin, its king.
One must assume that the messengers were also responsible for
delivering the valuables. They were messenger-errand-persons who
carried a message requesting to be rescued from the Syro-Ephriamitic
League, and carried the payment for such a rescue. As a result, the
Kingdom of Judah continued as an Assyrian vassal state.

10) Envoys With A Message To Avert Warfare

2 Chronicles supplies a message between the Egyptian
Pharaoh Neco and King Josiah which is missing from the 2 Kings 23:29
account:

> . . .Neco king of Egypt went up to fight
> at Carchemish on the Euphrates and
> Josiah went out against him. But he
> sent envoys to him saying, "What have
> we to do with each other, king of
> Judah? I am not coming against you
> this day, but against the house with
> which I am at war; and God has
> commanded me to make haste. Cease
> opposing God, who is with me, lest he
> destroy you."
>
> (2 Chron. 35:20b-21)

Josiah, an ally-by-necessity of Assyria (which stood between his
kingdom and the rising, threatening Babylonia) felt it better to help

Assyria, for he considered it a preferable overlord to either Babylonia or Egypt for Judah. He did not heed Neco's warning, and was killed in battle for his folly.

e. The Messenger As Errand Person

After Jericho was taken, all but Rahab and her family were placed under the ban, i.e., the consecrating and dedicating of all the spoils and booty of war to the deity (Yahweh in this case). Achan broke the rule of the ban by taking certain items and hiding them in his tent.

> So Joshua sent messengers, and they ran to the tent; and behold, it was hidden in his tent with the silver underneath. And they took them out of the tent and brought them to Joshua and all the people of Israel, and they laid them before the Lord.
> (Josh. 7:22-23)

Joshua (i.e., the book) appears to use 'messenger' in a totally different way; 1) as spy and 2) as errand-person (trusted). The preceding chapter has demonstrated, however, that such functions were not foreign to messengers.

f. Assassination

1) The Errand To Affect Revenge Through Assassination

In the battle at Gibeon Joab and his brother Abishai lost their brother Asahel who was killed by Abner. Abner had made peace with David and had brought Israel to make a covenant with David at Hebron. Joab and the army were away at the time on raids. Upon returning and reporting to David, Joab found out that Abner had been given safe passage by David. He protested David's action and left in anger.

> When Joab came out from David's presence, he sent messengers after Abner, and they brought him back from the cistern of Sirah; but David did not know of it.
>
> (2 Sam. 3:26)

Abner was taken by the messengers to Hebron where he was assassinated by Joab. By messengers here are meant those charged with the mission of bringing Abner back. Since David was unaware of their mission, one sees that they were probably sworn to secrecy. Like the conspiracy at the court of Ramses (*infra* Chapter I) messengers were involved in assassination plots.

2) David And Bathsheba: A Dilemma And Message Of Instructions To Assassinate

Joab was sent with the army to wage war agasinst the Ammonites and to besiege Rabbah. David remained in Jerusalem where late one afternoon he saw Bathsheba making her ablutions.

> So David sent messengers and took her; and she came to him, and he lay with her. And the woman conceived; and she sent (messengers) and told David, "I am with child." So David sent word to Joab (by messenger), "Send me Uriah the Hittite." And Joab sent Uriah to David.
>
> (2 Sam. 11:4-6)

David had intended for Uriah, the husband of Bathsheba, to be seen entering his own house. This would have given the impression that Uriah had slept with his own wife, or had violated one of the rules of Yahweh War (Holy War) under which David's troops in the field operated. When her pregnancy began to show, David reasoned, there would be no reason for the public to doubt that Uriah was the father of the expected child, and that he (David) would be in the clear. The plan backfired, however, for Uriah refused to enter his house for religious reasons (stated above). Moreover, David's own spies/messengers were among many who could testify to this piety. So:

> In the morning David wrote a letter to Joab, and sent it by the hand of Uriah. In the letter he wrote, "Set Uriah in the forefront of the hardest fighting and then draw back from him that he may be struck down and die."
>
> (2 Sam. 11:14-15)

The above messenger activity shows that messengers kidnapped Bathsheba; carried a message to David that she was pregnant; and were sent to the battlefield from the court. Even a high-ranking officer was used to carry a letter-message containing instructions to another (Joab) as to how his (Uriah the letter-carrier messenger!) own death was to be affected.

3) A Messenger Is Sent To Assassinate A Prophet

Benhadad, king of Damascus, mustered his army and besieged Samaria during a time when there was great famine there. One day the king of Samaria was walking along the top of the wall when a woman called upon him to adjudicate a situation which involved necessary cannibalism due to a paucity of food. Elisha the prophet's life was immediately threatened by the king out of exasperation (2 Kg. 6:24-31)

> Elisha was sitting in his house, and the elders were sitting with him. Now the king had dispatched a man from his presence; but before the messenger arrived Elisha said to the elders, "Do you see how this murderer (i.e., the king) has sent to take off my head? Look, when the messenger comes, shut the door fast against him. Is not the sound of his master's feet behind him?"
>
> (2 Kg. 6:32-33)

This messenger whose task was the assassination of the prophet Elisha is identified simply as the "captain on whose arm the king leaned . . ." (2 Kg. 7:2), and is similar to the Egyptian King's-Messenger.

g. Political Matters

1) The Message Of Overture

David went to Hebron--as an agent of the Philistines--and was anointed king over Judah by order of its elders. It was at Ziklag that David heard of the death of Saul.

> When they told David, "It was the men of Jabesh-gilead who buried Saul, "David sent messengers to the men of Jabesh-gilead, and said to them, "may you be blessed by the Lord, because you showed this loyalty to Saul your lord, and buried him.'"
>
> (2 Sam. 2:5)

It thus appears that David's first official act as king of Judah was to employ messengers to cement a relationship with the loyalists of the slain Saul. The message was an overture to transfer their loyalty to him; but ever so subtly.

2) Messengers Opening Diplomatic Relations With David

After David had become *nagid* of Israel (by treaty) and king of Judah at Hebron (by anointing), and while yet a Philistine agent!, he and his mercenary army took the Canaanite stronghold Jebus, and began to rebuild and restructure it as his capital. "And Hiram king of Tyre sent messengers to David, and cedar trees, also carpenters and masons who built David a house (2 Sam. 5:11)." These messengers were mostly envoys or ambassadors, and were the first necessary link between monarchs of two countries who had entered into some kind of relationship of state.[13]

3) Establishing An Embassy: The Opening Of Diplomatic Relations

The study of the evidence for the ANE messenger (Assyria) demonstrated that messengers were a signal of well-meaning and good intentions on the part of intercoursing kingdoms. For a similar reason David had also sent his envoys to Hanun upon the latter's ascension to the Ammonite throne (*infra*, the present chapter). Accordingly, ". . . Hiram king of Tyre sent his servants to Solomon, when he heard that they had anointed him king in place of his father; . . ." (1 Kg. 5:1; MT 1 Kg. 5:15)

4) Envoys From Babylon

When Sargon II was killed on a campaign, his son Sennacherib ascended the throne. During the period Babylon had been subjected to vassalage by Sargon. In Babylon, Mardul-apal-iddina (the biblical Merodach-baladan), with the help of Elam, defied Assyria's hold: "At that time Merodach-baladan the son of Baladan king of Babylon, sent envoys with letters and a present for Hezekiah; for he heard that

Hezekiah had been sick (2 Kg. 20:12)." "This was part of a concerted plan," writes John Bright, "for we know that Merodach-baladan sent envoys to . . . other kings also, . . ."[14] These envoys carried letter-messages to various kings; messages which invited the opening of diplomatic relations, and an alliance for mutual military defense.[15]

5) The Letter-Message Of Jehu

Linked with the above theme of assassination, but at the same time a matter of political import, and thus to be treated here, is Jehu's plan to liquidate the Omride Dynasty.

> Now Ahab had seventy sons in Samaria. So Jehu wrote letters, and sent them to Samaria, to the rulers of the city, to the elders, and to the guardians of the sons of Ahab, saying, "Now then, as soon as this letter comes to you, and there are with you chariots and horses, fortified cities also, and weapons, select the best and fittest of your master's sons and set him on his father's throne, and fight for your master's house." So he who was over the palace, and he who was over the city, together with the elders and the guardians, sent to Jehu saying, "We are your servants, and we will do all that you bid us. We will not make anyone king; do whatever is good in your eyes." Then he wrote to them a second letter, saying, "If you are on my side, and if you are ready to obey me, take the heads of your master's sons, and come to me at Jezreel tomorrow at this time." And when the letter came to

them, they took the king's sons, and
slew them, seventy persons, and put
their heads in baskets, and sent them to
him in Jezreel.

(2 Kg. 10:1-7)

Thus were wiped out all of the possible heirs to the Omride Dynasty.
Jehu also sent messengers throughout Israel inviting all of the Baal
worshipers (i.e., of the god Baal Melkart) to a great worship feast.
Once these worshipers had assembled themselves inside the Baal
temple, Jehu's eighty hand-picked men slaughtered them all, and
turned what was left of this temple into a latrine (2 Kg. 10:18-27).

6) Nehemiah: Messages Between Nehemiah And His Enemies

Nehemiah, governor of Judah, had set his people to the task of
rebuilding Jerusalem and its walls. His enemy in Samaria, Sanballat,
and his Transjordanian enemy, Tobiah, felt that the presence of
Nehemiah detracted from their former power over the territory of
Judah. Accordingly, and in league with Geshem the Arab who had
designs on southern Judah, every time Nehemiah succeeded in
improving the situation in Jerusalem, these three attempted to harrass
him and thwart his plans. According to Nehemiah

Sanballat and Geshem sent to me,
saying, "Come and let us meet together
in one of the villages in the plain of
Ono." But they intended to do me
harm. And I sent messengers to them
saying, "I am doing a great work and I
cannot come down. Why should the
work stop while I leave it and come
down to you? . . . In the same way
Sanballat for the fifth time sent his
servant to me with an open letter in his

> hand. In it was written, "It is reported
> among the nations, and Geshem also
> says it, that you are building the wall;
> and you wish to become their king,
> according to this report . . ." Then I
> <u>sent</u> to him, saying, "No such things as
> you say have been done, for you are
> inventing them out of your own mind."
>
> (Nehemiah 6:2-8)

Tobiah and Sanballat had many in Jerusalem who openly supported them. Nehemiah had enemies both within and without Jerusalem. He states:

> Moreover in those days the nobles sent
> many letters to Tobiah, and Tobiah's
> letters came to them. For many in
> Judah were bound by oath to him, . . .
> Also they spoke of his good deeds in
> my presence, and reported my words to
> him. And Tobiah sent letters to make
> me afraid.
>
> (Neh. 6:17-19)

h. Conspiratorial Matters

1) The Message Of Conspiracy

Ishbosheth (Ishbaal), the surviving son of Saul, and Abner, Saul's commander of the army, quarreled over Rizpah the concubine of Saul. Abner rebuked him and vowed to give Saul's house over into David's hands.

> And Abner sent messengers to David
> at Hebron, saying, "To whom does the
> land belong? Make your covenant with
> me, and behold, my hand shall be with
> you to bring over all Israel to you." And
> he said, "Good; I will make a covenant
> with you; but one thing I require of
> you; that is, you shall not see my face,
> unless you first bring Michal, Saul's
> daughter, when you come to see my
> face." Then David sent messengers to
> Ishbosheth, Saul's son, saying, "Give
> me my wife Michal, whom I betrothed
> at the price of a hundred foreskins of
> the Philistines." And Ishbosheth sent
> (presumably messengers) and took her
> from her husband Paltiel the son of
> Laish.
>
> (2 Sam. 3:12-15)

Shortly thereafter Abner addressed the leaders of Israel to support David.

2) Messengers Of Disobedience

Hoshea, king of Israel became the vassal of Shalmaneser, king of Assyria, and paid tribute annually to him.

> But the king of Assyria found treachery
> in Hoshea: for he had sent messengers
> to Sais, and offered no tribute to the
> king of Assyria, as he had done year by
> year; therefore the king of Assyria shut
> him up, and bound him in prison.
>
> (2 Kg. 17:4)

The two most tell-tale acts of disobedience of a vassal, the sending of messengers to another power(i.e., the signal of opening diplomatic relations through an embassy), and the cessation of sending tribute to the overlord or suzerain, led to the eventual conquest and exile of Israel in 722/1 BCE.

3) The Letter-Message To Defame Naboth

Because it was located near his palace, King Ahab of Israel wanted the ancestral vineyard of Naboth the Jezreelite. He offered to give Naboth another vineyard, or to pay him outright for it so that he could make of it a vegetable garden. It was the inheritance of his ancestors, and Naboth had to refuse the king's offers. Ahab was displeased and he pouted. When Jezebel his wife was told, she had him eat and enjoy life; she promised to give him the vineyard he wanted.

> So she wrote letters in Ahab's name and sealed them with his seal, and she sent the letters to the elders and nobles who dwelt with Naboth in his city. And she wrote in the letters, "Proclaim a fast, and set Naboth on high among the people; and set two base fellows opposite him, and let them bring a charge against him, saying, 'You have cursed God and king." Then take him out and stone him to death. And the men of the city, did as Jezebel had sent word to them.
>
> (1 Kg. 21:8-11a)

Jezebel received a message from the elders and nobles to the effect
that all had been carried out as had been instructed. She informed
Ahab who took possession of the vineyard immediately.

i. Additions: The Message And Beyond

1) A Messenger Speaks On His Own Initiative

During the reign of Hezekiah king of Judah, Sennacherib king
of Assyria came up against the fortified cities of Judah. Hezekiah sent
messengers with messages of apology to Sennacherib at Lachish.
Sennacherib demanded tribute from him, and sent the Rabshakeh with
a great army from Lachish to Jerusalem. There they were met by high-
ranking members of the king's court (2 Kg. 18:13-18).

> And the Rabshakeh said to them, "Say
> to Hezekiah, "Thus says the great king
> of Assyria: On what do you rest this
> confidence of yours? Do you think that
> mere words are strategy and power for
> war? On whom do you now rely, that
> you have rebelled against me? Behold,
> you are relying now on Egypt, that
> broken reed of a staff, which will
> pierce the hand of any man who leans
> on it. Such is Pharaoh king of Egypt to
> all who rely on him. . .'
>
>   (2 Kg. 18:19-21)

Once the Rabshakeh had delivered the king of Assyria's message, he
began to speak on his own initiative, for he continued:

> Come, now make a wager with my
> master the king of Assyria: I will give

you two thousand horses if you are able
on your part to set riders upon them.
How can you repulse a single captain
among the least of my master's
servants, when you rely on Egypt for
chariots and horsemen?

(2 Kg. 18:23-24)

The Rabshakeh continued to dialogue with Hezekiah's representatives; a dialogue which was interspersed with more messages from the king of Assyria. He received no reply from the people standing upon the wall before which he and his host stood. What is most important and of great interest is the fact that this message shows that some messengers elaborated on a message with their own words. Messengers thus appear to have enjoyed a certain freedom to respond beyond the verbatim message. This freedom was witnessed earlier when the Egyptian letter-carrier explained to the Assyrian king how his master could not have known of his (the Assyrian's) illness, and the obvious powers of freedom granted to the Egyptian King's-Messenger who displayed the same characteristics as the Rabshakeh.[16]

2) A Messenger Elaborates Further Upon Delivery Of A Message

Ahab defeated the Damascan coalition headed by Benhadad. For three years thereafter they observed a cease-fire. 1 Kings 22:13ff., however, finds Syria and Israel poised for war. Ahab and his southern ally, Jehoshaphat of Judah, inquired of the court, guild prophets (in their role as counselors) for signs of success and words of encouragement. Ahab, however, remembered that he had not heard all of the available prophetic counsel; he sent for the disagreeable Michaiah ben Imlah.

And the messenger who went to
summon Michaiah said to him,

> "Behold, the words of the prophets
> with one accord are favorable to the
> king; let your word be like the word of
> one of them, and speak favorably."
>
> (1 Kg. 22:13)

This example provides another instance of a messenger in the Hebrew Scriptures going beyond the delivery of a message. He appears to have taken it upon himself to instruct Michaiah as to what he should say.

j. Family Affairs

1) The Message Of A Long-Lost Son To His Father

When famine in the land forced Joseph's brothers to go to Egypt, he made himself known to them. He inquired of his father's well-being and then told his brothers: "Make haste and go up to my father and say to him, 'Thus says your son Joseph, God has made me lord of all Egypt; come down to me, do not tarry; . . .'" (Gen. 45:9).[17]

2) The Message Designed To Affect Forgiveness

After Joseph and a considerable host of mourners had buried Jacob in the cave at Machpelah (Gen. 50:13) he returned to Egypt. Then:

> When Joseph's brothers saw that their
> father was dead they said, "It may be
> that Joseph will hate us and pay us
> back for all the evil which we did to
> him." So they sent a message to Joseph,
> saying, "Your father gave this
> command just before he died, "Say to
> Joseph, Forgive, I pray you, the
> transgression of your brothers and

> their sin, because they did evil to you."
> And now, we pray you, forgive the
> transgression of the servants of the
> God of your father."
>
> (Gen. 50:15-17b)

The account does not make clear whether this message was uttered at one time by Jacob, or whether it was a desperate fabrication by the brothers. Moreover, Joseph's reply shows that this forgiveness did not have as its basis his father's alleged request.

3) Message-Request For An Audience With The King

Absalom son of David had been banished to Geshur in Aram. David granted a petition by Joab to have Absalom brought back. Two years after his return Absalom had not been to see his father. One day he sent Joab to David with the following message.

> "Why have I come from Geshur? It
> would be better for me to be there still.
> Now therefore let me go into the
> presence of the king; and if there is
> guilt in me, let him kill me." Then Joab
> went to the king and told him;
>
> (2 Sam. 14:32b-33a)

k. Courtship: The Message Of Suit

After the death of Nabal some ten days after a drinking spree (1 Sam. 25:36-39c):

> . . . David sent and wooed Abigail, to
> make her his wife. And when the
> servants of David came to Abigail at

> Carmel, they said to her, "David has
> sent us to you to take you to him as his
> wife." . . . And Abigail made haste and
> mounted on an ass, and her five
> maidens attended her; she went after
> the <u>messengers</u> of David, and became
> his wife.
>
>   (1 Sam. 25:39d-42)

David's messengers performed a courting function by carrying a
message of suit. In Chapter II, this activity on the part of messengers
was observed among the Ugaritans.

1. Healing

1) The Message Requesting A Cure

Namaan commanded the army of the king of Syria, and was a
leper. A young woman from Israel was working in the Syrian court
under the supervision of Namaan's wife. She told the wife that Elisha
the man of God in Israel could cure Namaan's leprosy. Namaan was
told all this by his wife. He in turn told the king of Syria.

> And the king of Syria said, "Go now,
> and I will send a <u>letter</u> to the king of
> Israel." So he went (as a messenger for
> the king of Syria, but also on his own
> behalf) taking with him ten talents of
> silver, six thousand shekels of gold, and
> ten festal garments. And he brought
> the letter to the king of Israel, which
> read, "When this letter reaches you,
> know that I have sent to you Namaan

> my servant, that you may cure his
> leprosy."
>
> (2 Kg. 5:5-6)

The king of Israel became perplexed and feared that the king of Syria was trying to goad him into a quarrel.

> But when Elisha the man of God heard
> that the king of Israel had rent his
> clothes, he sent (a messenger) to the
> king saying, "Why have you rent your
> clothes? Let him come now to me, that
> he may know that there is a prophet in
> Israel."
>
> (2 Kg. 5:8-9)

2) The Message Of Instructions To Affect The Cure Of Leprosy

In the above case the prophet--a sometimes suspected messenger himself--had sent a messenger of his own. When Namaan arrived at Elisha's house Elisha did not deal directly with him, but ". . . sent a messenger to him, saying, "Go and wash in the Jordan seven times, and your flesh will be restored, and you shall be clean." (2 Kg. 5:10).[18]

m. Business: The Response To A Message; An Invitation To Trade

Hiram king of Tyre sent messengers to Solomon when he heard that he had been anointed king (1 Kg. 5:1; MT 1 Kg. 5:15). Solomon replied by envoy.

> You know that David my father could
> not build a house for the name of the

Lord his God because of the warfare
with which his enemies surrounded him
... but now the Lord my God has given
me rest on every side; there is neither
adversary or misfortune. And so I
purpose to build a house for the name
of the Lord my God, ... Now therefore
command that cedars of Lebanon be
cut for me; and my servants will join
your servants, and I will pay for your
servants such wages as you set; ...

(1 Kg. 5:2-6)

Hiram received Solomon's message joyfully, for it said in effect that
not only was his neighbor to the south going to remain peaceful toward
him, but that he was most anxious to begin commercial intercourse
with Tyre as well.

And Hiram sent to Solomon, saying, "I
have heard the message which you have
sent to me; I am ready to do all you
desire in the matter of cedar and
cypress timber."

(1 Kg. 5:8)

Hiram went on to state just how and where the timber would be
delivered, and asked Solomon to provide food for his household in
return. Thus began Solomon's massive building projects. Note, too,
that Hiram hears the message sent to him.

n. Real Estate: The Message Of Justification Of Land Occupation

Jephthah was a judge in Israel. Earlier he (like David) had
been an outlaw and bandit-raider. He was asked by his people, the

Gileadites, to lead them against the existing Ammonite threat. After bargaining with the elders, and after making vows at Mizpah, Jephthah was elected *nagid*.

> Then Jephthah sent messengers to the king of the Ammonites and said, "What have you against my land?" And the king of the Ammonites answered the messengers of Jephthah, "Because Israel on coming from Egypt took away my land, from the Arnon to the Jabbok and to the Jordan; now therefore restore it peaceably." And Jephthah sent messengers again to the king of the Ammonites and said to him, "Thus says Jephthah ...
>
> (Jud. 11:12-14)

The message which followed was essentially a recapitulation of all the efforts of Israel under the leadership of Moses to pass through certain lands legally, and without strife. It ends: "But the king of the Ammonites did not heed the message of Jepthah which he sent to him." (Jud. 11:28). Jephthah had in essence sent a message of justification of land occupation.

o. Commodities: The Message To Get Rid Of Unwanted Goods

After the ark had been returned to Israel by the Philistines-- amid great pomp and ceremony--it came to rest for a time in the field of Joshua of Betshemesh. Some seventy curious inhabitants of Bethshemesh died as a result of looking into or handling the ark while it was there. Thereupon the leaders of Bethshemesh "sent messengers to the inhabitants of Kiriat-jearim, saying, "The Philistines have returned the ark of the Lord. Come down and take it up to you" (1 Sam. 6:21). This message may contain a very unfavorable view of the ark tradition, and is similar to that position which is reflected in the Book of Judges. That is, the ark is conspicuously absent from the accounts contained in that book (save one parenthetical reference).

p. A *nagid* And His Successor: Saul's Messages Concerning David

When Saul's depression and mental illness became more and more severe, he demanded a musician to soothe his frayed nerves. His servants recommended one of the sons of Jesse. "Therefore Saul sent messengers to Jesse, and said, "Send me David your son, who is with the sheep" (1 Sam. 16:19). After David had become a servant of Saul, and had also become his armor-bearer, Saul sent a message to Jesse. "Let David remain in my service, for he has found favor in my sight" (1 Sam. 16:22). Thus, at the introduction of David into the HS record, messengers are involved.

Later, a more mature David was playing the lyre in the presence of Saul. Saul had a seizure and threw his spear at David who was successful in evading it and effecting an escape. "That night Saul sent messengers to David's house to watch him, that he might kill him in the morning" (1 Sam. 19:11). Michal, David's wife, helped him to escape and arranged objects in his bed to make it appear as if he were still in it.

> And when Saul sent messengers to take David, she said, "He is sick." Then Saul sent the messengers to see David, saying, "Bring him up to me in the bed, that I may kill him." And when the messengers came in, behold, the image/*teraphim* was in the bed, with the pillow of goat's hair at its head.
>
> (1 Sam. 19:14-16)

David fled to Samuel at Naioth in Ramah. Saul was informed of his whereabouts and sent messengers to bring him back. These messengers fell under the influence of the ecstatic frenzy of the group of prophets over whom Samuel was presiding. They began to prophesy, and forgot about their original mission. "When it was told to Saul he sent other messengers and they also prophesied. And Saul sent messengers again the third time, and they also prophesied" (1 Sam. 19:21). Eventually Saul also went to Ramah to ascertain personally why his messengers had failed to accomplish their missions. He, too, had an ecstatic experience which gave rise to the question, "Is Saul also among the prophets?" (1 Sam. 19:24)

With these examples there is literary evidence that messengers became prophets (i.e., of the ecstatic type). As in the Book of Joshua, 'messenger' is used synonymously with 'spy' and 'errand-person.' They don't appear to have been commissioned to say anything in Saul's name; they were merely expected to execute certain orders of the king/*nagid*.

At an even later date David had to flee from Saul once again in order to save his life

> . . . as Saul and his men were closing in upon David and his men to capture them, . . . a messenger came to Saul, saying, "Make haste and come, for the Philistines have made a raid upon the land."
>
> (1 Sam. 23:26c-27)

Receipt of this message caused Saul to abandon his search for David, and go to fight the Philistines (the main reason he had been elevated to *nagid* in the first place). The sender of the message is unknown. However, the message is contained within an aetiological account which explains the name Rock of Escape (1 Sam. 23:28).

2. *'bd*

Often the Hebrew word *'bd*, servant, is translated as messenger in English. Sometimes *'bd* and *ml'k*, messenger, are used synonymously and/or interchangeably in some of the historical narrative material examined herein. In 1c3 above the envoys who were sent to Hanun king of Ammon by David are called in Hebrew *'bdyw* (his servants and not envoys). The English 'envoy' is an interpretation of the <u>function</u> of the servants sent by David. In 1d1 above Benhadad tells Ahab "I will send my servants (*'bdy*) to you tomorrow . . ." These servants are to function as messengers whose job will be to search Ahab's house and the houses of his servants to take away whatever pleases them (1 Kg. 20:2-12). *'bd* and *ml'k* are used again synonymously in k. above. The servants (*'bdy*) of David came to Abigail, "who went after the messengers (*ml'ky*) of David . . . (1 Sam. 25:39d-42). Thus, continuing the thematic unpacking, the *'bd* was involved in (alleged) Spy Activity (David's Sending His Servants To Ammon); Military Matters (The Message To Goad Another Into Battle); and Courtship (The Message Of Suit).

3. *rkb, rkb ss, rkb hss, rkb ssym*

Attention has already been called to the Reconnaissance-Messengers of 2 Kings 7:14-15 with reference to spy and reconnaissance activity (above 1c4), and also the results of a prophet having sent a prophet-messenger with a message to overthrow a dynasty in 2 Kings 9:17-19 (above 1a5). The emphases were different, however, and a view of the same texts from a different angle is now necessary.

The expressions *rkb* (rider) and *rkb hss* (horsemen) appear in connection with conspiratorial matters also. As Jehu and his party were returning to Jezreel, Joram king of Israel was anxious to find out how the battle for Ramoth-gilead had gone. He commanded the watchman "Take a horseman (rkb) and send to meet them. . . So a man on horseback (rkb hss) went to meet him, and said, "Thus says the king, . . ." (2 Kg. 9:17-18). Both the activity and the tell-tale formula are unmistakably associated with messenger activity. A second rkb ss was sent because the first did not return to the king (2 Kg. 9:19). rkb, rkb hss, rkb ssym, and rkb ss are then associated with the themes of Spy-Reconnaissance and Conspiratorial Matters.

4. *hmgyd*: Message Stating That The Overthrow Is Successful

Once Absalom revolted against King David his father, his rebellion gathered strength "And a messenger came to David saying, "The hearts of the men of Israel have gone after Absalom (2 Sam. 15:13)." The Hebrew word translated 'messenger' here is *mgyd*. It is a participial form of the *hiphil* verb pattern of the root *ngd*. It means to inform or tell. Thus, *mgyd* is the one who informs or tells. This is essentially what a messenger who delivers a message does, so the English is once again an interpretation. The theme is Conspiratorial Matters.

5. *hmrglym*

a. Military Matters: Joshua Sends Spies To Jericho

After Jericho had fallen into the hands of Joshua and his host, "Joshua said to the two men who had spied out the land," to collect the prostitute Rahab and her family. "So the young men who had been spies went in and brought them out (Josh. 6:22-23). The Hebrew word which is translated "who had spied out" and "who had been spies" is *hmrglym*. It is a participle form of the verb *rgl* (spy[out]). *hmrglym* and *ml'kym* are seen to be synonymous in Joshua 6:25b. Speaking of the resourceful Rahab it states: " . . . and she dwelt in Israel to this day, because she hid the messengers (*ml'kim*) whom Joshua sent to spy out (*lrgl*) Jericho."

b. Conspiratorial Matters: Message To Overthrow A King

Two years after Prince Absalom was allowed to return to Judah from banishment to Geshur in Aram, he sent a message to King David his father. This message is discussed above in 1j3 and is contained in 2 Samuel 14:32b-33a. It caused David (never known to have been a stern parent) to forgive Absalom's insolence and to allow him free movement in the kingdom once more. Several years later he asked David's permission to go to Hebron--at that time still a tribal religious center--to fulfill a vow which he had made while still in Aram. The king gave his permission.

> But Absalom sent secret messengers throughout all the tribes of Israel, saying: "As soon as you hear the sound of the trumpet, then say, 'Absalom is king at Hebron."
>
> (2 Sam. 15:10)

In 2 Samuel 15:13 one reads that this revolt was successful, at least temporarily.

Once again, *mrglym* appears with reference to messengers. As with spies, the Hebrew *mrglym* gives the same sense of clandestine activity. "Secret messengers" is more descriptive an interpretation than a translation.

6. Obscure And Debated Expressions Which Signal The Presence Of Messengers

Several ways of finding messengers in the Hebrew Scriptures have already been discussed. Recall the presence of the terms ml'k, 'bd, rkb ss (and allied expressions), *mgyd*, and *mrglym*; a random reading of various books of the Hebrew Scriptures while searching for the formula "Thus says (or said) NN"; and several expressions which are almost fail-safe indicators. There are several expressions connected with the messengers of the Hebrew Scriptures, however, which merit further study and comment.

a. *ml'kyk*

  Mitchell Dahood argued that more recent versions of Isaiah 23:2b were correct in rendering *ober yam mil'uk* as "your messengers passed over the sea."[19] To be sure, the text presents problems. Dahood cited the Dhorme Bible's translation: "*Tes messagers franchissaient les mers*," and the RSV's translation (cited above) as having been influenced by 1QIsa *ml'kyk*, "your messengers" as the emendation of MT *mile'uk*, and *'brw*, "they passed over," from MT *'br*. The RSV places a note below that according to one ancient manuscript a different translation is found. In all likelihood the reference is to 1QIsa which reads *ml'kyk*. The note continues, however, that the Hebrew text reads "who passed over the sea, they replenished you." This Hebrew reading is the bone of contention. Dahood held that Dhorme's and RSV's readings were superior to the MT reading, but he argued for greater precision in the rendering of the accepted emendation, *mal'akayik*. He maintained that "a greater degree of precision in reading *ml'kyk* could be achieved by heeding the parallelism with *soher*, 'merchant' and by taking into account Canaanite usage."[20] Dahood reasoned that although etymologically *mal'ak* means 'one sent,' the one who commissions the *mal'ak* is Sidon the merchant. Thus, thought Dahood, *mal'akayik* would have been best rendered "your salesmen." He supported this translation by stating:

> This inference seems to be supported by the publication of Virolleaud of some economic texts from Ras Shamra in which *mlakt* repeatedly occurs in the sense of "trading mission, business abroad."[21]

  The study of the extra-Hebrew Scriptural and Hebrew Scriptural messenger has demonstrated that this emendation is unnecessary unless one continues to maintain a myopic view of, and

apodictic definition of the term 'messenger.' 'Messenger' so this study
shows amply suffices as the emendation of MT *mile'uk*. Salesmen, if
that is indeed a plausible rendering, can also be messengers, for the
proof lies in the manner in which they were commissioned.

b. *md'*

Another expression pertinent to this study of the evidence of
the messenger is *md'*. Of interest is the suggestion that *md'* at
Qoheleth 10:20 be interpreted as 'messenger.'[22] It is thus debated
whether *md'* comes from *yd'*, 'know,' 'recognize.' An alternative
reading of this verse without resorting to unnecessary emendation may
prove to be a better reading without destroying sound methodology.
The passage would then read: "Thus with your messenger (or in the
presence of your messenger) do not curse the king: and do not curse
the rich in your bedchamber."[23] The RSV translates: "Even in your
thought, do not curse the king." I argue that the translation 'messenger'
is plausible because 'messenger' (employed here in verse) is indeed a
strong candidate for *md'* in light of the remainder of the verse, a verse
concerned with the transmitting of one person's words to another. The
contents of the whole verse, then, become a similar piece of advice to
that given to envoys by the Egyptian Ptah-hotep.

c. *nssr*

The beginning of Hosea 8:1ff. reads in Hebrew: "*el hkk sfr
knsr 'l byt yhwh*." Thr RSV translates: "Set the trumpet to your lips,
for a vulture is over the house of the Lord." H. Tur-Sinai read a
Hebrew *nssr* or *nssr* for MT *nsr* on the basis of Arabic *nassar*
meaning 'herald.' the one who blows the trumpet.[24] The passage would
then read: "Set the trumpet to your mouth, as a herald over the house
of the Lord. . ."

d. *mazkir*

Very little is known of David's political machinery. According to John Bright all we have to go on are two lists of his cabinet officers. These are found at 2 Samuel 8:15-18 and 20:23-26.[25] Of the several officers mentioned, the most important for producing evidence of the messenger is the title '*mazkir*.'

In "*Sofer und Mazkir*" J. Begrich argued that "*Sofer und Mazkir gehören . . . zu den hohen Beamten des Reiches . . .*"[26] The problem, then, must be solved with a view towards the duties of the "upper crust" of court officials. In all of his appearances the *mazkir* is never found alone. According to Begrich:

> *Er erscheint in Gemeinschaft mit dem 'aser 'al habbayit und dem sofer als Gesandter Hiskias an den assyrischen rab-saqe, führt mit ihnen die Verhandlungen und erstattet mit ihnen dem König Bericht (II Reg. 18: 18; 37). Er wird zusammen mit dem sofer und dem sar ha'ir von Josia abgesandt, den Tempel wieder in Stand zu setzen, . . . (II Chr. 34:8)* [27]

Thus, *mazkir* appears at least four times with *sofer*. One of the major problems confronting the researcher is that before the meaning of the uncertain *mazkir* can be ascertained, one must solve the riddle of the relationship of *mazkir* to *sofer*, their order of importance in the cabinet, and determine the character of their predecessors' offices. Begrich questioned the ordering of the officials as they appeared on the lists of 2 Samuel 8:15-18 and 20:23-26, and suggested that three separate lists had been confused by the editor of this text.[28] The titles themselves he saw having as their predecessors the Egyptian titles, the *ss* of the king, and the *whm. w* of the king, i.e., the scribe and the 'speaker' of the king. These titles dated from the period of Ramses IX (100 to 150 years before David). Begrich was certain that *whm. w* and *mazkir* were synonyms.

> *Das ägyptische Wort bezeichnet den 'Mitteiler,' 'Melder,' 'Sprecher' und wird deshalb auch gern mit 'Herold' wiedergegeben. Es steht dem nichts im Wege, das hebräische mazkir genau so zu übersetzen.*[29]

Begrich and Bright agree that *mazkir* is an official court title which is found from the time of David onwards; that the position was borrowed by the David administration to fill a position made necessary by the fact of a growing empire (with which Saul never had to concern himself); that *mazkir* and the Egyptian *whm. w* are synonyms bespeaking identical positions; and that the best translation for *mazkir* is 'royal herald.'

e. Miscellaneous Envoys

In Nelson's concordance to the RSV 'envoy' appears nine times in the Old Testament (both singular and plural).[30] The same Hebrew word does not appear in MT, however, each time 'envoy' appears in the RSV translation. For example MT Proverbs 13:17 has *mal'ak*, 2 Chronicles 35:21, *mal'akim*, Jeremiah 27:3, *mal'akim*, Isaiah 30:4, *mal'akayw*, and Isaiah 33:7, *mal'ake*, whenever 'envoy' appears in the RSV. Moreover, 2 Kings 20:12 and Isaiah 39:1 of MT are bereft of any word which would designate one as any type of messenger. For the missing envoy Rudolf Kittel proposed--on the basis of the demands of the following sentences--*sarisim*, 'any chief officer' for 2 Kings 20:12.[31] At Isaiah 39:1 Kittel proposed to emend *separim*, 'letters,' to *soperim*, 'scribes,' and also called attention to the addition of *kai presbeis*, 'and envoys/ambassadors,' by the LXX.[32] Thus, in all of the above cases it is understandable why 'envoy' is a plausible candidate for the corresponding MT expression.

At Isaiah 57:9 is found in MT the expression *sirayik*, which RSV renders 'envoys' also. The Qal (*Pa'al*) form, *sir*, is not used. A *Hitpa'el* form, *histayyer* at Joshua 9:4 means 'prepared for a journey.' Thus, *sir* is a person sent on a journey, *ergo* a messenger/envoy.

Finally, 2 Chronicles 32:31 of MT contains the word *bimlise*, which the RSV also translates as either interpreter, orator, or ambassador/envoy.

f. Summary

It has been observed that several additional expressions provide evidence of human messengers in the Hebrew Scriptures. These are generally found in places where a first reading of a given MT might not have readily yielded such evidence. Thanks to the efforts of Barr, Begrich, Bright, Dahood and Kittel, as well as to the discovery of 1QIsa and Egyptian texts dating from the time of Ramses IX, a much more clearly outlined picture of the human messenger of the Hebrew Scriptures has been made possible. Our knowledge of the types of the ANE messenger is now more complete than it has been at any previous time.

7. Analytical Summary

Few of the examples provided were of complete messenger activity. An ideal example of complete messenger activity was contained in 1 Samuel 25:1-13. Likewise, a broken message was seen to have some of the ingredients missing such as the legitimizing formula "Thus says MM" whereas a full message included the formula. Nevertheless, it was seen that both incomplete messenger activity, and the broken message were fully intelligible.

Biblical human messengers carried messages of two form types: messages to those of equal standing or status to the sender, and messages to those of subordinate status to the sender. The messages to those of equal standing reflected this standing in the choice of language employed. Most such messages were highly formalized and called for *parallelismus membrorum*. They were also bereft of imperatives. And where imperatives were inescapable they were neutralized by the situation at hand. The messages to subordinates, on the other hand, were highly punctuated by imperatives. Sufficient examples were provided to demonstrate this fact. In addition, questions of reproach or scorn were not foreign to the messages sent to subordinates. In a similar manner, the commissioning of a messenger was seen to also contain these imperatives. In all, the purpose of the imperatives was to maintain an effective control over subordinates who were located at some distance as if they were standing personally before the sender. This truth was in consonance with the already demonstrated fact that the messenger extended the power and person of the sender temporally and geographically, and that the message allowed the sender to communicate--even in the same tone of voice--as if he or she were there in person. The imperatives, or the absence of them, were seen to be the greatest single factor in determining the tone of a message.

Messengers came from all walks of life, and from all social levels. Jacob's messengers to Esau were most probably his servants; Joseph's messengers to the aged Jacob were his own brothers. The spy-messengers of Joshua were military men; the messengers of Saul who carried portions of a carved up ox were villagers. The messengers of David to Hanun of Ammon were most probably noblemen who served as envoys. Likewise, the messengers sent to David and Solomon by Hiram king of Tyre were also envoys. A general-grade officer, Uriah the Hittite, served as David's letter-bearer and carried a message which contained instructions for his own assassination, while another general-grade officer, Joab, served as Absalom's messenger to David. Young priests (or definitely the sons of priests) became messengers in the spy-messenger network which kept the temporarily-deposed David abreast of the status of Absalom's revolt; and a member of the sons of the prophets was Elisha's messenger to Jehu. The "captain on whose arm the king leaned" was the messenger sent to assassinate the prophet Elisha, and the commander of the Syrian army served as a letter-carrier of his king to Israel on a mission of mercy.

Messengers were seen to have taken the liberty of elaborating on the messages they delivered by engaging in free dialogue with the recipients of the message. The king of Israel's messenger to the prophet Michaiah ben Imlah told Michaiah that he should speak favorably of the predicted outcome of the impending battle over Ramoth-gilead. A really free hand was exercised by the Rabshakeh, messenger to King Hezekiah from the Assyrian monarch King Sennacherib. The Rabshakeh, it was noticed, exercised prerogatives unknown (i.e., by example) of any of the messengers which have been examined in this study.

The contents of the messages which were sent and received were just as variegated as the messengers who delivered them. A son who had attained fame and prosperity wanted his father to come and settle in a new home near him. After the aged father's death and burial a message was delivered to the famous son in his deceased father's name requesting that he forgive fully his brothers for having dealt treacherously with him when he was a youth. Messages requesting to pass through a given country with assurances from the sender that no vandalism would result from this passage were sent to the rulers of various countries which lay along the route which the Moses host wished to travel. In times of military danger, messages were sent to various clans and/or tribes informing them that their numbers and arms were needed to beat back an enemy, or to meet a threat to their continued existence. During these crises messages were sometimes sent to hopeful rescuers by a besieged party with instructions as to how best the rescuer could defeat the besieging forces after having observed a weakness in the strategy employed by the opposing force. A message designed to win the affections of a woman and to cause her to accept a proposal of marriage was delivered to the widow of a former antagonist who had died suddenly. Politically, messages were sent to Ammon to ensure continued peace with the son of an ally now recently deceased; it resulted in a declaration of war between the two kingdoms, and involved other kingdoms before it was finally over. Tyre sent messages to its southern neighbor at Jerusalem inviting peace between them on at least two occasions which for the Jerusalem parties resulted in the building of living quarters for the two kings, and a temple for one of them. A message in letter form was written in the name of a king by his wife. It instructed several unprincipaled people to accuse falsely a nobleman in public of having cursed deity and king. The king received the late nobleman's coveted property; the nobleman was stoned to death. Another message in letter form was hand carried by the man concerning whom the contents gave orders to others as to how his assassination was to be carried out. Messages were sent by one monarch to another in an attempt to goad the other into warfare; another sent by an Egyptian king attempted to accomplish the opposite. Still another message's contents held a plea from one king to another begging to be rescued from a league which was now laying siege to his city.

No major differences were to be noted between the messengers of the Hebrew Scriptures and their greater ANE counterparts. The same was true of the respective messages--which differed only in specific content, not in characteristics. In fact, this study was approached from the natural point of view that the human messengers of the Hebrew Scriptures were also *de facto* ANE messengers; they had enjoyed simply a great deal more potential notoriety because of the famous literary anthology in which they had become enshrined. Aside from the obvious intention to avoid unwieldliness, this is the only reason why the evidence of the human messenger of the Hebrew Scriptures was confined to a separate chapter.

Receipt of the foregoing messages had an effect and impact on the local and subsequent history of Israel, Judah and their neighbors which is to this day the subject and object of intense study. The messenger played a central role in the communication process of the world of the Hebrew Scriptures; the messages which were delivered authored history as we today understand that term, both religious and secular history. Had these messages not been delivered, had all of these messengers been somehow stayed from their commissioned duties, we would certainly not have a history of Israel worthy of our attention and study.

SUMMARY OF PART I

At the outset I stated that we moderns had come to know very little about messengers and the roles they played collectively in helping to shape the history of the ANE, or just where they were located in the chain of human communication. The more we knew about messengers, I theorized, the more we would know about the ANE, both generally and specifically in a way heretofore never attempted. The evidence contained herein verified that theory.

To begin, I collected and studied many examples and types of ANE messengers. My sources were as variegated as the types of messengers available. Messengers performed many kinds of functions, came from all walks of life, were of both sexes, and were an integral part of ANE political and social life. Messengers were also favorite literary characters. ANE life whether existential or imagined, found it most difficult to function well without the various kinds of messengers. The study's purpose, in addition to the preceding, was to enable me to make a definitive statement about the ANE messengers and their role in ANE society for a period which exceeded the length of time of any single ANE empire or political and social period. For nearly three thousand years, according to the literature studied herein, the understanding of what a messenger was and did as viewed by the inhabitants of the ANE was everywhere the same. I demonstrated then concluded that the messenger was one, human--or extra-human according to some literature--male or female, who either delivered verbatim messages either orally or in writing, or both, to the person(s) for whom the message was intended, or that the messenger performed a specific task or service. Both the delivery of a message and the performance of a task had the purpose of extending personally and geographically the power of the person(s) who had dispatched the messenger.

A similar study of various messages, mainly but not exclusively letters, enabled me to demonstrate and conclude that a message was a communication of information in either oral or written form, or both simultaneously, transmitted through a messenger. This message was often, though not exclusively, the main errand of the messenger. Receipt of a message signified that the power of the sender had indeed been geographically extended. The immediate situation was usually changed as a result of receipt and acknowledgement of the contents of a message. That is, the message resulted oftentimes in a history-making event. In addition, the study of the messenger and message provided valuable information about the political and social history of the ANE between ca. 3000 and ca. 30 BCE, as well as informed one of the nature and importance of one of the main types of ANE human communication techniques. One could now speak with clarity and certainty about the messengers and messages of the ANE as never before.

The evidence of the messenger phenomenon in the ANE provides quite a different prism through which much information already available on the ANE may be refracted. By causing the messenger to stand out in bold relief, and combining many such occurrences of references to messengers, a picture emerged which demonstrated that there was no aspect of ANE life which did not depend on them. Their ubiquity and stratification into types such as the ambassador, the envoy, the emissary, the herald and the harbinger demonstrated that the messenger was not a study of solely one class of ANE society. This study was a way of gaining a more balanced view of that society over an extended period of time.

The contributors to, and the framers of the Hebrew Scriptures, to focus on a body of literature relatively familiar to many westerners, found the communication-facilitating activities of the messenger to be indispensible also. Approaching the historical narrative material of this literature, I conducted a thematic study of the evidence of messengers. One immediately saw from the study just how active messengers were in ancient Israelite society as well. They were so ubiquitous that I found it difficult if not impossible not to pose the question of whether their omission from the narratives of the Hebrew Scriptures would cause the net literary result to be worth reading. The understanding of what a messenger was, and how messengers functioned in the ANE was exactly the same as that mirrored in the historical narrative material of the Hebrew Scriptures. I did not expect it to be otherwise--though many would still argue that the Hebrew Scriptures are a totally unique literature.

A study such as the preceding has many uses, and provides many reference services. The most obvious of them have been stated and demonstrated. But the study also stimulates thought about less obvious matters as one reads, say, the Hebrew Scriptures. Let us take for example the crossing of territorial borders. How was permission to cross territorial borders obtained or denied? How was passage through another's territory planned and executed? We often assume that one travelled easily throughout the region because of the image of Abraham (a literary construct) travelling from Haran to Egypt. The 'Message To Effect Passage', as I term it, forces one to slow the picture almost to a halt and to realize that one did not cross foreign borders with guaranteed ease. As one reads through the HS about other such border crossings, it would be well to pause and reflect on the role of the messenger and message in what was most surely a part of the actual border crossing process.

A comparison of the HS evidence with that of the preceding extra-biblical evidence demonstrates that there were concerns and activities that the ANE messenger addressed, or engaged in which do not find their counterparts in the historical narrative material of the HS. One example is the vizier, or prime minister of Egypt during the reign of certain pharaos. The Joseph-the-viceroy material in Genesis comes readily to mind. Literary-critical considerations, however, cause us to immediately disqualify the Joseph Narratives as unreliable for proper comparative analysis. The *mazkir* of b6d of Chapter III herein appears to have been a position and title borrowed from Egypt by the Jerusalem Court, but we are told precious little about the actual duties of this *mazkir*. Why the vizier-type is, or only appears to be, missing from the Jerusalem Court officials' list would supply much information about administration in the petty empire of Solomon and to a lesser extent David. It forces one to raise questions about that period in the history of Israel heretofore unasked.

The evidence contained in this part may be turned on an unclear aspect of HS studies and provide more clarity to that aspect. The application of this evidence to that aspect is contained in PART II of the present work.

PART II

**"kh 'mr yhwh:' THE EVIDENCE FOR THE
GREAT INDIVIDUAL PROPHET OF THE HEBREW
SCRIPTURES AS MESSENGER**

PART II
INTRODUCTORY
The Great Individual Prophet
of the Hebrew Scriptures as Messenger:
Some Necessary, Preliminary Considerations

The purpose of this part of the book is to point the evidence presented in PART I in one specific direction in order to demonstrate one of its many possible uses. Specifically, what follows is designed to stimulate some serious thought concerning references one constantly encounters to the great individual prophets of the Hebrew Scriptures as messsengers, to their oracular utterances--and oftentimes <u>every</u> utterance attributed to them--as messages, and to raise the question of the derivation of such references. Here I point to them because any serious, learned opinion concerning prophets being viewed and understood as messengers must be formulated in light of the evidence contained in PART I, <u>and</u> must round out such work. Questions must be raised concerning what caused the GIPs to be referred to as messengers, and about what caused their sayings to be termed messages. It must be asked whether the many references to the 'message' of a certain prophet in the works of modern scholars and/or theologians stem from and thereby embrace a technical term employed by modern inquirers, or whether 'messenger' as employed by them is based on earlier facts from ancient literature, especially the Hebrew Scriptures themselves. This may be accomplished by critiquing 'message' as employed in the works of well-known and influential scholars <u>who work in</u> the Hebrew Scriptures, and by comparing their use of 'message' with its understood <u>use in</u> the Hebrew Scriptures, a use already studied in great detail in PART I. A fresh study long overdue, therefore, in an age which repeats much which has already been concluded uncritically and calls it fresh work, is an inductive one which determines whether any material contained within the Hebrew Scriptures justifies an identification of <u>any</u> of the great individual prophets and any saying attributed to that prophet with messenger and message as those terms would have been understood and employed in ancient Israel and in the greater ancient Near East.

In addition to the foregoing concerns and obligations, one must take into account the expressions 'commissioning formula,' 'messenger formula,' and 'messenger speech,' expressions produced by the form-critical school's analyses of the prophetic *corpus* of the Hebrew Scriptures. The fruits of that school's investigations must not be overlooked when searching for candidates who promote allegations and produce categories of literature about prophetic messengers and prophetic, messenger speech, allegations and categories used thankfully, but uncritically by many contemporary scholars.

Coming full circle, what must be undertaken is a full-scale study of the great individual prophets compared with the ANE historical messengers point by point, and their prophetical sayings studied point by point with the messages of the ANE. In this manner only can the issue of whether the GIPs of the HS were messengers be settled properly and satisfactorily.

After acknowledging this problem (the first step in the scientific method), I understand that we are standing at the beginning of a long but necessary journey. Granting that, we are justified in asking for a map to help chart the best, safest, and most expeditious route. Otherwise, we may be found guilty of the charge of having engaged in idle chatter which could lead to a fool's errand.

The Three-Stage Factor

According to Claus Westermann,[1] the literature suggests that views concerning prophetic speech are divisible into three periods, before, during, and after the eighteenth century of this era. Before the century the prophetic *corpus* was refracted through the prism of faith, and was viewed as consisting of homogeneous literary units. "The prophetic book was equated with the word of God."[2]

Anthropocentric research emerged during the eighteenth century and was fully developed by the following century. It revealed a living, flesh and blood person behind the prophetic books. As one would expect, the emphasis shifted almost entirely toward ascertaining the "genuine" words of a given prophet. The remaining words were left in a questionable light with regard to origin, importance, and authenticity. Only the deity's word(s), or only prophetic man's word(s) were the extremes created thereby.

A third stage brought both extremes together and assigned equal value to both. It was emphasized that the deity's word(s) had come forth through a person, the prophet. Not only this, that word had been transmitted by hearers and disciples of the prophets as well as others who were affected by their words. A long line of transmission tradition was found, therefore, in the completed prophetic books according to this view. Tradition, the third factor, however, is usually still omitted when prophetic literature is considered.

'Message' and Modern Scholarship: A Sampling

'Message' is employed frequently by contemporary scholars when referring to the complete works of the great individual prophets. 'Message' so employed implies that the three-stage factor is not assumed to be applicable--or that it is simply being ignored. An implied homogeneous whole position similar to the pre-eighteenth century is still found in many contemporary scholarly discussions, especially as those discussions pertain to the prophets Amos through Ezekiel.

The historian of Israelite religion(s), Georg Fohrer, entitles a section of one of his works 'The Content of the Prophetical Message.'[3] The section is replete with numerous vague and/or generalized uses of the implied title 'messenger' for the individual prophets, implied by their having a 'message.' Accordingly, he writes:

> . . . Yahweh was considered powerful
> as the saviour and deliverer of Israel,
> helping the nation and the individual
> when they were in need, and according
> to the message of some of the
> prophets, even redeeming the guilty

> and the morally depraved existence of
> man.[4]

The prophet--presumably as messenger--can <u>change</u> his 'message.' Fohrer holds:

> Ezekiel's ministry can be divided into
> three periods . . . After a short period
> of silence following the fall of
> Jerusalem Ezekiel <u>changed</u> his
> <u>message</u> (not Yahweh!) to one of
> conditional salvation.[5]

If we were dealing with messengers as understood in the ANE for a protracted period of time, we would have here a case that would differ from that of any other messenger in the region at the time covered herein (ca. 3000-30 BCE)! At any rate, we observe how loosely and uncritically the term 'message' has been employed consistently by Fohrer.[6]

The historian John Bright also includes vague uses of 'message' in reference to the utterances of various prophets of the HS in his famous work.[7] Discussing the prophets of the late eighth century in Judah, he entitles one section "The National Emergency and the Prophetic Message.'[8] In this case he is writing about the activities of the prophets Isaiah of Jerusalem and Micah of Moresheth. Other sections are entitled 'The Prophet Isaiah: His Career and Message,'[9] and 'The Message of Micah.'[10] Concerning Isaiah, Bright writes that he " . . delivered a <u>message</u> that was first of all a denunciation fully in the tradition of Amos."[11]

Isaiah's early encounters with Ahaz, king of Judah, were fruitless. In the face of impending destruction at the hands of the Syro-Ephriamitic League, Isaiah cautioned Ahaz to remain steadfastly by the Covenant and to trust Yahweh. "Instead," wrote Bright,

he sent tribute to Tiglath-pileser and
surrendered his independence. Isaiah,
his advice scouted, handed over to his
disciples a record of what he had said
as a witness for the future (ch. 8:16-
18), and withdrew.[12]

Does withdrawing mean that as an alleged messenger Isaiah's
messenger service was closed for business, to open only when he
wanted to work? We may raise the question: If the prophets were
indeed messengers, did they work only (i.e., deliver messages) when
they felt so inclined, and quit summarily when it so pleased them?
Bright does not appear to question this, for in discussing the continued
career of Isaiah he wrote: "After his rebuff in 735-733, Isaiah
apparently made no attempt to influence national policy as long as
Ahaz reigned."[13]

It appears that Bright is using the term 'message' to mean a
summary or abstract of the combined oracles, utterances and symbolic
activity of the prophets which were brought to bear on a specific
problem at a specific time. It appears further that Bright views the
prophets as directing their own activity and responding to the stimulus
of the *status quo*. 'Message' so employed by Fohrer the historian on
Israelite religion(s) and Bright the historian on Israel does not appear
to point to a deliverer of such a message in the name and stead of one
who had commissioned another to deliver *verbatim* correspondence
to yet another. Bright differs from Fohrer, however, in that his
emphasis of 'message' is strictly on the words of a given prophet as the
words of a man.[14]

The preceding authors represented historical perspectives. A
theological perspective should also be included in these considerations
to show that this vague use of 'message' is not restricted to use by
historians on Israel, or on Israelite prophetic religion alone. This third
perspective is found in the work of Norman Snaith who states of the
prophets: "Their message is recognized by all as marking a
considerable advance on all previous ideas."[15] He states further:

"There are two aspects in which their message is unique, differing in each case from the ethical ideas of the Greeks."[16] As with the uses of 'message' by Fohrer and Bright, 'message' employed by Snaith could be substituted better by such such a word as either thought or ministry.

'Message,' 'Ministry,' and 'Thought': Synonyms?

An image appears to be forming that 'message' is being used synonymously with ministry or thought or some other such term. Fohrer on Hosea writes: ". . . we cannot distinguish well-defined periods in Hosea's ministry, but it is possible to make out a gradual transformation of his message."[17] Here, as employed, 'ministry' and 'message' could be synonyms for thought, but no messenger's presence or activity is evident. Yet Fohrer continues: "Hosea's message (thought; ministry?) is dominated by the severe tension between Yahweh's conduct toward Israel and the conduct of Palestinian Israel toward Yahweh, . . ."[18]

'Oracle' and 'Message': Synonyms?

Germane to the preceding question is the seemingly synonymous use of oracle and message to refer to the prophetic utterance. Again, Fohrer as spokesperson holds:

> According to the belief of the period, all oracles--including prophetic oracles--had to be communicated in poetically-structured form. There is therefore no genuine prophetical saying not in the form of poetry.[19]

This statement implies that those other than the prophets could utter oracles, and that those oracles, too, were considered legitimate as long as they were poetic. Oracle so used by Fohrer, it would appear, is synonymous with message. But here, remembering Israelite religious practice, we must raise the question: Does this also mean--providing that an identification of oracle with message is affected--that, say, priests--who also delivered oracles--are likewise to be called messengers, and all their sayings to be called oracles or messages from Yahweh?[20]

Summary

The use of 'message' by scholars such as Bright, Fohrer and Snaith--these uses are symptomatic of most scholars who write about the great individual prophet of the Hebrew Scriptures, and in no way are restricted to uses by these three scholars solely--reflect extremely ambiguous senses of the term. They imply--and their trusting readership assumes itself informed accordingly--that there is no question whatsoever that the great individual prophets of the Hebrew Scriptures were messengers and that their utterances--apparently all of them--were messages, or that their contemporaries understood them to have been such.   These 'messages' could presumably be identical with the word(s) of Yahweh and thus reflect a pre-eighteenth century stance when so thought of by an author. All but one of the examples taken from Fohrer's work fell within the first category.

Bright's examples readily fall within the second category, the view that the genuine words of the prophets were identical with his (Bright's) use of message. With Bright one gets the impression that the prophet was in charge of his actions at all times, that every word and gesture were well thought out, and that there was never an accidental slip of the lip; only the prophet's word was the message.

Moreover, message could be used synonymously with words such as ministry, oracle, and thought according to the manner in which 'message' was employed by all three scholars. This is how the examples taken from Snaith's work could be summarized. But we have also seen that there were several instances where Fohrer employed 'message' in a similar manner, and we would encounter no difficulty in including Bright's examples in this discussion as well.

Thus, a quest for an understanding of what makes one hold that a prophet is a messenger and what constitutes a message is not forthcoming from a mere use of 'message' by modern scholars.

Moreover, the works of modern scholars do not even reflect the later stage in the understanding of the development of prophetical speech forms. I am confident that if these scholars had had available to them a study such as the evidence contained in PART I they would have been far more careful in their selection of words employed in reference to the prophetic <u>corpus</u> of materials.

CHAPTER IV

The Historical Prophet
of the Hebrew Scriptures as a Messenger:
Origin, Development and Decline:
An Inductive Study

This study distinguishes between the prophet's functions as an oracle-giver, a deliverer of sermons, and his role as an alleged messenger. It views these as three separate functions (or possible functions) of the same person. The prophet's functions as oracle-giver and deliverer of sermons--or for that matter his role as advisor or counselor!--are not the focus of this study, nor are those functions in need of being clarified here. Since all of these functions could overlap, however, a distinction needs to be made. Here we focus on the problem of the prophet considered to be a messenger.

The Semitic languages having been my most steadfast ally thus far in uncovering the presence of messengers and messenger activity--oftentimes heretofore unacknowledged as demonstrated by Chapter III herein--I turn to biblical Hebrew for the same assistance initially with reference to a biblical view of the historical prophet as messenger.

The Hebrew *mal'aki* means my 'messenger.' It is also the title of a post-exilic book of prophecy known as the book of Malachi. The first verse of Malachi may be read either "The oracle of the word of the Lord to Israel by Malachi.", or ". . . by my messenger." At 3:1a one reads: "Behold, I send my messenger to prepare the way before me. . ." This messenger is the messenger of the covenant (3:1b). He serves as a herald. Malachi 2:7 tells one that even the priest is "the messenger of the Lord of Hosts." The little book ends with a promise that Elijah the prophet will be <u>sent</u> to prepare both parent and offspring for the "great and terrible day of the Lord . . ."(4:5). Malachi 4:5 (HS 3:23) also uses the verb *shlh*, to send, in reference to Elijah the prophet. This verb is characteristically useful in ascertaining biblical texts which are concerned with the sending forth of a messenger.[1] Thus, here is a prophetic book which appears to refer to a prophet as "my messenger"--and the reader is left to presume that *yhwh* is the one who refers to him as such. A messenger is spoken of as being sent to prepare the way, and Elijah may even be identified with this messenger. Lastly, the priest is also spoken of as a messenger who instructs.[2] The book of Malachi, then, is pregnant with references to messengers, prophet and priest are so named.

Martin Buss,[3] however, doubts the authenticity of an historical Malachi. He holds that a prophetic utterance, whether the source was known or was anonymous, received special handling. No extant words of a prophet were excluded if at all possible. "In the Old Testament, almost all oracles are placed under a name, even such an artificial one as Malachi, . . ."[4] He saw the name Malachi as being possibly taken from the statement in verse 3:1. The majority of critical, biblical scholars agree. Thus, there is no historical prophet Malachi to investigate, while the references to the legendary Elijah are of equally little assistance for this present study.

Second Chronicles 36:15-16 says of the Israelites: "The Lord, the God of their fathers, <u>sent</u> persistently to them by his messengers,. . . but they kept mocking the <u>messengers</u> of God, despising his words, and scoffing at his prophets, . . ." These verses seem to indicate that prophets and messengers are synonymous. Indeed, in the post-exilic period a movement toward the identification of the prophet and priest! as messsengers was made. But closer scrutiny of this particular verse will indicate that it is not poetic in structure. No synonymous parallelism is evident which would allow one to argue here that messengers and prophets are synonyms. In addition, prophets as messengers does not appear to have been the pre-exilic view of one of their functions. From the vantage point of hindsight, the Chronicler and his generation certainly could have developed an understanding that both were synonyms. This study is interested in ascertaining what the pre-exilic, great individual prophets were **not** understood to have been by their contemporaries, not what their later interpreters and commentators thought of them. Bereft, therefore, of such certainty from any extant, pre-exilic documents stating so, I cannot soundly employ these two verses in my quest to ascertain whence the view of the historical prophet as a messenger. Yet, the view that historical prophets were messengers remains steadfast in some circles, and the foregoing discussion has not altered that fact. I must therefore look elsewhere.

Jeremiah 26:12 states that he "spoke to all the princes of the people, saying, "The Lord sent me to prophesy against this house and this city all the words you have heard." He punctuated his statement in vs. fifteen by stating "for in truth the Lord sent me to you to speak all of these words in your ears." It would appear that Jeremiah is claiming messengership. He is depicted as claiming to have been sent with a specific task of speaking specific words to a specific people. These are some of the characteristics of secular messengers which have been discussed at length in Chapter I of the present work. Second Chronicles 36:12 says of Zedekiah, king of Judah, that in the final days of the kingdom, "He did not humble himself before Jeremiah the prophet, who spoke from the mouth of God." This passage also seems to imply that Jeremiah was a prophet-messenger.

Like Jeremiah, Ezekiel is depicted as having said that *yhwh* sent him to the people Israel. He, too, it would appear, is viewed as a messenger (Ezek. 2:2,4).

Isaiah of Jerusalem asked to be sent by *yhwh*. When the latter had asked whom he should send as his representative, Isaiah volunteered. *yhwh* responded with the formula of one who commissions messengers, "Go, and say to this people: . . ." (Isaiah 6:8-9) which contains the characteristic imperatives of such a formula (above, Chapter III). The implication is that Isaiah functioned as a messenger.

Amos states to Amaziah that although he was formerly occupied with two professions, "the Lord took me from following the flock, and the Lord said to me, "Go, prophesy to my people Israel" (Amos 7:15). The formula of commissioning, with its characteristic imperatives is present once again.

Jonah received the commission "Arise, go to Nineveh, that great city, and cry against it: . . .(Jonah 1:2a). The formula is the same as that for Amos and Isaiah. Jonah must also travel a great distance to fulfill his task, a feature of the ANE messengers already discussed in Chapter I.

Thus far, a view that certain historical prophets were messengers appears to be shaping up in the prophetical literature of the Hebrew Scriptures--and indeed in reference to certain pre-exilic prophets. Against the backdrop of the ANE and HS human messenger types, I have been able to point up legitimate similarities with the prophets so named as well as with others of the Hebrew Scriptures. In none of the above cases, however, has the historical prophet claimed for himself the title messenger, nor has the book containing utterances ascribed to him claimed this title for him. But such a book does exist.

Haggai, the post-exilic prophet is said to have been sent by the Lord their God (Haggai 1:12). "Then Haggai, the messenger of the Lord, spoke to the people with the Lord's message, 'I am with you, . . .'"(vs. 13). Finally, there exists a prophetic book--though late--which clearly reflects the view that Haggai, an historical prophet, was sent as a messenger with a specific message. It is stated emphatically. The evidence contained in Chapter III also demonstrates that messages as short as the one which Haggai is shown to have delivered were not unknown, or uncommon in the ANE.

Here, then, are several examples from the prophetic books. The historicity of the GIPs is not in question, even that of Jonah although that book is laden with much legendary material, and the books provide an introductory glimpse into what may reflect a HS view of the historical prophet as a messenger. I must examine the HS thoroughly at this point, however, to ascertain whether the view of the prophet being a messenger is truly reflected within its pages. With reference to this investigation, the only statement which will not be challenged is contained in Haggai 1:12, but comments about even that verse will be made at the appropriate juncture of the following discussion.

1. The Spokesman/Respondent/Answerer at Mari

The biblical prophets had their counterparts in other portions of the ANE. Texts from the middle Euphrates city of Mari in Mesopotamia are particularly helpful in this respect, for they contain accounts of men and women who addressed heads of government in the name of their god(s) just as the Israelite prophets addressed many Israelite and Judahite kings. These prophetic figures from Mari, called spokesmen, (let us also say spokespersons) respondents, or answerers, came without having been summoned by anyone, and always addressed a specific problem or event.[5] With reference to the HS prophet, James Sanders maintains:

> The Hebrew word for prophet, *nabi'*, probably means spokesman. That is, unlike <u>seer</u> or <u>gazer</u>, *nabi'* seems to emphasize not some mystical aspect of the role of the prophet but his actual function in the life of the covenant people.[6]

Concerning those Mari personalities Sanders adds: "Apparently their appeal to authority was also some ancient sacred context."[7]

A letter-message from Aleppo, dating from the eighteenth century BCE, from an ambassador of Zimri-lim (1780-1746), king of Mari, to his lord speaks of an *apilum*, "answerer." Numerous letters from this period testify to the presence of the *apilum*, or *muhhum* and his feminine counterpart, the *muhhutum*, all of whom functioned at, and are associated with specific sanctuaries and/or temples.[8] Fohrer can therefore write of them: "They belonged to a class of men and women who received mandates from the deity with whose temple they were associated through omens, dreams, or visions and ecstatic experiences, which they transmitted in the form of oracles.[9]

These prophets seldom addressed the head of state directly. Rather, they spoke to a high-ranking member of a cabinet and demanded of that official that a certain mandate from the deity be transmitted to the head of state. Thus the Mari prophet and prophetess did not directly address the king. Instead, they commissioned <u>their</u> messenger (in the form of the official) to deliver a <u>message</u> to the head of state. The Mari texts contain examples of the commissioning formula which is identical to the commissioning process practiced all over the ANE. One text in which the Mari prophet speaks contains this formula: "*Now go, I send you. Thus shall you say to Zimri-lim, saying: . . .*"[10]

One letter-message to Zimri-lim showing how the spokesperson employed officials as messengers commences: "Speak to my lord: Thus says your servant Itur-asdu: On the day on which I sent this letter of mine to my lord, Malik-dagan, a man from Sakka came to me and reported as follows . . ."[11] Itur-asdu was an official. He sent this letter-message which was to be recited before the king. In it he repeated an account told to him by this man from Sakka who was a prophet. Malik-dagan the prophet claimed to have been sent by the god Dagan, for he stated his credentials, i.e., that Dagan had commissioned him: "Now go. I have sent you; to Zimri-lim you shall say as follows:. . ." after which followed this message. "Send your emissaries to me and give me a complete account. Then I will cause even the sheiks of the Benjaminites to wriggle in a fish-trap and place them before you."[12] Itur-asdu ends his message (of recounting the prophet's message, plus his own addition) by stating that "This is what the man saw in his dream and said to me."[13]

These ancient, non-biblical texts concerning the *apilum, muhhum,* and *muhhutum,* and containing the commissioning formula, are of invaluable assistance in helping one to see an aspect of the role of the biblical prophet which we might not have fully understood otherwise. The HS prophet was viewed as transmitting mandates from his deity to people in responsible positions of government in Israel. Unlike his or her Mari counterpart, however, the HS prophet also addressed common people, in addition to a much more variegated audience. The explanation for this major difference lies in the fact that "the biblical prophet was a covenant mediator; for in the Mosaic theology the covenant was with the people directly."[14]

The HS view especially the earlier prophets of the books of Samuel and Kings in the same light as these prophets from Mari. They were understood as persons who bore words "from the deity to the king relevant directly to a moment of crisis in government" (in its fullest responsible sense).[15] I am here referring to such figures as Nathan, Gad, Elijah, and Elisha, to name but a few. Like their Mari counterparts, the words of the HS prophets were frequently threats which came, they said, from a displeased deity.[16] They would be viewed, then, "as precursors of the giants of the classical period of prophecy from ca. 750 to ca. 540,"[17] (i.e., the GIPs) and this in light of the spokespersons, respondents, and answerers from Mari.

The similarities between the Mari prophet and the HS prophet are summed up thusly:

> The parallels to a certain type of Israelite prophecy are unmistakeable. The *apilum* or *muhhum* corresponds to the *nabi'*; like the *nabi'*, he used the form of the short prophetical saying. He demanded that the divine command be transmitted to the king without regard for whether it pleased the king. He criticised the king's conduct without regard for the fact that vassals of the king learned of his criticism. He delivered admonitions and warnings.[18]

2. Inquiring of the Lord

The practice mentioned in the HS of "inquiring of the Lord" may have great significance for an understanding of how the historical prophet may have been considered by some as a messenger. Before prophets as such are ever mentioned for the first time (chronologically) in the HS, early on indirect allusions to oracle-givers of what must have been the Arab *kahin* type are made. Genesis 25:22c states that Rebekah "went to inquire of the Lord" concerning the two struggling children within her womb. Likewise, Exodus 33:7b's "And every one who sought the Lord would go out to the tent of meeting, which was outside the camp." reflects a similar activity with Moses as the oracle-giver. The laws of Exodus 21:6 and 22:8,9, and 11 pertain to specific cases which should be brought before the deity for adjudication. They also suggest that an oracle-giver was present to interpret the will of the deity to the litigants. To these may be added "the terebinth of the soothsayers" of Judges 9:37 and the "terebinth of the oracle-giver" of Genesis 12:6. Sufficient information exists, especially before the appearance of the prophet."[19] The oracle or mandate was acquired either mechanically (i.e., through the casting of lots, or through the reading of the entrails of animals and/or birds), or through the oracle-giver who served as the deity's "mouthpiece."

It is but a small step from the above view to the one contained in 1 Kings 22:5ff. King Jehoshaphat of Judah was on the verge of joining King Ahab of Israel in a war against Syria. Before committing himself, however, Jehoshaphat suggested to Ahab that he "Inquire first of the Lord." Some four hundred guild, court prophets responded: "Go up; (against Ramot-gilead) for the Lord will give it into the hand of the king" (1 Kg. 22:6). Here it is specifically the prophets who deliver the Lord's "answer," or "reply."

The Rabshakeh's message from Sennacherib, king of Assyria (2 Kg. 18:13-36; Isa. 36-39) so unnerved Hezekiah, king of Judah, that he sent several high-ranking messengers to the prophet Isaiah of Jerusalem. Contained in their message is the following sentence. "It may be that the Lord, your God, heard all the words of the Rabshakeh, whom his master the king of Assyria has sent to mock the living God, and will rebuke the words which the Lord your God has heard; therefore lift up your prayer for the remnant that is left (2 Kg. 19:4)." This is a far more sophisticated form which involves asking a prophet to "inquire of the Lord," for it is done indirectly by the use of a conditionally-phrased sentence. Prayer is now the vehicle whereby the prophet is to inquire. Isaiah 19:6-7 contains the prophet's reply. It is prefaced by the formula "Thus says the Lord." It is a reply of reassurance.

In Isaiah 7:10-11 one reads the following: "Again the Lord spoke to Ahaz, 'Ask a sign of the Lord your God; . . .' Here one sees that the deity is entreating Ahaz to inquire of him. Ahaz, however, deigns to do so (vs. 12), and Isaiah responds in spite of his (Ahaz's) refusal to inquire with his famous Immanuel sign of verse 14. This is indeed a twist of circumstances, for in all of the above accounts the initiative has been on the part of the inquirer. In turn, the response from the deity has been favorable generally. When one refused to "inquire of the Lord" the Lord's response proved to be unfavorable. At any rate, we appear to be well into an area wherein historical prophets were believed to have been the vehicle through whom the deity made his mandates known, mandates which may have been solicited or unsolicited.

The idea of "inquiring of the Lord" being associated with the historical prophet is certainly clear in an example which involves the prophet Jeremiah. Zedekiah, king of Judah, sent two trusted men to the prophet with the following message: "*Inquire of the Lord for us*, for Nebuchadnezzar, king of Babylon, is making war against us; perhaps the Lord will deal with us according to all his wonderful deeds, and will make him withdraw from us. (Jer. 21:2)" There is here an absence of circumlocution and inuendo like that contained in the message of King Hezekiah to the prophet Isaiah of Jerusalem; Zedekiah specifically asked for an oracle from the prophet.

Commenting on Jeremiah's reply, J. Lindblom appears to identify oracles with messages, and implies thereby that the prophet Jeremiah is a messenger when he states:

> The prophets were traditionally oracle-givers; and this function was never abandoned during the whole history of prophecy. Jeremiah immediately received a 'word,' i.e., a revelation from Yahweh and formulated an oracle introduced by the common formula, 'Thus says Yahweh.'[20]

It has been demonstrated, however, that the presence of such a formula alone does not cause one to be a messenger, nor cause the utterance to be a message (Chapter III). It has likewise been demonstrated in the same study that oracle and message are not synonyms. It is thus not surprising that Lindblom must explain further: "True there is a vision implied, there is also an oracle, but the oracle and the message are two separate parts of the vision."[21] According to Lindblom, then, it is the _oracle_ and not the _message_ which is introduced by the formula "Thus says Yahweh." If this is true, 'Thus says Yahweh' should be termed the _oracle formula_ instead of the _messenger formula_. To throw even further doubt on the matter, Lindblom then adds: "As is often the case in the prophetic writings, the original oracle has been edited and somewhat enlarged. But there is no doubt about the essential content of the original oracle."[22] This statement is true, but it in no wise helps one gain a clearer understanding of the origin of the view that the historical prophet was a messenger. Lindblom's statements only muddy waters which have already been long muddy and polluted. In addition to confusing the issue of oracles vs. messages, they leave open the possibility that the formula 'Thus says Yahweh'--which is one of the major reasons why many consider the prophet to have been a messenger in the first place--may even have been simply part of the editing process, and not a part of the original utterance--which is to be considered as either an oracle or possibly as a message.

Thus, no clear-cut evidence is forthcoming from an inquiry into the practice of "inquiring of the Lord" as to whether it is the basis for understanding the view of the historical prophet as a messenger.[23] "Inquiring of the Lord" is indeed a practice with which the HS credit the historical prophet. This credit is as an oracle-giver, however, and not as a messenger, as that term has been established and demonstrated throughout PART I.

3. The Council of Yahweh[24]

In addition to the prophet "inquiring of the Lord" and delivering his reply by oracle, several pre-exilic prophets have been associated by modern scholars with the council of Yahweh. These scholars claim that prophets stood in Yahweh's council, were addressed by Yahweh, and were sent from his presence with mandates to groups or to individuals. It would appear, then, that an investigation of this claim could conceivably throw more direct light on the view of the historical prophet as a messenger. The "person who enters heaven" stage has been reached.

The first HS prophetic use of the heavenly council idea involves the prophet Michaiah ben Imlah (1 Kg. 22:1-38). Michaiah was the final prophet summoned at King Jehoshaphat's request to prophesy concerning the outcome of an intended battle with Hadadezer of Syria. Ahab had warned Jehoshaphat that Michaiah never prophesied good concerning him. Having been instructed to do so, Michaiah gave a favorable oracle. Ahab, however, warned him to tell the truth. The result was a prophecy of doom (1 Kg. 22:17). Upon completion of the doom prophecy Michaiah added:

> Therefore hear the word of the Lord: I
> <u>saw</u> the Lord <u>sitting on his throne</u>, and
> all the <u>host of heaven standing beside</u>
> <u>him</u> on his right hand and on his left;
> and the Lord said, 'Who will entice
> Ahab, that he may go up and fall at
> Ramoth-gilead . . .? Now therefore
> behold, the Lord has put a lying spirit
> in the mouth of all your prophets; the
> Lord has spoken evil concerning you.
> (1 Kg. 22:19-23)

This passage is the <u>only</u> passage in which a prophet claims to have had an experience in the council of Yahweh. There appear, however, to be other statements within the HS which may be later developments on this use in 1 Kings 22:19-23. These occur in Isaiah, Genesis, Deutero-Isaiah, Job, Psalms and Daniel.

Snaith, commenting on Isaiah 6:1-5, states that these verses "form a bridge from the pre-eighth century ideas of holiness to the new covenant given by the eighth century prophets."[25] In addition to this theological function, Isaiah 6:1 tells that seraphs were also among the members of the heavenly court.

Also employed by modern scholars as a clue to the belief in a heavenly council is the statement in Genesis 1:26. It states: "Let <u>us</u> make man in <u>our</u> image, according to <u>our</u> likeness," and is interpreted as the deity speaking to other heavenly beings. Genesis 6:2 contains the statement: "the sons of God saw that the daughters of men were attractive;" which might also point to whom some of the heavenly beings were believed to be.

One of the more perplexing occurrences associated with the idea of a council of Yahweh is the three-fold "Comfort!"(masculine, plural, imperative of Isaiah 40:1), whereas one of the most vivid images of Yahweh's council is provided by the prologue to the book of Job. Job 1:6 states: "Now there was **the** day when the sons of God came to present themselves before Yahweh, and the adversary also came among them." One not only gains entry into the council through this scene, one learns that the council met on a specific day and was not continually conducting business. This point of a specific time should be kept in mind as the study continues.

Fohrer's observation of what may be considered judgment within the divine council itself is noteworthy:

> Most are comfortable with the prophet's claim of having been privy to the divine council, but few ever think of their dissenting within the body. Psalm 82, however, represents a judgment discourse of Yahweh (spoken by a cult prophet) in the "divine council," comprising invective, admonition, and threat just as the judgment speeches do.[26]

According to Fohrer, this pre-exilic poem, which incorporates Canaanite mythological material, attacks the Canaanite pantheon and proclaims Yahweh's universal lordship.[27] This view implies that the gods of the nations make up the heavenly council. This, then, is a fairly composite, albeit sketchy, picture of the divine or heavenly council of Yahweh into which certain historical prophets are said to have gained entry.[28]

Where the prophets and the council of Yahweh are concerned, Kingsbury writes: "Completely explicit records of the prophetic experience with the council of Yahweh do not exist, nor are they to be expected."[29] He noticed five major elements in Michaiah's account: (1) King Yahweh was seated on a throne; (2) He was surrounded by heavenly creatures; (3) All this was seen by the prophet who; (4) retailed what he had seen; and (5) This scene, believes Kingsbury, because it takes place on the threshing floor, is to be connected with an annual agricultural feast allowing one to ascertain the time of the vision.[30] The time was the turn of the year (1 Kg. 20:26) in the northern kingdom (i.e., Spring).

Isaiah of Jerusalem also recounts a vision of Yahweh and his council (Isa. 6:1-13). This account also contains the same five elements.[31]

Ezekiel's vision(s) when analyzed also yield(s) the same five elements.[32]

In all of these visions the accounts are fairly clear. In several remaining prophetic books less explicit references to prophetic encounters with the council of Yahweh are also pointed out. These include the five visions of Amos (Amos 7:13; 4-6; 7-9; 8:1-3; and 9:1) which yield three of the five elements; (1) seeing Yahweh; (2) hearing him speak; and (3) the time of the vision is the period of harvest.[33]

Two of the five elements are found in Jeremiah's temple speech (Jer. 26:1): (1) he heard Yahweh's words; and (2) the sermon was delivered at the time of the New Year's festivals.[34]

Deutero-Isaiah is also believed to have had an encounter with Yahweh's council, and is the last HS prophet for whom modern scholarship claims such an encounter.[35]

It will be noticed that of the five (or less) common elements a special time of the year is common to all of them. My earlier reference to the book of Job showed that the council met on a specific day. With this in mind, Kingsbury correctly observes:

> After Yahweh had inquired of the
> adversary concerning Job and the
> latter had denounced him, Yahweh

granted him permission to test Job. It
was not until "the day" came again that
there was a report on the results of the
testing. This picture, then, is a picture
of Yahweh and his council which met
on a specific day and on that day fixed
the destiny for the next period of
time.[36]

The fate of humans was decided at the annual meetings of the heavenly
council. These meetings were always held at the time of the New
Year's celebrations. These conclusions are drawn from two important
Babylonian rituals: (1) the rite wherein Marduk gained power to
decide the destinies of the coming year, and (2) the divine assembly
met to decide the fates of men.[37] It was thus the prophet's role to find
out what fates had been fixed and announce them to the waiting
congregation. One would begin looking for evidence here which
pointed to the prophet probably prefacing his remarks with some
formula, including "Yahweh has decreed the following." Kingsbury
thus concludes:

The above data will not account for
every prophetic oracle. It was,
however, the basic experience which
set the prophet as cult person over
against the priest and also other
prophets as cult persons. One
experience in the council of Yahweh
may have given rise to all of the
prophet's "Thus Yahweh has said." It
may have been that the experience was
a repeated one.[38]

Kingsbury's study grappled effectively with the time at which the heavenly council supposedly was convened, the purpose for which it was believed to have been convened, and the Babylonian rites with which the council of Yahweh and its purposes are similar. Of equal importance for this study are his final remarks. This experience, we are told, set prophet as cult person against priest and other cult prophets. This problem mushroomed to the point where a certain prophet disputed the utterances of another although both prophets' utterances were perhaps prefaced by standard legitimizing formulae. Kingsbury's article also left unanswered the question of the number of experiences with the council a given prophet would have had to have had when compared with the number of oracles he delivered; oracles which were probably prefaced with a legitimizing formula. Thus, if the HS were inclined to contain a view of the prophet as a messenger on the basis of his alleged council experience, the view was complicated and confusing, and little can be gained from it except a view of one ancient form of sophisticated fortune telling. Yet, the insistence by numerous scholars that certain prophets stood in the council cannot be abandoned easily.[39]

a. Messenger Duels?

There are examples of heated debates and disagreements among certain of the prophets of the HS. When Ahab and Jehoshaphat asked for a prophetic oracle concerning a campaign against Hadadezer of Syria, Zedekiah, one of the guild prophets, stepped forward and promised victory. Michaiah ben Imlah when summoned promised defeat and death for Ahab on the same occasion (1 Kg. 22:13-28).

The prophet Hananiah opposed Jeremiah when the latter counseled Judah to give in to the Babylonians (Jer. 27). Hananiah, on the other hand, gave an oracle of hope and salvation; he predictd that the 597 BCE deportees would return from a Babylonia which would not be able to hold them captive. Baruch's account (Jer. 28), says Fohrer, "shows the bitterness of the conflict between prophets proclaiming antithetical *messages* in the name of Yahweh."[40]

The prophet Ezekiel disputed the arguments of his prophet contemporaries. They held that Yahweh had forsaken neither his promise nor his people. This had been the same argument of the prophet Hananiah who had argued his case on the basis of Israel's legitimate, authoritative traditions also. Yahweh would bring the 597 BCE exiles back within a two year period (Jer. 28:2-4).[41]

Michaiah, Zedekiah, Hananiah, Jeremiah, Ezekiel and his contemporaries were all members of the same covenant community. If the prophets (for the sake of argument) are here viewed as messengers from Yahweh, it is a situation wherein messengers must be viewed as claiming that other messengers were delivering false messages from and in the name of the one who had commissioned them. Their disputes, however, point to grave differences of hermeneutics. Some prophets' claims to have stood in the council of Yahweh, whereas others had not, may contain a portion of the reason for such duels. Jeremiah's intimation of this in Jeremiah 23:18 is a case in point, and cannot be ignored. However, the prophets' claims of experience with a heavenly council (or claims made for them) are so inconclusive that I must look further for historical cause for their being viewed as messengers, especially if one is to demonstrate that they were so viewed by their contemporaries.

b. True vs. False Prophets: True vs. False Messages?

The duels or disputations between certain prophets all claiming to speak the true words of Yahweh have led some scholars to place the prophets into one of two groups; true or false prophets. If these groups are valid and the prophets are proven to indeed be messengers, one is then forced to consider the additional problem this presents; true versus false messengers as well. But with the use of the term "false prophets"--specifically the "name prophets" Zedekiah and Hananiah--one immediately encounters a problem; the Hebrew text does not know the term "false prophet!" The HS, therefore, *never* discuss them. The term comes, rather, from a Greek language text/translation which speaks of *pseudoprophétes* in Jeremiah 6:13; 26:7, 8, 11, 26; 27:9; and 28:1. According to von Rad:

> *Die Verbindung Jahwehs mit seinem Volk stand in Israel nicht auf einer einlinigen Sukzession von Offenbarungsmittlern. Gerade die Inspiration der Propheten, die uns als Schriftpropheten bekannt sind, war institutionell keineswegs gebunden, und es war also nur eine Frage der Zeit, bis einmal die Bescheide aufeinanderprallten und Offenbarungsträger gegen Offenbarungsträger stand.*[42]

There exist numerous causes for this development. Israel's own history offers one reason why matters could grow and worsen to the point where fellow prophets denied each other's utterances, spoken in the name of the same deity.

When Queen Jezebel, wife of King Ahab of Israel, set out to suppress Yahweh worship by championing the cause and cult of her Tyrian Ba'al Melkart, the prophets of Yahweh in Israel of the North received the brunt of her attack and became major targets for persecution. Many capitulated under a real fear and under expressed orders gave favorable oracles, and said whatever they had been told to say (1 Kg. 22:1-28). Others, like Michaiah, stepped outside this circle of prophetic puppets and refused to be so intimidated by neither court officials nor by their fellow frightened prophets. One result was a schism within the prophetic ranks which never healed.

That the Hebrew text does not fall into the Septuagintal (or at least one of the Septuagint's version's) trap of name-calling is significant. It would have been difficult for the Israelite and Judahite communities to decide between two dueling prophets. The problem could conceivably be solved by "inquiring of the Lord" to give a sign or oracle. But that sign or oracle would have been delivered by a prophet! Therein would have been found the problem of credibility. The Hebrew text, rather, provides both accounts and makes no judgment of individual cases. But I have pressed ahead too rapidly. Why were prophets disputing one another's utterances anyway?

The above historical situation involving Jezebel's open war on Yahweh's prophets would only explain a dispute between northern prophets, and then for only a limited historical period. The prophetic disputes occur also in Judah and in Babylonia some two centuries later than the northern disputes. Are there, then, other instances in the biblical text which would point to the embryonic causes of these disputes? To supply an answer I turn first to the book of Deuteronomy. Deuteronomy 7:7 ff. establishes the relationship between Yahweh and his people; prosperity, sanctification and salvation are assured. In Deuteronomy 12:9 ff. one reads that Israel is in a good land and is secure from her surrounding enemies. Deuteronomy 20:4 ff. states that Yahweh fights Israel's battles and causes Israel to be victorious. Deuteronomy 18:15 gives the reason for the presence of the prophets in Israel. Because Israel at the mountain of Yahweh feared the awesome encounter with him, she asked that Moses intercede on her behalf. This Moses did so effectively that a prophet like him was to appear to continue this form of relationship between Yahweh and his people after Moses. But even here one notices that it is taken for granted that unauthorized persons might conceivably claim a prophetic function. A checking and balancing measure was instituted. If what they said did not come to pass, Israel did not have to trouble herself. I will explain why this was so.

Numbers 11:24 ff. is also helpful for my inquiry. Seventy elders were called to the tent of meeting where a portion of the prophetic spirit of Moses was bestowed upon each of them. After this experience the seventy began to prophesy we are told. Von Rad writes that this account also served the aetiological function of explaining why (to a later audience) there were so many different types of prophetic guilds spread all over Israel.[43] The account also attempted to address the question (also presumably late) of why there were those who prophesied, but were known to be a member of no known guild! One reads, therefore, that a portion of the spirit of Moses "spilled" upon two members of the camp who were not a part of the authorized tent of meeting group. These two also began to prophesy by the same spirit. Thus, the HS avoid using a term such as false prophet because they could explain the appearance and utterances of *any* prophet. The HS are not embarrased by antithetical oracles. Many of their interpreting champions, however, are.

I must discuss the cause of the disputes between prophets. One would think that the major cause was some specific religious or social problem. This, alas, is not the case. In fact one learns: "*Es handelt sich nicht . . . um den Kultus, nicht um das Vergeltungsdogma, nicht um das Verhältnis der Fremdvölker zu Jahwe. Allein die Frage nach dem Schicksal des eigenen Volkes steht zur Debatte und auch da nur die Frage: Heil oder Gericht.*"[44] The crux of the dispute is this. In Deuteronomy 13, if what a prophet states does not come true, Israel is to have no fear; it is a test (not a false prophecy!) from the Lord. There is no possible way that the prophetic utterance could therefore be in error (i.e., be considered false). This clean-cut, flawless form of prophesying had an official and corporate-controlled character. In the dispute between Jeremiah and Hananiah, however, the error according to Jeremiah of a prophecy not being fulfilled is proof that that prophecy was not legitimate. For him, this is the test. Deuteronomy's "prophet" can only function within the framework of a corporate structure--there are no individuals--which because of the prevailing theology forces him to deliver favorable oracles of salvation and sanctification--or to repeat the process of "inquiring of the Lord" until a favorable oracle is possible. As a prophet, Jeremiah's stance is free and individual, but most importantly, historical. This is not to say that the Deuteronomic view is unhistorical; it says, however, that Deuteronomy's particular philosophy of history is stunted and growthless. Yahweh indeed in history gathered a people to himself, gave to them his laws and commandments, a thriving land, protected it and them from surrounding enemies, fought their battles, and Yahweh was constantly in their midst. Therefore, prosperity, sanctification and salvation characterized this people forever. This is Jeremiah's main problem with such a *Heilsgeschichte*. It acknowledges Yahweh working in history *once* for a specific purpose which was expected to remain in force forever. History for Jeremiah was a continuum, and Yahweh continually worked in it. Only one who operated outside the corporate mentality could perceive this. Michaiah ben Imlah, Micah of

Moresheth, and Ezekiel are all understandable in this light. It is the light of process thought.

What remains is to determine which form of prophetic receipt of a communique most probably guaranteed that a given oracle was valid (according to the HS). Jeremiah challenged the process whereby opposing prophets claimed to have received revelations through dreams, through ecstasy, or through visions. "*Was sie kündigen*," writes von Rad, "*ist chason libbam: wir würden sagen: Halluzination*."[45] What a dreamer retails is simply a dream; one who grasps the "word" (*dabar*) of Yahweh speaks fact. This difficult-to-grasp "word" is divorced from the corporate-controlled channels of acquisition (i.e., the state-controlled religion) and is relegated to the transcendental realm where it is impossible to be manipulated by mantic techniques. For Jeremiah the difference is clear; if a prophet has not stood in the council to acquire Yahweh's "word" his prophecies are without relevance. One will know this because the proving ground for a given prophecy (however acquired) is the realm of history--not the retrocentric and static history as viewed by Deuteronomy--the dynamic history in which Israel finds herself "now."

The Hebrew Scriptures, then, imply that there were correctly and incorrectly informed prophets *without ever stating so*. The evidence is presented by both duels between prophets and the history of Israel subsequent to 540/39 BCE.

4. The Prophet and Symbolic Actions

Often accompanying the utterances of certain prophets were symbolic actions which appear to have been designed to buttress the spoken words of the prophet. "They are, so to speak, parables in action," writes Lindblom.[46] A brief sampling of these actions must suffice here;[47] Hosea's marriage(s) and naming of his children (Hos. 1:2-9); Isaiah of Jerusalem wearing a yoke (Jer. 27:1-3, 12b); and Ezekiel baking bread (Ezek. 4:9-17). These were deliberate acts designed for a specific purpose, that of punctuating their utterances. In the effort to ascertain whether the historical prophet was viewed as a messenger, one must take note of this fact and practice to ascertain whether it was a characteristic of ANE messengers in general. This I shall accomplish in the final chapter.

5. The *rîb*, or Controversy, or Lawsuit of the Prophets[48]

The Hebrew Scriptures view the prophet as a respondent (in the spirit of Moses) for both Yahweh and his people. From the council of Yahweh where the fates were decided, certain prophets claimed to have come to deliver mandates to Israel in the midst of her daily routine. The prophet is viewed as a mediator between Yahweh and Israel also. There is a small number of prophets, however, concerning whom one scholar opines: "It is very fruitful to view the whole ministry of the several judgmental prophets in the light of the covenant lawsuit."[49] According to this view:

> The prophet, as the messenger or emissary from the heavenly council, stands forth, as it were, and proclaims the convening of the court in the marketplace of man. In the session the prophet is the principle court officer. God is, of course, the judge. But God is also the plaintiff bringing accusations against the people.[50]

Note Sanders' cavalier use of <u>messenger</u> and <u>emissary</u> as well as the multiple roles assigned to both prophet and deity here. Yahweh's major complaint is that certain responsible individuals, groups, or Israel as a whole, have violated some portion of the covenant agreement. Yahweh demands redress.

It would advance the view of the historical prophet as a messenger greatly if such a forensic function could also be documented for extra-Israelite ANE messengers.[51] See also the four appendices concerning the forensic function of certain eighth-century prophets in the present work.

6. Persecution of the Prophets

Above (3a), I stated that Jezebel persecuted the prophets of Yahweh and made their lives miserable. This she did because she planned to make the cult of the Tyrian Ba'al the leading, or the official cult in Israel.

Amos prophesied in Bethel at King Jeroboam II's private sanctuary. He was made unwelcome and was told to leave, to return to Judah and there to do his prophesying. Amaziah the priest forbade him to prophesy ever again in Bethel (Amos 7:12-13). One assumes that Amaziah had the king's authorization in this matter.

Michaiah ben Imlah was imprisoned on rations of bread and water because he "forthtold"(not foretold) the doom of King Ahab in his planned battle against Hadadezer of Syria. Before being imprisoned, however, Zedekiah, one of the guild prophets who challenged Michaiah's prophecy, struck him in the face. Michaiah was then given over to the authorities and was mentioned no more (1 Kg. 22 ff.).

Eliakim (Jehoiakim), king of Judah and vassal of Pharaoh Neco, replaced Josiah on the throne. He spent a great deal of time and money on the building of a new palace for himself. The prophet Uriah ben Shemaiah prophesied against both the king and his city. Jehoiakim received news of these negative prophecies and sought the prophet's life. Shemaiah learned of this fact and fled to Egypt where he sought safety. He was pursued there, however, by the agents of the king, was captured, and was brought back to Jerusalem by force. The vassal king had him executed (Jer. 26:20-23).

The prophet Jeremiah was persecuted by the Jerusalem populace (consisting of priests, guild prophets, and people in general) shortly after his temple address. This assembly had seized him and the priests in particular were calling for his death (Jer. 26:7-11). On this occasion the elders of the land defended him and no harm came to him. But for challenging the official theology of divine providence, however, the unpopular Jeremiah was tried twice and was imprisoned frequently.

These are by no means all of such incidents involving the persecution of certain prophets recorded in the HS. The foregoing examples, however, suffice to show that sometimes the prophet's utterances caused him to suffer harrassment, persecution, and even death. Do the HS view these occurrences as an occupational hazard of the "office" of prophet?

7. The Quoting of an Earlier Prophet: The Short, Direct Prophetic Utterance

The prophets who came after Ezekiel should be viewed as *epigoni*.[52] These later prophets either quote or take their lead from the pre-exilic prophets. Isaiah 40:27-31, which shows Israel's fearfulness and lack of trust, can be compared with Ezekiel's rehearsal of the same situation in Chapter 37. Likewise, Isaiah 43:12 stresses Yahweh's relationship with Israel in her time of purity, when she worshiped Yahweh alone, and takes its lead from Jeremiah 2:2-3. Other examples are seen in Isaiah 43:18 and Jeremiah 16:14-15; Isaiah 48:3-8 and Jeremiah 44; the colophon of Isaiah 48:22 (which also appears in Isa. 57:21 and 66:24) and Hosea 14:9. In fact, the general attitude of most exilic and post-exilic *epigoni* may be summed up as follows.

> The prophet uses the language of the pss. at many points. He has familiarity with liturgical language . . . depended on the use of biblical phrase and allusion. Here, though not only here, he reveals his knowledge of that . . . aspect of the psalmody which finds its place also in the "confessions" of Jeremiah, . . .[53]

The post-exilic prophets were not the only ones to quote earlier prophets. When the elders came to Jeremiah's defense they quoted from the preserved words of Micah of Moresheth:

> Micah of Moresheth prophesied in the days of Hezekiah king of Judah and said to all the people of Judah: '. . . Zion shall be plowed as a field: Jerusalem shall become a heap of ruins, and the mountains of the house a wooded height.' (Jer. 26:18)

Here is an example of the fact that earlier prophecies were collected and remembered in certain circles--here among the elders of the land. This quoting of the prophet Micah appears to have been quite spontaneous, which might reveal the fact that such utterances were short and direct and would facilitate being memorized. It is possible that this example, coupled with the later (i.e., post-exilic) practice of alluding to an earlier prophet's words, point toward the HS's acceptance of the short, direct utterance of the prophet (as opposed to the long, well-thought-out texts contained in the various prophetic books) and the short, direct message of the messenger in the same or similar light.

8. The Writing Down of the Prophetic Utterance

The writing down of the prophetic words, especially the judgment or doom pronouncements is connected to the purpose of writing in general in the ANE. I find the following statement by Martin Buss particularly illuminating.

> Writing could be employed in the ancient world for several standard purposes. It is thus used for letters . . .

spells, and laws, all of which are attested in the Old Testament. It may be noted that written spells appear typically in the negative form of curses. In prophecy, the operation of written curses is emphasized repeatedly; indeed, the use of writing is mentioned primarily for words of woe, partly to give them added threatening power and partly to seal them for a later occasion since they are not accepted by the hearers. Such a tendency helps to explain the survival of doom prophecies from pre-exilic times and specifically the relatively firm written tradition of Hosea's negative sayings as in chas. 4-14.[54]

There is thus a kind of execration text mentality underlying the writing down of the prophetic oracles. Sometimes the prophet wrote down his own oracles. Thus, E. Würthwein is correct in stating that: "Wooden tablets for brief writings may be meant when the prophets Isaiah and Habakkuk are instructed to write down a prophetic oracle" (Isa. 30:8; Hab. 2:2).[55] Würthwein goes on to state that some suggest that the inconsistent arrangement found in some biblical books may be due to prophetic utterances having been written down on pottery fragments before being collected into books.[56] This information, however, is inconclusive.

There is now an explanation as to why the prophecies of the historical prophets were written down. Some messages in the ANE were written down in letter form also. In addition, there are (in the HS) two alleged messengers who wrote down their own (alleged) messages and delivered them, as opposed to two people who were involved in the message delivering and recording process.

9. The Demise of Prophecy

A certain situation must exist into which the prophetic type steps. "Its starting point is the belief that particular utterances of men are in reality the word of God and as such can claim for themselves especial authority."[57] This is the kernel of the whole problem with which this book deals. Other than both ancient **and** modern acceptance uncritically of suggestions that prophets were messengers, suggestions which have come from a number of quarters, just what *evidence* is there? Does the whole interest in the prophet as messenger speak more to the ones who want and/or need to accept such an allegation more than it does to any personal claim made by any of the great individual prophets with whom we are especially interested here? Why people, ancient and modern, can arrive at a mental state wherein they are willing to believe, or be convinced that a person speaking is not speaking his or her own words still needs adequate explanation. As I continue I shall make some contribution to the solution of this problem. But I digress.

Of the several kinds of words spoken by humans ranking as divine words, the prophetic saying (*dabar*) is the most relevant for my investigation. This prophetic *dabar* was valued highly by some. It was written down, preserved, and passed on. Even at a late date, the recitation of such a *dabar* was efficacious in the saving of another prophet's life (Jer. 26:18 ff.). The *dabar* of one prophet could also be directed against the dabar of another. Hosea 1:4-5 corrected the earlier prophetic dabar of Elisha (through one of his disciples) to Jehu in 2 Kings 9:1-12. This was possible because "the authority of the divine word from the past was subject to that of the present."[58]

Although the HS give a picture of a succession of the prophetic *dabar*, they do not conceal the fact that the succession was often broken. In Zephaniah 3:2 one reads: "She (Jerusalem) listens to no voice, she accepts no correction. She does not trust in the Lord, she does not draw near her God." Interpreting this (and the interim period of 21 years for Jeremiah's silence) John Bright, the historian, suggests that after Manasseh had taken the throne "Hezekiah's reform was cancelled completely and the voice of prophecy silenced; those who protested--and apparently there were those who did--were dealt with severely (2 Kg. 21:16)".[59]

If one searches for succinct explanations as to why and when the prophetic *dabar* of the HS ceased to be spoken, Fohrer offers a reasonable explanation.

> Ezra's reform finally set the mainstream of Yahwism on the course that turned its back on the insights and principles that had previously prevailed, above all on the message of the prophets. Here we are dealing with more than a reshaping of Israelite Yahwism--a new religion was in the making.[60]

Bright sees the beginning of the end having occurred much earlier in Israel's history. On the law scroll found in the temple at Jerusalem he writes:

> The official promulgation of a written law, in fact, marked the first step in that process which progressively elevated the law until it became in post-exilic times the organizing principle of religion, and, at the same time, the first step in the concomitant process whereby the prophetic movement, its word rendered progressively superfluous, ultimately came to an end.[61]

One specific prophecy sows the seeds containing the death knell of prophecy in Israel. Zechariah 13:3-6 holds:

> And if anyone again appears as a prophet, his father and mother who bore him shall pierce him through when he prophesies. On that day (i.e., the Lord's day) every prophet will be ashamed of his vision when he prophesies; he . . . will say, 'I am no prophet, . . .'"

So much had prophecy deteriorated as a viable, marginal, social option for influencing national policy that Deutero-Zechariah can write of prophets and unclean spirits in the same sentence (Zech. 13:2b).

In light of the preceding, Eissfeldt wrote: ". . . the spring of prophetic inspiration dried up. Finally, in about the third or second century, the prophetic charisma comes completely to an end, as is shown by 1 Macc. 4:46 and other passages, and it makes way for apocalyptic erudition . . .[62]

Thus, the Hebrew Scriptures witnessed both the rise and the fall of the prophetic movement in ancient Israel. They thereby allude to the fact that the prophet (especially if viewed as a messenger) was instrumental and participated in only one of several forms of revelation, and then only for a limited period of time. Apocalypticism is thus viewed as prophecy's natural successor.

10. Summary

In attempting to view the great individual prophets as messengers, what comes out of the preceding examination of existing evidence must be judged as inconclusive when compared with the categorical statements of post-biblical scholarship and commentary.

The investigation began with the discovery that not every HS prophet could be termed historical; that the name Malachi, for instance, was placed over a *corpus* of anonymous prophecies. This practice in itself was not unusual, for a similar practice was in effect for Isaiah 40-66 and Zechariah 9-14. But since there is no Malachi-the-man to investigate, it would not have aided my study to pursue the matter further.

In other cases, too much legendary material was intertwined with the historical narrative material to allow one to write definitively of, say, a historical Elijah or Elisha to my study's advantage. Despite this fact, the HS preserve enough information to warrant an investigation into the question of whether the historical prophets of the HS were and had been considered messengers and by whom. Haggai, the post-exilic prophet, is specifically called "the messenger of the Lord," (Hag. 1:12). This is the only indisputable HS example which involves an undisputably historical prophet. It still remains to be determined *who* held him to be the Lord's messenger, the correct understanding of *who* is meant by *Lord* here, and in both cases *why*?

Since ascertaining whether the GIPs were viewed as messengers is my main task, I could not ignore the fact that much of the same terminology connected with historical messengers of the ANE was also employed by the HS when recording the careers of the GIPs. Nor could I ignore the fact that these individual prophets employed some of this same terminology when providing autobiographical information, or in their utterances in the name of Yahweh. Jeremiah therefore exclaimed: "for in truth the Lord sent me to you to speak all these words in your ears" (Jer. 26:15); Ezekiel said Yahweh sent him to the people Israel (Ezek. 2:2,4); Isaiah of Jerusalem claimed to have volunteered to go to Israel as an envoy (Isa. 6:8-9); and Amos stated that Yahweh told him to go to Israel and prophesy (Amos 7:15). One should be aware of the rhetorical device of editors at work in these "autobiographical" excerpts, however.

The terminology was so strikingly similar that, when coupled with the indisputable statement of Haggai 1:12, an investigation into the origins, development and subsequent demise of the phenomenon of prophecy in ancient Israel (and thereby any view of the prophets as messengers) was essential.

In order that my investigation not take place in a vacuum, I pursued a brief study of the spokesperson at Mari. Numerous similarities between what one readily knew about the HS prophet were seen to be applicable also to the Mari spokespersons. Above all, they were both understood as persons who laid a certain charge at the foot of a person or persons to correct some injudicious act or to correct a faulty worldview. This was done by appealing to some ancient sacred authority. These Mari prophets were some of the forerunners of the great individual exponents of prophecy in Israel between 750 and 540 BCE.

Investigation of the HS practice of inquiring of the Lord was undertaken because it was but one step away from showing how the HS could have come to view the historical prophet as a messenger. The prophet was believed to be in touch with the other world somehow, and was thought to be able to give the deity's reply to the inquirer. This process of supplying the deity's reply to the inquirer possibly involved numerous mechanical devices. The reply to the inquiry was generally favorable. Negative replies were repeated until they turned out to be positive. Although I found this practice alluded to in the HS long before the appearance of any prophet in Israel, I found that it involved the historical prophet as well (Jeremiah 21:12). Curiously, the response following these inquiries was consistently referred to as an *oracle*. J. Lindblom, among others, commented that this oracle was not identical to the message of a given prophet, but conceded that both oracle and message were part of a given prophetic vision. According to this view, it was the oracle not the message which was introduced by the so-called messenger formula. I concluded that an investigation of the practice of inquiring of the Lord in Israel did not allow one to state conclusively that it was the basis for the view that the HS prophets were messengers.

If inquiring of the Lord was inconclusive, the claim made by numerous modern scholars that certain prophets had stood in the council of Yahweh or in a heavenly council, was at least to bear some fruit. It was claimed that these prophets, during a session of this council, were addressed by King Yahweh who sent them from his presence with specific mandates to groups or to individuals. In addition to the above mentioned similarity between the terminology of the historical messenger, and the frequent prefacing of prophetic remarks by 'Thus says the Lord' with the introduction of the council of

Yahweh, one now witnessed a claim that the historical prophet had been sent an unspecified distance to fulfill the duty of delivering the mandate of Yahweh. This travelling of a certain distance one also noticed among the characterisitcs of messengers of the ANE in Chapter III. However, this suggestion of travel was accompanied by a problem-producing fact which Kingsbury's work had supplied. The council was believed to have been convened but once a year. If this view were correct, its impact on, and significance for my discussion was seen in the fact that if the HS viewed these historical prophets who were to have stood in the council as Yahweh's messengers, they could have been messengers only once a year, theoretically. This fact left numerous other instances of the use of 'Thus says the Lord' woefully unaccounted for. The problem persisted.

The HS, however, are not slaves to 20th century logic, and in addition to the above problem, they show that historical prophets disagreed with one another publicly as to whose utterances in the name of Yahweh were valid and/or invalid. Duels or disputes were recorded of several prophets involved in conflict with one another. Many of these disputes involved the issue of the council of Yahweh and the claim that some of the prophets had not been therein. A transition in pre-exilic prophecy and ascertaining the credentials of a prophet had been set in motion. Throughout this transitional period a shift from the orthodox theology was noticed; a theology which had guaranteed Israel security from surrounding enemies, prosperity, sanctification, and salvation forever, (all of which found their point of confluence in the favorable oracles of the orthodox cult prophets), to a prophetic view which challenged this theology. At issue again was the method whereby a prophet received Yahweh's revelations, and the great individual prophets denied that their adversaries were the recipients of valid revelations. The HS in characteristic fashion recorded both views.

Accompanying many of the prophets' utterances were symbolic actions which could have no other purpose than to buttress or augment in some way those utterances. These actions ranged from wearing a yoke to baking bread. The HS viewed the prophets as persons who punctuated their utterances by symbolic actions. Unfortunately for this investigation, the symbolic actions pointed more to the intellectual level of the audience who witnessed these actions and for whom they were designed, than they (the actions) were helpful in solving my problem of whether the HS prophetic literature provided definite evidence of the great individual prophets either being viewed by their contemporaries as messengers, or the HS themselves making such an explicit claim.

The *rîb*, or controversy, or lawsuit was also linked to the prophet's allegedly having stood in Yahweh's council, for upon his alleged return he announced that Yahweh had convened his court to try Israel for her waywardness. According to the HS, the GIPs had forensic functions as well.

Frequently the HS prophet was the victim of persecution; sometimes at the hands of fellow prophets, sometimes at the hands of rulers, priests, and/or the general populace. Oftentimes the prophets were identified with the contents of their unpopular utterances and suffered harrassment, physical abuse, and even death.

The prophetic utterance which had already been preserved in oral form for quite some time was oftentimes written down; sometimes, the evidence strongly suggests, by the prophet himself. In addition, the prophetic doom oracle was written down in an attempt to add threatening power to it in a manner similar to the significance of writing execration texts on pottery vessels. They were sealed for a later period since most were ignored at the time of delivery. This attitude on the part of the prophets' contemporaries to their utterances provides one of the strongest reasons why the question of who viewed the prophets as messengers is raised. The question of when such a view came into existence is also linked to the practice of writing down prophetic utterances for a later time. It is, then, this issue of time, coupled with the foregoing, which provided the main reasons for my study.

Just as the HS produced and contained enough material to allow some to allege that the GIPs were messengers, they also produced enough information to show that this alleged messenger's days were numbered! Just as they (the HS) chronicle the rise of the prophetic movement, they also chronicle its demise. Several scholars have offered opinions as to why prophecy in Israel declined. They agree generally, however, that it declined because the post-exilic community forged a new religion (or performed a radicalectomy on the old one(s) which ultimately witnessed the prophet's disappearance from the Israel of the HS. The HS, too, contain in Zechariah 13:2b-6 a final judgment on prophecy and prophets; oddly enough by a prophet.

The view of the HS prophet (in general) as a messenger may be likened to an incomplete mosaic of a seemingly familiar scene. Through the bits and pieces of similarity of expression and activity which make up this incomplete mosaic, the reader (like one beholding the mosaic) gets the impression that the incompleted portion can be easily filled in by comparing it with what is already recognizeable. To be able to fill in what is incomplete pays tribute more to a fertile and nimble imagination than to empirical certainty by way of demonstrated evidence. When one carefully scrutinizes the evidence, the only examples of the HS specifically naming prophets as messengers are "Haggai the messenger of the Lord" (Haggai 1:13), and Malachi 3:1 where one reads that Yahweh is to send his messenger, by whom is most probably meant the legendary Elijah. One may only say with certainty that the HS view the post-exilic prophet Haggai as a messenger. How and why Haggai is so viewed, and at such a late date in the history of the prophetic movement in Israel, we are not told. We may speculate, but we do not know.

Modern scholarship's use of 'message' did not produce enough hard data to support a claim on the part of modern scholars that the HS, GIPs were messengers. A thorough study of what evidence there existed in the HS themselves produced only one late, but irrefutable reference to an historical prophet being a messenger. Even that one cameo occurrence raises more questions than it supplies answers to my inquiry. Thus, both sources, the general modern and the Hebrew Scriptural, proved most inconclusive. Form-critical analysis and elaboration of the prophetic books has caused the most categorical statements to be made concerning the prophet's alleged messengership. I turn now to the form-critical designations of 'commissioning and messenger formulae' and 'messenger speech' to ascertain whether even here such categorical statements are warranted and tenable (especially beyond a mere descriptive function).

CHAPTER V

The 'Commissioning Formula,'
the 'Messenger Formula,'
and 'Messenger Speech' in the
Prophetic Books of the Hebrew Scriptures

Edmond Jacob, writing on the issue of how and why the prophetic oracles of the HS have their present form, noticed that many prophets "formulate their oracles in just the same way as a messenger transmits a message that has been entrusted to him; . . ."[1] He observed further that passages such as Numbers 22:16; Judges 11:12; 14:22; 1 Kings 20:3; 22:27; 2 Kings 18:28, which relate messages, "have the same form as prophetic oracles."[2] Jacob has reversed the actual situation unfortunately, for it is some of the prophetic oracles which appear to have been formed along the same lines as regular communication techniques of the ANE. They have certainly been presented that way. Characteristic of the modern scholar's attitude toward the prophets and their utterances, Jacob adds : "When the prophets introduce their discourse by the words "Thus saith Yahweh," they imply the transmission of a message received without any addition of their own; and in other respects they take care to distinguish the Word of Yahweh from their own words."[3] The strength of Jacob's statements will be probed below.

1. The 'Commissioning Formula'

When Elijah was (depicted as being) instructed what to tell Ahaziah, several imperatives were used in the instructions contained in 2 Kings 3. "*Arise, go up* to meet the messengers . . . and *say* to them . . .," undoubtedly corresponds with the style of the commissioning of a messenger, while what follows resembles the contents of a message to subordinates as discussed in PART I.

Likewise, one reads in the book of Jeremiah where Yahweh is depicted as telling the prophet to "*Go* and *proclaim* in the hearing of Jerusalem," (2:1); "*Go* to the house of the Rechabites and *speak* with them, and *bring* them to the house of the Lord, into one of the chambers; then *offer* them wine to drink," (35:2); "*Go* and *speak* to Zedekiah, king of Judah and *say* . . ."(34:2). Isaiah of Jerusalem is told to "*Go*, and *say* to his people:" (Isa. 6:9); "*Go forth* to meet Ahaz . . . and *say* to him," (7:3-4), Ezekiel is told to "*eat* this scroll and *go*, *speak* to the house of Israel," (Ezek. 3:1). The instruction to Hosea is "*Go*, *take* to yourself a wife of harlotry, and *have children* of harlotry," (Hos. 1:2). Amos stated that the Lord told him to "*Go*, *prophesy* to my people of Israel." (Amos 7:15). Jonah is told "*Arise*, *go* to Nineveh . . . and *cry against it*;" (Jonah 1:2).

Concerning such formulae, Klaus Koch cautioned: "But it should not be too quickly assumed that the prophet's position was that of a special messenger, or that his profession was that of a messenger."[4] Koch's assertion is that anyone can be a messenger of the Lord. He does not question whether they ever were, he is widening the field. He merely argues that prophets, too, were not exempt from this category, (recall Elijah's disciple-prophet and his mission to Jehu) thereby raising the issue of whether prophets, in addition to their other functions, were intermittently placed in this capacity; and then suddenly![5] Koch, however, offers his thoughts on messengers gratuitously. He makes thereby no serious contribution to the solution of our problem. For the present his study is important because it underscores once again the fact that the frequent careless uses of the term 'message' of Amos, Hosea, *et al.* by scholars was misleading and deserved the challenge to its frequent use above (PART II INTRODUCTORY), for its presence implied also that the prophet was always a messenger and that every prophetic utterance was a message from Yahweh--both of which Koch calls into question by his statement.

The presence of one or more imperatives in an extant formula is witnessed in 2 Kings 1:15. "Then the angel (i.e., messenger) of the Lord said to Elijah, "*Go down* with him; *do not be afraid* of him" (the captain of the fifty sent by Ahaziah to take him captive). This was, as Koch correctly informs, "a speech . . . which concerns one man personally, it is not to be passed on."[6] It is therefore a private oracle and the so-called commissioning formula does not signal any sort of messenger-type activity. Isaiah 18:4; 21:16; and 31:4 likewise reflect oracles (private), Jeremiah 13:1 is a private oracle containing the imperative formula "*Go* and *buy* a linen waistcloth, and *put it on your loins*, and do not dip it in water; . . ." The imperatives found in Jeremiah 13:4 and 13:6 also serve as examples.

2. The 'Messenger Formula': An Overview

Although the introductory formula *kh 'mr yhwh* (Thus says the Lord or Thus Yahweh has said) begins many of the so-called prophetic messages, and is thereby generally recognized as signalling such a message, it is well to regard the words of Martin Buss. Discussing the analysis of literary forms in some prophetic books he observes: "There is even an absence of prophetic formulas--like "Thus says the Lord"--which has been regarded as useful aids for discovering divisions" in some of the prophetic books.[7]

The most prolific use of the formula *kh 'mr yhwh* in an exilic prophetic book occurs in Deutero-Isaiah (40-55), where it is found more often than in any of the individual prophetic books from Amos to Ezekiel, with the notable exception of the book of Jeremiah, where it occurs in excess of fifty times. The formula appears no more than twelve times in the words ascribed to Isaiah of Jerusalem. Examples occuring in Deutero-Isaiah include Isaiah 41:21; 42:5 (which contains an extended formula of the Rabshakeh (Isa. 36:4,13); 43:1,14,16; 44:2b; 45:1 (concerning Cyrus); 45:11 (considered by Köhler to be the only complete example of *Botenspruch* in the HS prophetic books);[8] altogether some twenty-one times. The proclamation formula "Hear this," "Hear O sons of Israel," is found some fifteen times in the book.[9]

The formula *kh 'mr yhwh* never occurs in Joel, Habakkuk, or Hosea. An alternate formula, however, appears in Hosea and Zephaniah as *n'm yhwh*, (says the Lord or a saying of the Lord or even an oracle of the Lord) in Hosea 2:13c; 16:21 which were accompanied by two examples of the proclamation formula at 4:1 and 5:1) and in Zephaniah (1:10; 2:9; 3:8,20c).[10] In the book of the prophet Nahum, *kh 'mr yhwh* occurs only once, at Nahum 1:12; *n'm yhwh* occurs twice (Nahum 2:13; 3:5). Micah 3:5 contains the only *kh 'mr yhwh* in the book. It is accompanied by one "Hear what the Lord says;" at Micah 6:1 which is a combination of the 'messenger formula,' and the 'proclamation formula,' and several proclamation formulae as part of a *rîb* or lawsuit (Micah 1:2; 3:9; 9:9b). The book of Obadiah contains one *kh 'mr yhwh* formula and two occurrences of *n'm yhwh* at verses 8 and 46. Trito-Isaiah (56-66) employs the formula *kh 'mr yhwh* eight times, and especially noteworthy is the occurrence at Isaiah 57:15: "For thus says the high and lofty One." The formula *kh 'mr yhwh* appears twelve times, and one of these in the form "says my God," at Isaiah 57:21. The proclamation formula is used once at 66:5.

The book of Isaiah contains three instances of the formula *kh 'mr yhwh 'ly* (Thus says [said] Yahweh to me" at Isaiah 18:4; 21:16 and 31:4). Here the formula is used as part of prophetic autobiographical material and marks private oracles only. *kh 'mr yhwh* also occurs in Jeremiah eight times for the same reason (3:6, 11; 13:1; 14:11, 14; 15:1; 17:19; 25:15).

The apocryphal book of Judith contains two interesting formulae which are germane to my study. In Judith 2:5 King Nebuchadnezzar called Holofernes, his general, and said to him;"Thus says the Great King, the lord of the whole earth." This formula is reminiscent of the formula found at Isaiah 42:5 and 36:4, 13. Here one notices that the so-called messenger formula is not followed by any kind of message from the king to any of his distant subordinates as would be expected, nor is it spoken by one who would deliver such an unexpected message. Likewise, one also notices the formula "So says (or Thus says) King Nebuchadnezzar, the lord of the whole earth." at Judith 6:4. Although this is the correct form, it appears here in the same position as the formula *n'm yhwh* appears in, say, the book of Jeremiah (*passim*) especially at 50:31, i.e., it appears at the end, not the beginning of a discourse as would be expected. The commissioning formula in Judith 2:6, however, is used correctly. It is possible that the forms degenerated after the demise of prophecy. Martin Buss could therefore observe correctly that: ". . .since the essential, or inner siutuation may be similar under a vartiety of external conditions, it is possible that a genre is used outside its ordinary or original position. The prophet can burst forth in a lament. A psalm can be sung outside the temple."[11] To this valid observation one may add that the prophet could have employed the 'messenger formula' in a similar manner, for it has been observed that not all messenger formulae automatically signalled 'messages' or messenger activity, even when employed by a given prophet.[12]

Thus, evidence in several prophetic books--and one apocryphal book--has been presented which demonstrates that not every occurrence of *kh 'mr yhwh* is followed by a so-called message, or that strictly speaking it is even to be called a messenger formula, for other formulae function in the same way whether it (i.e., *kh 'mr yhwh*) is present or not. What can be said with certainty is that at best the formula and its variants "are used when the importance and the reliability of a prophetic utterance are to be particularly emphasized."[13] This still does not tell us whether the formula was added by the prophets themselves or whether the formula was added by editors and redactors at a later stage in the development of the prophetic *corpus* of literature.

a. Variations on the 'Messenger Formula': The Addition of Material

As late as 1969 Klaus Koch could still state: "It is still undecided whether the prophets borrowed more than the legitimizing formula, Thus saith the Lord' (*kh 'mr yhwh*) from the messenger formula, which was then used in diplomatic circles."[14]

Friedrich Baumgärtel raised doubts about the connection between 'Thus saith the Lord' and the messenger formula which was very often extended to include certain titles in Jahweh's honor. These included 'Thus said the Lord Sabaoth' and 'Thus says the Lord, the God of Israel.'[15]

Koch, on the other hand, demonstrated that the inclusion of certain titles was found just as much in the mouths of royal messengers, e.g. 2 Kings 18:19 ("And the Rabshakeh said to them, 'Say to Hezekiah, "Thus says the great king, the king of Assyria:"), and was therefore by no means unknown in the messenger formula.[16]

Additions to the basic *kh 'mr yhwh* formula in the prophetic books are found at Isaiah 1:24; Isaiah 3:15; Isaiah 30:15; 38:5; and

45:11. The formula found at Isaiah 57:15 "For such says the high and lofty One. . ." reflects the extent of variations on the basic formula.

b. Allied Formulae

Not all of the prophetic oracles to the nation of Israel, or to individuals are preceded by *kh 'mr yhwh*. Some are preceded by no formula at all, but may or may not be concluded by other formulae. Therefore, the messenger formula is also the subject of a discussion by H. W. Wolff who noticed some important variations on the formula.[17] He holds that the formula "also accounts for the 'proclamation formula' that now begins the passage in (Hosea) IV:1a: "Hear the word of Yahweh, O sons of Israel."[18]

A much shorter form is found in Hosea 5:1 and in a variety of forms in such passages as Amos 3:1; 4:1; 7:16; 8:4; Micah 3:1, 9; 6:1; and Isaiah 1:10.[19] "As a fixed formula," continues Wolff, "hear the word of Yahweh (*sm'w dbr-yhwh*), with the addressee in the vocative first occurs in Jeremiah (2:4; 7:2; 19:3; 22:11; altogether 15 times) and Ezekiel (6:3; 13:2; 21:3; altogether 10 times)."[20]

The prophetic books which do not contain the formula *kh 'mr yhwh* do usually contain the proclamation formula in one of its various forms.[21] But those that contain neither *kh 'mr yhwh* nor *sm' dbr-yhwh* (or its variant) contain the formula *n'm yhwh* which is often found in conjunction with *kh 'mr yhwh* as in Isaiah 45:11-13c. Says Lindblom, "Every oracle can be described as a *n'm yhwh*, perhaps a 'whispering' of Yahweh, or even simply as a "Word of Yahweh."[22] In the prophetic books it is usually translated into English as "says the Lord," and Buss noticed that *n'm yhwh*: "moved from early songs and wisdom to law instruction and from there to prophecy. The usages . . . do represent several noticeable specializations of the opening formula. The phrase appears in Hosea 4:1 and 5:1, introducing legal procedure. As a mantic formula, a two-fold call occurs already in Num. 23:18, in prophecy the call appears as a rule in non-divine speech."[23].

One must therefore conclude that not only *kh 'mr yhwh*, but *sm' dbr-yhwh* and its variants, as well as *n'm yhwh* from a functional point of view, may all be considered 'messenger formulae.' The basic problem this work addresses, however, remains the same.

c. The prophecy of Disaster and the Position of the Formula *kh ʿmr yhwh* in the Prophetic Books

Since the pioneering efforts of Köhler,[24] Lindblom,[25] and Wildberger,[26] it has been recognized that the prophecy of disaster against Ahaziah (2 Kg. 1 ff.) has an affinity with the form of the message found throughout the ANE. The prophecy of disaster may be divided into two parts: the diatribe and the threat. The diatribe reproved the person addressed, and stated that his position was no longer tenable before the deity. In addition, it held that the fault was exclusively the fault of the person or persons addressed. The threat--especially the main section--gave notice that a disaster was about to be brought about by the deity.

The diatribe was not understood to be verbally inspired, for it contained the prophet's own words which were given his own personal thrust and stamp. Thus, von Rad could hold that the diatribe was of purely human origin. It was a reflection by a prophet which he voluntarily appended to the *dabar* of Yahweh.[27] In a similar manner, Wolff writes of a "passage of prophetic reflection."[28]

Klaus Koch called attention to the fact that the prophets before Jeremiah placed the formula *kh ʿmr yhwh* after a diatribe, as illustrated by 2 Kings 1:4, 16 and also by Amos 7:17. Koch, of course, assumes that this formula was actually in use in pre-exilic times by the prophets he designates. Here it shows that even Koch was aware that the formula was not employed uniformly--by whomever!

Over against Gunckel, Von Rad, Wolff and Koch, Claus Westermann objected to the term diatribe. He held that the term should have been emploied to characterize an independent literary type, and not be considered as one part of a greater literary whole. He extended his argument by maintaining that a diatribe could only be pronounced to a person directly, and could not be done through an intermediary as in 2 Kings 1:6 (Here the formula is located before both the diatribe and the *dabar*).[29] To this Koch objected on the grounds that the message (note the term) was delivered to a subordinate, thus corresponding exactly with the style of an official communication. He accepted Westermann's observation, however, that the term diatribe was not always a suitable description of the first part of the prophecy. Koch favored the term 'indication of the situation.'[30] He suggested further that the prophecy of disaster to the individual be considered as an isolated type.[31]

The debates notwithstanding, what one is able to say with some certainty is that when a prophecy of disaster, and what the majority of the above-named scholars accepted as a diatribe, both appear in the prophetic books, the diatribe preceds the prophecy and is separated from it by *kh 'mr yhwh* (e.g., Isaiah 10:20-27).

d. The Formula *kh 'mr yhwh* and the Editing Process

Since some of the individual prophetic books contain either few or no 'messenger formulae,' it may be questioned whether *kh 'mr yhwh* was originally a part of the delivered prophetic oracle, or whether it was an editorial, or at least later addition under post-exilic influence. It may also be questioned whether *kh 'mr yhwh* is a deuteronomistic trait carried out further during the exilic and post-exilic editing phases. A recent work entitled **Who Wrote The Bible?** offers some insightful arguments about the identity of the Deuteronomist and his program and period.[32] Von Rad singled out the following twelve examples as deuteronomic prophecies, i.e., forward-looking prophecies made with the advantage of hindsight--the only exact science!

1. Nathan 2 Samuel 7:13
2. Ahijah 1 Kings 11:29 ff.
3. Unknown Prophet 1 Kings 13
4. Ahijah 1 Kings 11:26 ff.
5. Jehu 1 Kings 16:1 ff.
6. Joshua 6:26
7. Michaiah 1 Kings 22:17
8. Elijah 1 Kings 21:21 ff.
9. Elijah 2 Kings 1:6
10. Anonymous 2 Kings 21:10

11. Anonymous 2 Kings 23:26
12. Hulda 2 Kings 22:15 ff.[33]

The purpose of these after-the-event prophecies (in the hands of the Deuteronomist(s) was to buttress a concept of history, for there exists correspondence between the prophecies and the historical events.[34] There must not have been a great deal of such prophetic sources in existence of which the Deuteronomist(s) could have made use. If there had been Von Rad observed: ". . . he (better, they) would not have cited three times--and against three different kings--the words "him that dieth . . . in the city shall the dogs eat, and him that dieth in the field shall the fowl of the air eat" (1 Kg. 14:11; 16:4; and 21:24)."[35]

Of the twelve deuteronomistic prophetic examples, eight (numbers 1,2,3,4,8,9,10, and 12) contain, or are closely preceded by the formula *kh 'mr yhwh*, which in light of the preceding, one must also suspect as being an after-the-fact addition by the Deuteronomist(s).

I have already pointed to the prolific uses of the formula *kh 'mr yhwh* in the book of Jeremiah and in Isaiah 40-55--one a pre-exilic prophet and the other an exilic prophet--and its absence from the books of Habakkuk and Hosea who were both pre-exilic prophets. The following examples strengthen my suspicions even more.

A "man of God," i.e., a prophet, came in consequence of a revelation from Judah to Bethel just as King Jeroboam II was standing by the altar to offer a sacrifice.[36] The man cried out against the altar and said: "O altar, thus says Yahweh, . . ." (1 Kg. 13:1-2).[37] The prophet appeared and pronounced an oracle of doom against the high places and the priests who officiated at them. What is noteworthy is the use of the formula *kh 'mr yhwh*, in light, especially of Lindblom's statement that: "The utterance of this prophet is of course based on events after they had happened."[38] This statement implies correctly an editing phase, which might take into consideration a later addition of *kh 'mr yhwh*.

In 701 BCE Sennacherib of Assyria attempted to subjugate Jerusalem.[39] The attempt was aborted and he and his forces suddenly raised the siege and returned to Mesopotamia. The sudden departure, interpreted by the Jerusalemites, gave rise to the belief in the inviolability of Zion. Isaiah of Jerusalem prophesied at this time. "The Isaiah legends," writes Fohrer, "together with the prophetical discourses they contain; which certainly do not derive from Isaiah but from a much later period" suggest that numerous occurrences of the formula kh 'mr yhwh contained within these "discourses from a later period" were likewise added much later (i.e., they were editorial additions).[40]

Later discourses find their companions in the more or less free epitomes of the original utterances of some of the prophets. A case in point is Jeremiah 19:14 ff. After crushing an earthenware vessel, Jeremiah stood in the court of the Jerusalem Temple and according to the source announced: "Thus says the Lord of hosts, the God of Israel, Behold, I am bringing upon this city and upon all its towns all the evil that I have pronounced against it, because they have stiffened their necks, refusing to hear my words." "This general and colorless speech," writes Lindblom, "was of course never delivered in this form. What we have is a brief epitome of an address uttered publicly in connection with the episode of the broken vessel."[41] Lindblom's observation does a service in that it once again allows one to call the presence of the 'messenger formula'--not so much the utterances following thereupon, which could, however, also be questioned--into question. Perhaps an original proclamation-type formula preceded the original sustained Jeremianic utterance: perhaps not. No one knows. On the other hand, the original may not have been preceded by any kind of formula, and may have only contained a n'm yhwh at the completion of the utterance. At any rate the original utterance has been transformed by the collector and/or editor. The kh 'mr yhwh may now be serving as a literary device, i.e., serving the double-duty function of signalling an utterance thought to be important at the time it was being preserved, and to call attention to it when it was being read at a later date.

Thus, the appearance in the HS prophetic material of the formula kh 'mr yhwh does't necessarily imply the presence of a prophet as a messenger, nor does its presence guarantee that it was an original part of a prophetic utterance before which it may now be located.

3. "Messenger Speech": Its Characteristics

Many religious and political "offices" which appear in the history of the settled people Israel are shown to have at one time been exercised by the sole figure Moses. Moses is depicted as lawgiver, priest, judge, military commander, and prophet. Therefore it is not surprising to find in Exodus 3:14b I AM saying to Moses (the shepherd): "*kh t'mr lbny ysr'l 'hyh slhny 'lykm*" ("Thus shall you say to the people of Israel I AM sent me to you.") One recognizes here the combined 'commissioning formula' and the 'messenger formula' of the prophetic books. One reads in Numbers 11:16 ff. that Moses is also the 'founder' of Israelite prophecy. What follows (in the Exodus account) is a new development. It is an announcement of what *'hyh* is about to do, i.e., create a people, an *'m*.

The great individual prophets represented a new development in Israelite prophecy. From their point of view the optimistic oracles of the professional salvation prophets bespoke a faulty hermeneutic which resulted in their inability to deliver the valid *dbr* of Yahweh. Passages such as Amos 7:14, Micah 3:5, 11; and Jeremiah 23:9-32 reflect how seriously these prophets denounced their colleagues, the professional guild prophets.

The main function of the prophets was to receive revelations from the other world and to utter them as oracles to the people of their own world. Essentially, in such oracles the prophet, like Moses, announced what Yahweh was about to do.

The great individual prophets prophesied in full possession of their faculties, and not in an ecstatic frenzy. They delivered their oracles publicly and often in poetic form. Some have called these publicly-delivered, poetically-formed oracles "messages." And that is the rub.

a. Prophetic *dbr* and the *dbr-yhwh*

"In the time of the classical prophets," wrote J. Lindblom, "the identity of Yahweh's word and the words of a true prophet was self-evident and indisputable."[42] This situation is not as self-evident as Lindblom would have us believe, and it may indeed be disputed.[43] The statement which follows this ill-chosen sentence, however, is noteworthy. Here Lindblom correctly notes that the statement contained in Haggai 1:12 shows that in the post-exilic period "we meet with expressions which show that men were aware of a possible distinction that should have been made between what was taken to be Yahweh's word(s) and those of the prophet."[44] If any community needed to make such a distinction it would indeed have been the post-exilic community; they were farther from the source. Fohrer is much closer to being correct when he writes: "Even the sayings formulated by the prophets in their own right and not ascribed to Yahweh claim a similar power (i.e., a magical power)."[45]

A distinction between "Yahweh's word" and the prophet's word is found in Hosea 6:5 (a pre-exilic prophet): "Therefore I have hewn them by the prophets, I have slain them by the words of my mouth, and my judgment goes forth as the light." Once again the distinction is even evident in Fohrer's comment on this example. "Despite the warnings of the prophets and the word of Yahweh, the people remained rebellious down to the time of Hosea."[46]

It is thus important when reading the prophetic literature contained in the HS to know when a given prophet is speaking and when that prophet is supposed to be speaking the word(s) of Yahweh if 'messenger speech' is to be singled out. To complicate matters, however, there are portions of prophetic literature which do not refer to Yahweh at all, so that it is oftentimes difficult to determine whether the "speaker" is to be Yahweh or the prophet. Buss is aware of the difficulty involved when he writes: "Admittedly, the substantive distinction between the two types can be upheld only if one credits to divine speech no more than those sayings in which the divine "I" explicitly occurs."[47]

1.)   The Literary Material Enshrining the Prophetic Utterances: A Summary of the Main Types

Not every word of the prophet was considered a *dbr* of Yahweh. It is therefore necessary to determine what kind of prophetic material contained in the various prophetic books is predisposed to being considered *dbry-yhwh*. Prophetic material may be generally summarized as:

      1. prophetical sayings
      2. prophetical accounts
      3. imitations of rhetorical
         forms deriving from
         other fields such as
         liturgy, argument,
         historical analysis. [48]

The prophetical sayings include:

      1. prophetical oracles
      2. sayings proclaiming
         disaster or threats
      3. sayings proclaiming
         deliverance or
         assurances
      4. invectives
      5. admonitions and
         warnings

From what has been stated above, these five types are all well-suited to contain the *dbr-yhwh* and either follow, or are preceded by the legitimating formulae.

    The prophetical accounts by their very nature may be excluded from being candidates for 'messenger speech.' They include:

      1. narrative seer sayings
      2. accounts of visions
      3. accounts of auditions

4. accounts of visions and
   auditions
5. accounts of symbolic
   actions

The imitative forms show that the altered situation of the prophet required forms as yet uncommon for their proclamation. These included the dirge, the psalm and the lament.[49]

Thus, although it differs in length and content from book to prophetic book, it is the prophetical saying which must be the object of this part of my investigation.

2.) Original Prophetic Utterances and Summary Reproductions: Prose vs. Poetry

Ancillary to the issue of prophetic *dbr* vs. *dbr-yhwh* is the issue of the presence of short, poetic oracles versus long, prose narratives in the prophetic books. Just as it was necessary to summarize the forms of prophetic speech in order to ascertain which utterances were best suited to be termed 'messenger speech,' in analyzing the utterances which follow the formula *kh 'mr yhwh, n'm yhwh* and/or *sm' dbry-yhwh* a distinction must be made between the original prophetic utterances and later reproductions, and/or abstracts of those utterances which use the same formulae. The purpose of an examination would be to determine whether they are poetic (original?) or prose (reproduction/abstract?)

In opposition to the belief that the product of ecstatic experiences was the short oracle, J. Lindblom held that sketchy images and forms would seem to be more probable as a product of ecstatic experience.[50]

According to Martin Buss: "Gunckel noted that prophetic words are either short or fall into smaller utterances in which the prophet turns hither and yon, in other words, that no lengthy coherent exposition takes place."[51]

Likewise, Georg Fohrer, discussing the two major divisions of prophecy, corresponding to the two types of religious background, nomadic and settled area religions, wrote:

> . . . the poetic form of O.T. prophetic discourse may owe more to the deliberate and artistically composed speech of the seer than to the ecstatic stutterings of the *nabi*. It seems to be the case that no Israelite prophet purporting to speak in the name of Yahweh could gain a hearing unless he clothed his speech in poetic form.[52]

As to the reason for the use of the poetic form, he added:

> Though the O.T. contains no explanation of this fact, the *kahin* was often so intimately associated with a deity or demon that delivered of a seer discourse in meter was considered the mark of a person associated with the powers of the supernatural world. The ability to speak in poetic form was a remnant of this association.[53]

It is most probable that the prophetic sayings, especially those following the various introductory formulae, would be in poetic form. Those prophetic sayings which are in prose and follow upon the introductory formulae could then be immediately suspect as paraphrases. Lindblom points out such paraphrases throughout the prophetical material.[54] He warns the reader that "such summaries and abstracts are for the most part in prose."[55] Since this is demonstrably the case, he states that "critics have often maintained that the prose portions of the prophetic utterances are not authentic simply because they are prose. This is a mistake."[56] As to how this quandry is solved, Lindblom observed:

> The authenticity or otherwise of a prophetic saying is proved by its content, not by its form. If a saying is in accordance with a given prophet's general mode of thought, we are not justified in rejecting it, even if it is in prose. The prose form may of course be original; but usually it is a sign that an original prophetic utterance has been paraphrased.[57]

3. The Stages Through Which The Prophetic Saying Passed Before Delivery

The prophetic saying passed through at least four stages:

1. The first stage, and thus the ultimate source of prophetical activity, was a moment of deep personal contact with God, in which the "spirit" or "word" of Yahweh came upon the prophet.

2. The second stage was the prophet's interpretation of this experience.

3. As the third stage there was added the rational processing of the experience.

4. The fourth stage, which paralleled
the third, was reduction of the
'message' (N.B.!) to artistic
form.[58]

It is the first of these stages which lends itself least to necessary
analysis.

b. The Prophetic Saying And 'Messenger Speech'

Of the different types of prophetic literature the prophetic
saying has been shown to be the type which should contain the *dbr-yhwh*. This *dbr-yhwh* was generally recognizeable because it was
preceded by a legitimizing formula which was usually *kh 'mr yhwh*,
but which could also be *n'm yhwh* or even *sm' dbr-yhwh*. *kh 'mr
yhwh* is called, form-critically, the messenger formula and is generally
believed to signal 'messenger speech.' 'Messenger speech,' too, is a
form-critical designation. According to Claus Westermann: "prophetic
speech as the speech of a messenger has definite and evident forms
that make it into a messenger's speech."[59] To discover such messenger
speech he suggested that a three-step process be followed. 1. *All*
prophetic speech forms are to be examined first of all as to whether
they are and intended to be messages and how they are to be
understood as messages.[60] This statement follows upon an earlier one
in which he observed that:

Not every ordinary speech that is
prefaced by "thus says the Lord" (or the
like) turns out to be a messenger's
speech: rather it can be assumed from
the outset that the prophetic speech as
the speech of a messenger has definite
forms that make it into a messenger's
speech.[61]

Westermann's cautious statement helps one see, however, how careless such a statement as Lindblom's (which is symptomatic of this kind of sweeping statement made by numerous scholars) really is when he states:

> All that a prophet has to proclaim, based on divine revelation, is regarded by him as something that Yahweh has spoken to him. It is held to be a 'word' (*dabar*) from Yahweh. This becomes apparent from the manner in which the prophets designate their messages, particularly from the formulae by which they introduce and conclude them. One of the most common of these is the typical oracle formula 'thus says Yahweh,' . . . [62]

Therefore Westermann, in an attempt to avoid such careless language, advised further: 2. It must be asked whether the two-part message corresponds to the prophetic speech. And as to the third part, 3. One must ask whether and how a speech whose very nature requires directness (as the reproaching speech) is altered in order to become a message.[63] The two-part message to which Westermann alluded contains (1) the report and (2) a summons. The report is generally in the perfect while the summons is in the imperative. Genesis 45:9 contains an example of a message embedded in historical narrative. In the example: "God has made me lord of all Egypt;" corresponds to the report in the perfect, while "come down to me, do not tarry." is the summons in the imperative.[64]

In the prophetic books, Amos 7:16-17 is seen by Westermann to be an account which contains prophetic messenger speech. Dividing it into the major parts of its form, he arrives at the scheme (1) summons to hear; (2) accusation (which corresponds with the perfect); (3) introduction to the announcement by the messenger formula; and (4) announcement of judgment (in the personal address which corresponds with the imperative). Exploited schematically, Amos 7:16-17 is as follows:

> Summons to hear: Now therefore hear the word of the Lord.
> Accusation: You say, "Do not prophesy . . ."
> Messenger formula: (Therefore) thus says the Lord:"
> Announcement: "Your wife shall be a harlot . . ."[65]

By this reasoning, passages such as Amos 1:3-3:2; 3:12a; 5:16-17, and 8:3 have also been recognized as 'messenger speech.'[66] Isaiah 7:7-9, as a judgment oracle, is a very good example of 'messenger speech.' It is preceded by the messenger formula, is composed in beautiful verse, is brief, and contains the perfect and imperative parts. According to Fohrer, Jeremiah 2:2-3, 7-8, and 3:19-20 is likewise an example of messenger speech. It is preceded by *kh 'mr yhwh*, is poetic, is fairly brief, and even concludes with the formula *n'm yhwh*. The material which is located between the verses must be considered numerous additions to a basically short prophetic saying.[67]

One notices that each of these examples is preceded by the kh 'mr yhwh formula, and that all are judgmental prophetic sayings. The contents of the judgment sayings, however, are not consistent. "The various judgmental messages of the great prophets," writes Fohrer, "depicted judgment in many forms; differing views can be found within the writings of a single prophet."[68] Natural catastrophes; devastating wars and deportation, revolution and anarchy, and the Day of Yahweh were some of the ways that this judgment would be accomplished.[69] This explains why Westermann suggested that *all* prophetic speech forms had to be examined. But even with all his caution, Westermann realized that many messenger speech examples could be overlooked and that his examination had been restricted to HS examples for the most part. What had been conducted was an examination similar to the Mafia holding public hearings on members of its own group who have been indicted on charges of corruption, or to the internal affairs section of a given police department investigating alleged criminal activity of some of its brother officers. The examination had not been undertaken against the backdrop of a comprehensive study of the messenger phenomenon of the greater ANE (i.e., PART I of the present work). His study did succeed, however, in curbing the free assumptions made by careless scholarship with reference to how messenger speech in the prophetic books was to be sought. Alas, he made no suggestion as to what to do with 'messenger speech' when one indeed found it! Westermann realized further that:

> Among the messages (of the Old Testament prophetic books) there is a type that places the entire stress on the perfect part (is it the same as news?), and a type in which the meaning of the message comes in the imperative part. Besides these there is the transmission of commands and questions, of an inquiry through a messenger, a warning, a reminder, statements of cooperation, etc., messages in various realms of life are to be distinguished, such as personal, political, and above all, court life. All this deserves a comprehensive investigation that cannot be made here. A further question must be raised: Is the herald's call (or the proclamation by a herald) a form that is independent of the message or only a variation of the usual message?[70]

In summary, the form-critical categories of 'commissioning formula,' 'messenger formula,' and 'messenger speech.' which heretofore played such an important role in maintaining the belief that the HS prophet was a messenger, when subjected to rigorous analysis, provided very fruitful results.

The 'commissioning formula' was characterized by the same presence and use of imperatives as were the commissioning formulae employed by those who commissioned ANE messages to be delivered. Examples of the 'commissioning formula' were contained in 2 Kings 3; Jeremiah 2:1; 23:2; Isaiah 6:9, and were there found to be similar to the formula discussed in PART I. At this juncture I only wanted to alert the reader that such similarities existed, without embarking on any sort of comparative analysis. The presence of the 'commissioning formula' would be evaluated later.

The formula kh 'mr $yhwh$ is frequently called the 'messenger formula' by form-critics and scholars of biblical literature in general. It occurs often in prophetic literature as a whole, but does not occur at all in some prophetic books. kh 'mr $yhwh$ is similar to the formula "Thus says (or said) XX" which a messenger in the ANE often employed to legitimize the message which he or she delivered. In the secular world, not every time this formula occurred did a message follow. The Hittite kings frequently used this formula when providing autobiographical information (especially for their chronicles). In the post-exilic apocryphal book of Judith, the author had the king of the "Assyrians" also employ the formula, but again no message of any kind followed (Judith 2:25). The HS occurrences (especially in the prophetic books) oftentimes followed a similar pattern. In prophetic autobiographical accounts, the prophet is depicted as having employed the formula to state that Yahweh had spoken to him (cf. Isa. 18:4; 21:16; Jer. 3:6, 11; 13:1). Because the above uses are frequent, the form-critical scholar Westermann cautioned that one should look beyond the formula kh 'mr $yhwh$ to what followed in order to be certain that an alleged message followed, for not all occurrences of kh 'mr $yhwh$ could even be form-critically termed 'messenger formulae.'[71] The formula, the presence of which most relied upon, itself was not a reliable indicator of what was termed 'messenger speech.'

Other formulae within the prophetic literature functioned more reliably than *kh 'mr yhwh* as an indicator of alleged prophetic messages. Among these were the allied formulae *sm' dbr-yhwh* (Hear the word of Yahweh!), often called the proclamation formula (but never used by the herald as far as PART I has shown), and *n'm yhwh* (says the Lord, an oracle of the Lord, a saying of Yahweh), especially when *kh 'mr yhwh* was wholly absent from the text.

It is possible that *n'm yhwh* may have been the only pre-exilic legitimizing formula employed by some prophets according to the implication of Jeremiah 23:31. I concluded that one had to speak of the possibility of 'messenger formulae' rather than *the* 'messenger formula.'

It appeared that *kh 'mr yhwh* was most reliable as an indicator of suspected 'messenger speech' when it was immediately preceded by a diatribe. Such an example was found in Isaiah 10:20-27. This occurrence, however, proved to be unstable, for the formula *kh 'mr yhwh* precedes the diatribe in 2 Kings 1:4, 16 and Amos 7:17, and precedes both diatribe and prophecy (the alleged message) in 2 Kings 1:6, and would still be reliable in indicating the presence of alleged messenger speech.

The formula was employed in no consistent pattern, however, and because of uses and interpretations of prophetic literature by the Deuteronomistic and other schools, I suspected that many occurrences of *kh 'mr yhwh* did not necessarily imply the presence of the speech of a messenger, i.e., a message, and that it was often probable that the formula itself was added at a later stage in the development of the written prophetic *corpus*. What could be said with certainty was that the presence of *kh 'mr yhwh* signalled nothing which could be said to be a message. Rather it indicated in its patternless fashion that what followed its appearance was held to be important by those who later reworked the material. All indications are that *kh 'mr yhwh* belongs to the *interpretation* stage and not to the *presentation* stage of the GIPs themselves.

The GIPs, especially, delivered their sayings usually publically and often in poetic form following the method of the *kahin* and the *hanif*. This publicly-delivered, often poetically-constructed saying, when analyzed form-critically, has been termed 'messenger speech.' Due to the many forms of prophetic speech, that form which served as the best candidate for 'messenger speech' had to be separated from other existing literary forms. This separation produced (1) prophetical sayings; (2) prophetical accounts and (3) imitative forms. Of these, it was the prophetical saying which, of necessity, occupied my attention. The sayings were comprised of oracles, sayings proclaiming either threat and disaster, or deliverance and assurance, invectives, or admonitions and warnings. Once this distinction had been made, the sayings appeared to be extant in two principle types: those which appeared to be the words of a given prophet, and those which appeared to be summary reproductions of a given prophet's words. Moreover, some scholars advanced the view that only the original words of a prophetical saying were poetic, leaving every prosaic prophetical saying to be considered a summary.[72] Others held that the authenticity of a given saying was proved only by its *contents*, and that *form* was unimportant. Prose forms could also be original, but they were generally a sign that the original utterance had been paraphrased or summarized.[73] I did not embark, however, upon any attempt to recover the *ipsissima verba* of the prophets.

There remained the task of associating 'messenger speech' with the prophetic saying, for the prophetic saying was often preceded by the formula *kh 'mr yhwh, n'm yhwh*, or *sm' dbr-yhwh* just as were the alleged prophetic messages. What is definite, however, is the fact that the prophetic sayings were always associated with the various formulae, but I was still unable to demonstrate that these formulae always signalled even 'messenger speech.' The characteristics of such 'messenger speech' according to Westermann were that it contain a *report* and a *summons*. The report was to be generally rendered in the perfect, while the summons was to be in the imperative.[74] Genesis 45:9 and Amos 7:16-17 were viewed by Westermann as examples of 'messenger speech.'[75] James Ross reasoned that passages such as Amos 1:3-3:2; 3:12a; 5:4-6; 5:16-17, and 8:3 had also been recognized as 'messenger speech.'[76] According to Fohrer, Jeremiah 2:2-3, 7-8 and 3:19-20 were also examples. The material found between these verses he considered to be nothing more than numerous additions to an essentially short saying. A careful reading of the examples offered by these scholars belies three different views of what 'mesenger speech' is or was. Westermann's form-critical scheme of both Genesis 45:9 and Amos 7:16-17 is not applicable to the examples offered by the reasoning of Ross or Fohrer. Moreover, Westermann's Amos 7:16-17 example, so crucial for his demonstration of 'messenger speech,' is totally ignored and is glaringly absent from Ross's examples of 'messenger speech' in the Amos material. None of these scholars was looking at the same *thing*! Form-critically, Westermann's assertions were proven to have been the most sound. Although the prophetic material he selected for comparison with messages found elsewhere in the HS was highly selective and restricted (with the exception of the Mari material) to intra-HS examples only, and within this material mainly those examples which both had the two-part form, his study did succeed in showing how freely scholars had assumed 'messenger speech' was to be located in the prophetic books. Westermann also admitted that his (and thereby the form-critical school's) study had its limitations and called for further rigorous study of the problem.[77]

CHAPTER VI

The ANE Messages, Messages Contained Within the Hebrew Scriptures, the Proclamations and Announcements of the Herald and the Prophetic Saying of the Great Individual Prophet: A Comparison and Constrast

      The form-critical analysis of the prophetic books revealed a rich variety of prophetic utterances which were distributed over a variety of literary genres.[1] General understanding of prophetic literature is richer as a result of the contributions of form-criticism. But when form-critical analysis attempted to explain how the HS prophet was a messenger, it could only contend that there were noticeable similarities between certain prophetical sayings and the messages delivered by messengers of the ANE. Here the comparison centered on a rather small number of examples which were fairly identical in structure (i.e., form) to certain prophetic sayings. Although the methods of form-critical analysis exploited fully these similar forms, most of the examples were taken from the messages contained within the HS narrative material. The best of these examples was shown to be Judges 11:12 ff. (because formally it is similar to the "messenger speech" form found in prophetic literature--which came primarily as a result of **Israel's** misconduct). Not enough ANE, extra-HS messages of all types examined in PART I were employed by the form-critics to make their comparisons comprehensive enough, or less biased.

      Form-criticism also drew attention to the similarities between the messenger formula of the ANE messengers ('Thus says [or said] NN') and the prophetic formula *kh 'mr yhwh*. But even here, the form-critical analyses revealed that not every occurrence of *kh 'mr yhwh* automatically signalled that what followed was even qualified to be termed 'messenger speech' (i.e., the form-critical, literary category) and even less the speech of a messenger! It held that in the prophetic books "the message formula introduces the message consisting of a perfect and an imperative part which still offers a decision to the addressee."[2] Form-criticism also counseled that not **every** prophetic utterance which was preceded by *kh 'mr yhwh* was 'messenger speech,' and that **every** prophetic utterance should be scrutinized rigorously in order to determine whether or not it was **intended** to be 'messenger speech.' Thereby, the responsibility for ferreting out such 'messenger speech' was placed on the shoulders of the non-specialist reader, with form-criticism now offering at best a kind of makeshift guide to "assist" the reader. The result has been the ever growing misunderstanding about prophetic speech and those who have uttered it, which the present work addresses. It was obvious that form-criticism had reached its limitations with regard to its attempts to explain how the HS prophet was a messenger through its attempt to describe and explain 'messenger speech.' It had, however, made more than a noble attempt. Yet form-criticism demonstrated that numerous *lacunae* existed in attempts to explain messenger speech, and messenger formula. It observed correctly that most explanations had been theological, not literary-historical-critical. Form-critical studies also made it known that there were possibly other types of messages (than the two-part perfect and imperative type) and that it had only demonstrated **one** type. There were too many questions left unanswered about messages in general. Some of the really important unanswered questions were:

1. Should an ultimatum which is preceded by "thus says XX" be considered a message? (1 Kings 20:2-3)
2. Should the announcement of an event be considered a message?

3. Is the call of the herald or a
   proclamation which is
   delivered by him or her
   also a message?

The questions became legion, answers did not follow rapidly. The evidence contained in PART I, however, has supplied many answers to these questions, but a comparison and contrast of the ANE and HS messages as are contained in that work with the prophetic sayings of the HS great individual prophets may illuminate the problem much more. It is upon the illumination of the problem that a solution may be formulated.

1. The Message

A message is a communication of information, advice, direction, or salutation which is transmitted through a messenger. In the ANE the message was essentially the errand and function of a messenger. Its contents allowed situations to be initiated, maintained and controlled, or even terminated by one from afar as if that person were actually present. It is as if the commissioner of a messenger and sender of a message were in two places at once. The messenger was a prosthesis of the person in whose name and by whose authority he or she spoke; the message being identical to the original spoken word (even in terms of intonational stress patterns) was not. These ANE messages could be delivered either orally, in writing, or both simultaneously. By "oral" in PART I and herein is meant those messages which were gleaned from narratives concerning messengers who delivered them orally. By "written" is meant primarily letters. In truth, all of my research sources were naturally **written** ones.

2. The Short "Oral" Message, The Proclamation/Announcement, and the Short Prophetical Saying

The "oral" messages of the ANE messengers were characterized by their brevity. Such brief messages must have been designed to be remembered easily. Oral messages varied in length, but most must have been fairly brief. One need only look at Psalms 9-10; 25; 34; 37; 111; 119; 145; or Proverb 31:10-31 in the MT to see how certain mnemonic devices (in this case the acrostic) were employed to aid or facilitate memorization. Other such devices (poetic construction, meter, stress, alliteration) were also employed. Examples of the brief "oral" message include the following. The first column contains examples from the ANE messengers, the second column contains examples from the HS messengers of the narrative material, and the third column contains proclamations/announcements from HS, Ugaritic and Assyrian heralds.

ANE	HS	Herald
(Egyptian and Ethiopian vassals of Assyria revolting against their lord, Ashurbanipal) "Let a league be established between us and let us be a help to one another, If we divide the country among ourselves, then there shall not be another lord between us."[3]	(From Balak, king of Moab, to Balaam the seer) "Let nothing hinder you from coming to me; for I will surely do you great honor, and whatever you say to me I will do; come, curse this people for me." (Num. 22:15-17)	(Message/announcement to Eli the priest) "Israel has fled before the Philistines, and there has also been a great slaughter among the people; your two sons also, Hophni and Phineas, are dead, and the ark of God has been captured."
(Egyptian harem wives attempting to place	(The Moses host attempting to get to Canaan through Transjordan) "Let me pass through your land; we will not turn	(Cushite messenger's message to David concerning Absalom) "Good tidings for

the son of the
favorite among
them on the
throne of Ramses
III)
"Excite the peo-
ple, goad on the
enemies to begin
hostilities a-
gainst their
lord."[4]

(Message to
Wenamon from
Zakar-Baal
Prince of Byblos)
"Eat, drink, and
let not thy
heart feel ap-
prehension, Thou
shalt hear all
I have to say
in the morning."[6]

(Message from
the Hyksos king
to the Prince of
Thebes in order
to goad the lat-
ter into a
fight)
"My messenger
has come to thee
concerning the
splashing of the
hippopotami,
which are in the

aside into field or
vineyard; we will
not drink the
water of a well;
we will go the
King's Highway un-
til we have passed
through your terri-
tory."
(Num. 21:21-22)

David's message
to his envoys to
Ammon)
"Remain at Jericho
until your beards
have grown, and
then return."
(2 Sam. 10:5)

(Prince Absalom
to King David
after the latter
had allowed the
former to return
from exile)
"Why have I come
from Geshur? It
would be better
for me to be
there still, Now
therefore let me
go into the pre-
sence of the king;
and if there is
guilt in me, let
him kill me."

my lord the king!
For the Lord has
delivered you this
day from the
power of all who
rose up against
you."
(2 Sam. 18:31)

(Anat's announce-
ment to Baal)
"Receive Baal, the
glad tidings
I bring thee,
They will build
for thee a house
like thy brethren
and a court like
unto thy kin-
dred's."[5]

(Message to King
Ashur-nasir-pal,
king of Assyria)
"The city of Suru
which is in Bit-
Khalupe hath re-
volted, and they
have slain Khama-
ti, their gover-
nor, and Akhiaba-
ba, the son of a
nobody, whom they
have brought from
Bit-Adini, have
they set up as king
over them."[7]

pool in the city,
for they allow
me no sleep, day
and night the
sound of them is
in my ear."[8]

(The god Yamm's
request to have
the god Baal sur-
rendered to him)
"Give up, gods,
him whom you pro-
tect, on whom the
multitudes wait,
give up Baal and
his lackeys,
(even) Dagon's
son, (that) I
may inherit his
portion."[10]

(2 Sam. 14:32b-33)

(The men of Beth-
shemesh to the men
of Kiriath-jearim)
"The Philistines
have returned the
ark of the Lord.
Come down and
take it up to you."
(1 Sam. 16:19)

(Saul the **nagid**
to Jesse the
father of David
the youth)
"Send me David
your son, who is
with the sheep."
(1 Sam. 16:19)

(Same as above)
"Let David remain
in my service, for
he has found favor
in my sight."
(1 Sam. 16:22)

(Same as above)
"Nur-Adad, the
prince of the land
of Dagara, hath re-
volted, and the men
throughout the
whole of the land
Zamua have banded
themselves together
and they have built
a wall in the pass
of Babite."[9]

Analysis of the foregoing yields the following:

Column 1

1. Message to one of equal status
    a. entreaty b. desired end

2. Message to one of unequal status
   imperative
3. Message to one of unequal status
   a. imperfect b. imperative
4. Message to one of equal status
   a. perfect b. explanation
5. Message to one of unequal status
   a. imperative b. explanation

Column 2

1. Message to one of equal status
   a. entreaty b. compensation c. desired end
2. Message to one of equal standing
   a. entreaty b. desired end
3. Message to one of unequal standing
   imperative
4. Message to a superior
   a. complaint b. desired end
*5. Message to one of equal status
   imperative
6. Message to one of unequal status
   imperative
7. Message to one of equal status
   a. entreaty b. explanation

Column 3

1. Message to a superior: statement of a fact
2. Message to a superior: statement of a fact
3. General message: statement of a fact
4. Message to one of equal status: statement of a fact
5. Message to a superior: statement of a fact
6. Message to a superior: statement of a fact
7. Message to a superior: statement of a fact

Only number five of Column 2 corresponds in **components** with the form-critical description of 'messenger speech.' 'Messenger speech,' however, by its very nature, must take the form of a message to one of **unequal status**. By restricting oneself to the above two components only, existing form-critical descriptions of 'messenger speech' would have caused one to overlook the other eighteen messages.

The same brevity which characterized the "oral" messages of the ANE and HS (secular) messengers is noticeable among some of the sayings of the GIPs which are referred to as 'messenger speech.' As examples I note the following. The first column contains examples from the prophet Isaiah of Jerusalem. Column 2 contains examples from the prophet Jeremiah. The third column contains examples from the prophet Amos. Among the GIPs, only,these three prophets yielded short sayings.

| (Isaiah of Jerusalem to Ahaz, king of Judah concerning the Syro-Ephriamitic league which has threatened Judah) "It shall not stand, and it shall not come to pass. For the head of Syria is Damascus, and the head of Damascus is Rezin, And the head of Ephriam is Samaria, and the head of Samaria is the son of Remaliah. If you will not believe, surely you shall not be established." | (Jeremiah to Jerusalem) "I remember the devotion of your youth, your love as a bride, how you followed me in the wilderness, in a land not sown. Israel was holy to the Lord, the first fruits of his harvest. All who ate of it became guilty; evil came upon them, says the Lord." (Jer. 2:2-3)

(Jeremiah to Jerusalem) "Behold, I will lay | (Amos at Bethel) "An adversary shall surround the land, and bring down your defenses from you and your strongholds shall be plundered." (Amos 3:11)

(Amos at Bethel) "As the shepherd rescues from the |

(Isa. 7:7-9)

(Isaiah concern-
ing Moab)
"In three years,
like the years of
a hireling, the
glory of Moab will
be brought into
contempt, in spite
of all his great
multitude, and those
who survive will be
very few and feeble."
(Isa. 16:14)

(Isaiah to King
Hezekiah con-
cerning the fate
of Jerusalem in
the face of Assy-
rian attack)
"He shall not
come into this
city, or shoot an
arrow there, or
cast up a siege
mound against it.
By the way he
came, by the same
he shall return,
and he shall not
come into this city,
says the Lord. For
I will defend this
city to save it,

before this people
stumbling blocks
against which they
shall stumble;
fathers and sons
together, neighbor
and friend shall
perish."
(Jer. 6:21)

(To the women of
Jerusalem con-
cerning their sons)
"The dead bodies of
men shall fall like
dung upon the open
field, like sheaves
after the reaper,
and none shall ga-
ther them."
(Jer. 9:22)

(To the wise,
might, and rich
of Jerusalem)
"Let not the wise
man glory in his
wisdom, let not the
rich man glory in
his riches; but
let him who glories
glory in this; that
he understands and
knows me; that I am
the Lord who practices
steadfast love, justice,

mouth of the
lion two legs,
or a piece of
an ear, so
so shall the
people of Israel
who dwell in
Samaria be res-
cued, with the
corner of a
couch and part
of a bed."
(Amos 3:12)

for my own sake   and righteousness in
and for the sake   the earth; for in these
of my servant David."   things I delight, says
(Isa. 37:33-35)   the Lord."
                         (Jer. 9:23-24)

Evidence is frugal and scanty for both the "oral" message and the short prophetical saying of the GIP. This situation is more than likely due to the fact that both were delivered and were not usually recorded in writing. Analysis reveals that each follows the formula *kh 'mr yhwh*, and that two are concluded by the formula *n'm yhwh* (The first Jeremianic saying of the middle column and the final saying of the same column). All of the sayings take the form of a communication to one of unequal status, but instead of the expected imperatives, one finds generally statements of fact, entreaties accompanied by wishful results, or both.

3. The Written Message and the Sustained Prophetical Saying

PART I produced evidence of written messages delivered by the ANE messengers. These written messages are contained within Chapter II and are also intertwined in Chapter III with the activity of the HS, historical mesenger. However, I shall reproduce several here for comparative and contrastive purposes. The first column contains a letter message from Assyria. Column two contains two letter messages. The first is a letter from Lachish, while the second is from the HS. An Egyptian letter message is contained in the third column.

Message of the king   Thy servant Hoshaiah   To Horus, greeting,
to Sin-tabui-usur: hath sent to inform   On the first of the
It is well with me.   my lord Yoash: May   current month at
May thy heart be   Yahweh cause my lord   about the eleventh
cheered. Concerning   to hear tidings of   hour a disturbance
Sin-shar-usur, what   peace! And now thou   occurred in the
thou didst send.   hast sent a letter   village and on run-

How could he say
evil words of thee
and I hear anything
of them? Shamash
perverted his heart
and Ummanigash
slandered thee be-
fore me and would
give thee to death.
Ashur, my god,
withholds me.[11]

but my lord did not
enlighten thy ser-
vant concerning the
letter which thou
didst send to thy
servant yesterday
evening, though the
heart of thy servant
hath been sick since
thou didst write to
thy servant.
And it hath
been reported to thy
servant, saying,
"The commander of
the host, Coniah
son of Elnathan, hath
come down in order
to go into Egypt;
and unto Hodaviah
son of Ahijah and
his men hath he sent
to obtain . . .
him . . .[12]

(Letter-message
from Jehu to the
guardians of the
heirs of the Om-
ride Dynasty)
Now then, as soon
as this letter
comes to you, and
there are with
you chariots and
horses and
fortified cities

ning out we found a
crowd of the vil-
lagers who had
come to the assist-
ance of Polemon,
who is performing
the duties of over-
seer of the vil-
lage. When we in-
quired into the
matter they inform-
ed us that Apollo-
dorus and his son
Maron had assault-
ed Polemon; that
Apollodorus had
escaped but Maron
had been put into
prison; and that
the latter had
appeared before
Ptolemeus the
from king's cousin and
Strategos on the
1st. We thought it
well to notify the
matter for your
information.
Good-bye. The
3rd year, Mesore
2.[13]

also, and weapons,
select the best and
fittest of your
master's sons and
set him on his
father's throne . . .

These written messages are lengthy when compared with the "oral" messages. An examination of their form and component parts adds the following.

Column 1
Message to a subordinate
a. perfect b. resolution

Column 2
Message to a superior: statement of a fact
Message to a subordinate: Ultimatum

Column 3
Message to a superior
a. perfect b. resolution

None of them participates in the form-critical description of a message as discussed above.

There is also a sustained prophetical saying which may in many respects be compared with the longer written message. It is this length when comparison is made, which causes me to think that these longer prophetical sayings were also written (i.e., by the GIP, or dictated by him). Examples from Isaiah of Jerusalem and Jeremiah follow.

Isaiah 10:24-27)

O my people, who dwell in Zion, be not afraid of the Assyrians when they smite with the rod and lift up their staff against you as the Egyptians did. For in a very little while **my** indignation will come to an end, and **my** anger will be directed toward their destruction. And the Lord of Hosts will wield against them a scourge, as when **he** smote Midian at the rock of Oreb; and **his** rod will be over the sea, and **he** will lift it as **he** did in Egypt. And in that day **his** burden will depart from your shoulder, and **his** yoke will be destroyed from your neck.

(Jeremiah 7:3-15)

Amend your ways and your doings, and I will let you dwell in this place. Do not trust in these deceptive words: 'This is the temple of the Lord.' For if you truly amend your ways and your doings, if you do not oppress the alien, the fatherless and the widow, or shed innocent blood in this place, and if you do not go after other gods to your own hurt, then I will let you dwell in this place, in the land that I gave of old to your fathers for ever. Behold, you trust in deceptive words to no avail. . . I will cast you out of my sight, as I cast out all your kinsmen, all the offspring of Ephriam.

The following example is most important, because it purports to be a letter from Jeremiah to the exiles in Babylonia. Notice that it begins with the formula *kh ʿmr yhwh*, and like the previous ANE examples, it is a lengthy letter-message.

(Jeremiah 29:4-23)

Thus says the Lord of hosts, the God of Israel, to all the exiles whom I have sent into exile from Jerusalem to Babylon: build houses and live in them; plant gardens and eat their produce. Take wives and have sons and daughters; Take wives for your sons and give your daughters in marriage, that they may bear sons and daughters, multiply there and do not decrease . . . Do not let your prophets and diviners who are among you deceive you, and do not listen to the dreams which they dream, for it is a lie which they are prophesying to you in my name; I did not send them, **says the Lord**. . . concerning Ahab the son of Koliah and Zedekiah the son of Maaseiah, who are prophesying a lie to you in my name: Behold, I will deliver them into the hand of Nebuchadrezzar king of Babylon . . . because they have spoken in my name lying words which I did not command them, I am the one who knows and I am witness, **says the Lord.**

Analysis is as follows.

Isaiah 10:24-27
'Message' to one of unequal status
a. admonition b. resolution

Jeremiah 7:3-5
'Message' to one of unequal status
a. entreaty b. admonition c. resolution d. threat

Jeremiah 29:4-23
'Message' to one of unequal status
a. imperative b. admonition c. resolution

The longer prophetical saying is more closely allied to the ANE message than the short "oral" message is to the short prophetical saying, because both were longer and reflected more carefully thought out contents. A comparison reflects this relationship.

Column 1	Isa. 10:24-27
Message to a subordinate a. **perfect** b. resolution	'Message' to one of unequal status a. admonition b.resolution
Column 2	Jer. 7:3-5
Message to a superior: statement of a fact Message to a subordinate ultimatum	'Message' to one of unequal status a. entreaty b. conditional resolution c. threat
Column 3	Jer. 29:4-23
Message to a superior a. **perfect** b. resolution	'Message' to one of unequal status a. **imperative** b. admonition c. resolution

But still only Column 1's and 3's message forms contain the "perfect" of form-criticism's 'messenger speech,' while only the saying (i.e., 'message') of Jeremiah 29:4-23 contains a form-critical "imperfect." None contain both components. Yet there is absolutely no dispute that Columns 1-3 contain messages. The question remains whether the prophetic sayings (short and/or long) are messages and whether both the prophet understood himself to have been a messenger **and** he was considered so by his contemporaries.

4. The Poetic Prophetical Saying

a. The Short Poetic Saying

In the previous section one saw that the longer prophetical saying corresponded to the longer written messages of the ANE and that one of these longer sayings was itself a **letter**. The short saying corresponded to the "oral" message, and the "oral" message was clearly the type of verbatim message delivered by the ANE messengers. Georg Fohrer holds that prophetic oracles "had to be communicated in poetically structured form." and that there was "no genuine prophetical saying not in the form of poetry."[14] Many of the short sayings are poetic, and appear also to be the product of deliberation just as the longer sayings discussed above. Fohrer goes so far as to maintain that "no Israelite prophet purporting to speak in the name of Yahweh could gain a hearing unless he clothed his speech in poetic form."[15] Short poetical sayings are found in the book of Isaiah, Jeremiah, Amos, Zephaniah and Micah.

(Isaiah 1:24-26)

"Ah, I will vent my wrath on my
enemies,
and avenge myself on my foes.
I will turn my hand against you
and will smelt away your dross
as with lye

and remove all your alloy.
And I will restore your judges as at
the first,
and your counselors as at the
beginning.
Afterward you shall be called the
city of righteousness,
the faithful city."

(Jeremiah 2:2-3)

"I remember the devotion of your
youth,
your love as a bride,
how you followed me in the wilderness,
in a land not sown,
Israel was holy to the Lord,
the first fruits of his harvest.
All who ate of it became guilty;
evil came upon them,
says the Lord."

(Amos 2:4-5)

"For three transgressions of Judah,
and for four, I will not revoke the
punishment;
because they have rejected the law
of the Lord,
and have not kept his statutes,
but their lives have led them astray,
after which their fathers walked.
So I will send fire upon Judah,
and it shall devour the strong-

holds of Jerusalem."

(Zephaniah 2:9)

"Therefore, as I live," says the Lord
of hosts,
the God of Israel,
"Moab shall become like Sodom,
and the Ammonites like Go-
morrah,
a land possessed by nettles and salt
pits,
and a waste forever.
The remnant of my people shall
plunder them,
and the survivors of my nation
shall possess them."

(Micah 1:6-7)

"Therefore I will make Samaria a
heap in the open country,
a place for planting vineyards;
and I will pour down her stones into
the valley,
and uncover her foundations.
All of her images shall be beaten to
pieces
all her hires shall be burned with
fire,
and all her idols I will lay waste;
for from the hire of a harlot she
gathered them,
and to the hire of a harlot they
shall return."[16]

Analysis shows that all take the form of a communication to subordinates, with the following components. The saying of Isaiah is comprised of (a) punishment and (b) restoration; the saying of Jeremiah is a reminiscence; while that of Amos has (a) accusation and (b) punishment; and both the sayings of Zephaniah and Micah deal with punishment only.

b. The Sustained Poetic Saying[17]

Just as there are short poetical sayings, there exist also sustained prophetical sayings in poetic garb. The following Isaianic passage serves as example.

(Isaiah 30: 1-5)

"Woe to the rebellious children,"
says the Lord,
"who carry out a plan, but not
mine;
and who make a league, but not
of my spirit,
that they may add sin to sin;
who set out to go down to Egypt,
without asking my counsel,
to take refuge in the protection of
Pharaoh,
and to seek shelter in the shadow
of Egypt!
Therefore shall the protection of
Pharaoh turn to your shame,
and the shelter in the shadow of
Egypt to your humiliation.
For though his officials are at Zoan
and his envoys reach Hanes,

> every one comes to shame
> through a people that cannot
> profit them,
> that brings neither help nor profit,
> but shame and disgrace."

Analysis shows that the saying takes the form of a 'message' to subordinates with (a) woe and (b) results as the two components.

5. Mixed Sayings

Some of the prophetical sayings, whether long or short, poetic or prose, or a combination of these types, are mixed as they presently stand. That is to say, they begin as a *dbr-yhwh* and appear to end as a prophetic *dbr*.[18]Observe the following examples.

The sustained prophetical saying of Isaiah 10:24-27 has been discussed above. Notice that the *dbr-yhwh* portion contains three possessive pronouns in speech which runs to the words "their destruction." Following upon this is a section which contains third person narrative, and which appears to be prophetic *dbr*. The use of quotation marks in many English versions, however, gives the reader the impression that this is all one *dbr*, or *dbr-yhwh*, since it follows upon the expanded *kh 'mr yhwh* formula.

Similarly, at Jeremiah 2:2-3, the same phenomenon occurs. The *dbr-yhwh* proceeds to the words "not sown." There one also notices the personal pronouns. Following these, however, is the third person use in reference "to the Lord" and "his harevest." Yet this saying is cast as a *n'm yhwh*.[19]

With these sayings being candidates for prophetic 'messages,' this combination of *dbr-yhwh* and prophetic *dbr* forces one to be even more skeptical of 'messenger speech.' At any rate, no such mixture of *personae* among the short "oral" messages, or the sustained written messages of the ANE were chronicled. It is also now understandable why Westermann cautioned that not every occurrence of the 'messenger formula' was followed by a 'message.'[20]

The preceding discussion of mixed sayings drew attention once again to the issue of Yahweh's word(s) versus the GIPs' word(s). If one is to know when Yahweh is "speaking," and thereby to ferret out 'messenger speech,' all of the foregoing considerations are necessary and **must** be made,--but they still do not resolve all of the difficulties involved. Martin Buss has suggested that the differences between the *dbr-yhwh* and the prophetic *dbr*, if such is to be upheld, "can be upheld only if one credits to divine speech no more than those sayings in which the divine "I" explicitly occurs."[21] Yet one could continue to analyze prophetic speech form-critically as has been done thus far, and compare those results with the messages of the ANE messengers, or the previous results of form-criticism *ad nauseum*, and still be led to one inescapable fact; the burden of proof for those who maintain that there is a literary phenomenon called 'messenger speech' which demonstrates that the prophets Amos through Jeremiah were messengers lies with those who would assign **any** speech to Yahweh! Buss reminds all correctly that "the prophet is the actual speaker; "divine speech" is merely a term for those in which "I" other than the prophet's becomes stylistically prominent."[22] But even this first person "I" had become so intertwined with the third person "he" that it proved difficult to isolate it always once a move was made from the form-critical categories to a more thorough comparative investigation of the forms of alleged prophetic 'messenger speech' with actual messenger speech.

In appreciation of the art and discipline of form-criticism, but like that school of thought which has moved beyond the parameters of form-criticism to include rhetorical considerations, I conclude with Buss: ". . . prophetic speech and divine word are not separable genres existing independently, but that they are factors of style, perhaps even not necessarily rigid ones."[23]

The more this study proceeded beyond the traditional parameters, the more it became apparent that many statements concerning prophetic speech as the speech of a messenger needed clarification; that they (the statements) were plausible as long as no one stormed the citadel in which they were being given refuge. Once the siege machines of thorough comparative and contrastive analysis were directed against the walls of refuge, defense was shown to be futile as well as untenable. Yet, I am infinitely far richer as attacker than when I began, for I laid siege to a noble adversary!

Summary

The question of whether the HS, GIPs should be called messengers and whether they considered themselves messengers as well as whether their contemporaries understood them to be messengers, had to be approached with two complementary sets of concerns: (1) the types, forms, and characteristics of construction of representative prophetical sayings as compared with the types, forms, and characteristics of construction of representative "oral" and written messages of the ANE messengers, and (2) the activities of the prophets when performing their alleged messenger role as compared with the demonstrated activities and roles of messsengers of the ANE. Both **saying** and **person** had to be considered (not one to the exclusion of the other) if an accurate assessment was to be made. Chapter VI concentrated on the **saying**.

As to saying, further study extended the limits of the form-critical investigations. The literary comparison showed that just as the messenger had delivered a short "oral" message, the prophet as an alleged messenger, delivered what is believed to have been a brief "oral" saying. When the prophetic saying which contained the two necessary components of 'messenger speech' (i.e., a report in the perfect and a summons in the imperative) was compared with the analysis of some twenty-one examples of ANE short "oral" messages, 'messenger speech' corresponded (in two-component form alone) with only ANE short "oral" messages. The contents of the message showed it to be a message to one of unequal status, whereas the 'messenger speech' by its very form-critical nature, had to be directed toward one of unequal status since it purportedly came from a deity. The purpose of this examination throughout was to demonstrate how unreliable the term 'messenger speech' was when compared with uncontested, indisputable messages, and to show how many messages would have been overlooked had one simply relied on the form-critical criteria alone. **'Messenger speech' was neither equal to nor the equivalent of message.**

Just as there was evidence which enabled one to speak of "oral" message and "oral" saying, I presented evidence which allowed one to speak of written messages and sustained prophetical sayings. The written messages were in the form of letters, while the sustained prophetical sayings, because of their length, were suspected of having been written down also. In fact, one lengthy prophetical saying was indeed itself a letter (Jer. 29:4-23). Analysis showed that none of the written messages participated in the form-critical description of 'messenger speech.' The written messages and the sustained prophetical saying did have more in common, however, than the short "oral" message and the short saying of the prophets. Both the written messages and the sustained saying reflected more carefully thought out contents; they had not been spontaneously produced. Once again, when comparison was made, it was the 'messenger speech' which was most unlike messages of the ANE.

Aside from these differences, there were other types within the category of the prophetical saying which had no ANE counterpart. The short saying, which I compared with the short message, was found in two types: (1) the short **prose** saying and the short **poetic** saying. Several scholars had maintained that in order for a prophetic saying to have been considered genuine, it had to have been clothed in poetic garb. According to this view, 'messenger speech' had to be poetic. None of the short poetic prophetical sayings corresponded with the form-critical designation 'messenger speech,' but all of them did resemble (but were not identical to) messages to subordinates. There were also sustained poetical sayings which, likewise, did not correspond to the form-critical designation. Thus far my study has produced a comparison and contrast of:

      a. the short "oral" message and short "oral" prophetical saying which resembled each other in that both were brief and were intended as communications of information. No further conclusions could be drawn. They were not identical.

b. the short "oral" prophetical saying which was of two types: (1) prose and (2) poetic. Form-critically, 'messenger speech' required a perfect report and an imperative summons. Other scholarly opinions were prepared to maintain that, form-critical designations notwithstanding, only if a prophetical saying was poetic would it have been considered a genuine *dbr-yhwh*, i.e., an alleged message, at the time it was delivered by the prophet.

c. the longer prophetical saying which was similar to the written message of the ANE which was also of two types (1) prose and (2) poetry. What is maintained in b. above holds for this type as well.

Scholarly opinions are so divided on what constitutes 'messenger speech' on the one hand, while on the other, when the two main groups of these opinions (i.e., the form-critical opinion and the poetry-oriented opinion) are compared with authentic examples of messages from the ANE (both "oral" and written) the problem still remains. It may be stated confidently that in light of the present study to maintain that prophetic speech is or was the speech of a messenger simply because it vaguely resembles such speech on the surface of things is no longer tenable. 'Messenger speech' outside the HS has no literary and/or form-critical parallels. This was the inevitable result of the comparative study. The designation 'messenger speech' continues to be useful, however, in terms of dividing the various forms of literature contained within the prophetic *corpus* of materials. This designation should be understood as one of convenience which then allows one to speak of **this** type of prophetic utterance as distinct from

that type, i.e., merely to avoid confusion when speaking of types of literature. To place more stress on 'messenger speech' than it can and should bear, and to draw conclusions from it which cannot be defended successfully, leads one to faulty conclusions, and eventually to forcing one to explain the **mixed saying**!

The mixed saying is found among the categories of prophetical sayings which had been discussed during the comparison and contrast also. By mixed saying I meant that analysis had shown that such a saying began with a *dbr-yhwh*, but that a change of person occurred in the delivery, which caused the saying to end as a prophetic *dbr* with no apparent reason for the change. That is to say, the prophet appears to have begun delivering a prophetical saying which may not have contained the so-called divine "I," but at any rate which was intended to be understood as Yahweh"s word(s). In some cases the saying was immediately preceded by one of the legitimizing formulae, which led one further to believe that what followed were Yahweh's word(s). Suddenly, however, the reader intuits that someone else is speaking, and that they (the reader) have not been alerted by the speech that such a change has indeed occurred. Such is the nature of the mixed saying. In contrast, none of the ANE messages presented such a mixture of *personae*. The problem, however, may be traced to the editing process, or to the collecting phase of the production of the prophetic books.

To extricate oneself from this problem, which was in part brought on by form-critical investigation, the presence of the divine "I" was held by some investigators to be the best way of separating the prophet's words from Yahweh's words (which were contained purportedly within the prophetical sayings, i.e., that prophetic speech most likely to contain 'messenger speech.'). To do so, however, would only worsen matters (as has now been observed with the mixed saying), and cause more fruitless categorizing of prophetic speech mainly in an attempt to continue to "prove" that the prophets were messengers. Prophetic speech and 'messenger speech' (which could contain the divine "I") could not really be considered separable *genres* with separate existences. On the contrary, they had to be seen as factors of style.

CHAPTER VII

The ANE Messengers, the Messenger
of the Hebrew Scriptures, and the
Great Individual Prophet of the Hebrew Scriptures:
A Comparison and Contrast

When considering whether or not the great individual prophets should correctly be termed messengers, and in exactly what context, much needs to be taken into consideration. A plethora of factors (among them form-critical considerations) are involved which must be examined and discussed.

According to the Ezekiel tradition, the prophetic "messenger role" was only one of several roles that the prophet appeared to perform. Says Fohrer:

> In addition to reports of symbolic actions and ecstatic visions, the Ezekiel tradition contains many discourses, often of considerable length. The minatory forms are most heavily represented, with fifty-six discourses, as well as a great number of historical analyses, discussions, instructions, and allegories, which bear witness to the rationalistic and reflective element in Ezekiel's thought. Finally promises constitute a significant portion of the book. To these were added a series of later discourses deriving from various authors and periods.[1]

The same is true to a greater or lesser extent of all the traditions concerning the great individual prophets. Thus, if one wishes to speak of a prophet as a messenger, one must at least be prepared to understand that prophet as one exercising one of several **possible** roles he felt called upon to perform during the course of his activity. Still, however, one would have to present cogent arguments to demonstrate that a given prophet felt called upon to perform in such a way. Generally, the key to this alleged messenger role should be expected to be signalled by the presence of the formula *kh 'mr yhwh*. I have demonstrated, however, that it is not as simple a matter as this.

What has been severely lacking in previous studies is a comparison and contrast of the prophets (especially the GIPs) with the ANE and HS messengers at as many points as possible to ascertain just how closely or not the prophets come to participating in the activities, and sharing the characteristics of the messenger whose status is unquestioned. The purpose of such an exercise is to provide a much larger framework than usual literary-restricted types provide, within which I may expose more than has generally been known or acknowledged about the relationship of prophets to messengers.

1. Purpose

The purpose of the messenger was to extend temporally and geographically the existing power of another's either spoken word(s) (in the same tone of voice), deeds, or both as well as deliver the written form of such word(s). I offer as examples (all of which are found in the appropriate section of PART I) the letter-carrier from Egypt who was sent to the court of King Burnaburi-iash of Babylonia who delivered the written words of the king of Egypt (Babylonia); the personal messenger of King Hezekiah who by deed delivered the tribute to Sennacherib, king of Assyria, and who also did obeisance as a slave before the victorious Assyrian monarch (Assyria); and the harbormaster who, serving as messenger for the Prince of Byblos, delivered to Wenamon the message (in a tone of voice to match that of the prince's) "Get out of my harbor!" (Egypt)

According to Deuteronomy 18:5, Israel, fearing the encounter with the awesome Yahweh at Sinai-Horeb, allowed Moses to intercede on her behalf in order to seal the relationship between herself and her deity. The prophets (according to tradition) continued to maintain this relationship by interceding for Israel before Yahweh, after a portion of the spirit of Moses was divided among seventy elders of Israel--who, upon receipt of this spirit, began to prophesy (Num. 11:24 ff.). As intercessor within the cult, the prophet carried petitions before Yahweh from Israel, as well as mandates from Yahweh before Israel. This was generally accomplished by the oracle. Thus, the suspected role of the prophet as messenger would only have been a part-time role--if at all!

2. Status as Messenger

The status of the ANE, HS secular extension of another's words and deeds, and the one who proclaimed and announced tidings as a messenger was as an integral and indispensable part of the ANE culture. The inability of the messenger to function due to war, or natural catastrophe had an effect on the ANE societies which may be likened to a complete information blackout by the modern information media (printed, radio, television, computer). The rule of Cyrus the Persian was successful in large measure due to the firm control which he kept on the political situation through an efficient system of communications.[2] That system of communications is worth a study in itself. The system was maintained by messengers on a full-time basis. The frequent use of the messenger in the historical narratives contained in PART I, Chapter III shows once again how important messengers were to Israelite society, as well as to the authors, collectors, and redactors of the HS. Moreover, the herald of the HS was involved in proclaiming some of the most important tidings of the biblical record. Heralds announced that the two sons of the priest of Shiloh, Eli, were dead and that the ark had been captured by the Philistines(1 Sam. 4:17); that the rebel prince, Absalom, and his sympathizers were dead or defeated; David the king could return to the throne of Jerusalem (2 Sam. 18:31); and of great importance, they brought good tidings, and proclaimed peace and salvation; they proclaimed to Zion that her deity lived (Isa. 52:7). **Messenger** even appears as the title of some members of a given court. Reference is made to Dagan-abu, the messenger of *Ia-si-li-im*, the ensi of Tuttul (Sumer); and to the King's-Messenger (Egypt); as well as to Eagadada, the royal messenger (Sumer).

The status of the great individual prophet as a messenger is doubtful. Thus far this status has depended on a definition of such terms as 'commissioning formula,' 'messenger formula,' and 'messenger speech' which, since Ludwid Koehler's form-critical study *"Deuterojesaja (Jesaja 40-55) stilkritisch untersucht,"* of 1923, remain hypothetical, contradictory, form-critical designations at best.

3. Geographical Theater of Operations

Messengers exercised their functions in an area which began near the (now) Persian Gulf in southern Mesopotamia, and continued northward along the Fertile Crescent, turned westward into Anatolia, continued southward through Syro-Palestine, and then southwestward into Egypt definitely as far southward as the present-day Assuan (Aswan) Dams.

The great individual prophets operated chiefly in Palestine in both the kingdoms of Israel and Judah. Jeremiah continued to be active in Egypt after being taken there, and Ezekiel prophesied in Babylonia among especially the first group of deportees from Jerusalem (ca. 597 BCE).

4. Temporal Period of Operation

The period covered herein for the messenger ranges from approximately 3000 BCE (which coincides with the early **written** evidence of the existence of messengers) to the Roman occupation of Egypt, around 30 BCE. This does not mean that messenger activity did not exist prior to the first date, nor does it mean that after the latter date messenger activity ceased. My chief purpose in setting these limits on the evidence contained in PART I and on the present chronological discussion was to demonstrate that for a long and constant period of time prior to, during, and long after the appearance and demise of the office of prophet (i.e., *hozeh, ro'eh,* and *nabi'*) in Israel, that the understanding of **messenger** by the people of the ANE remained unchanged. It is this important consistency of understanding which the evidence of PART I demonstrated overwhelmingly, and which makes this comparison and contrast valid.

Chronologically, the first time that prophets are mentioned in the HS is in 1 Samuel 10:5. They are organized into a band and are inciting war against a Philistine garrison in the midst of Israelite territory. Another organized band of prophets is found at Ramah and are led by Samuel (1 Sam. 19:20). At the time (ca. 1020 BCE), Saul was *nagid*. These were, however, ecstatic prophets (i.e., chiefly the *ro'eh* and/or *hozeh*) whose ecstatic visions were brought on by the help of the harp, tambourine, flute and the lyre (1 Sam. 10:5b). The *nabi'* type of prophet, who is the subject of this inquiry, dates from approximately 750 BCE (Amos) to approximately 580 BCE (Ezekiel).

5. Types

Men of various military ranks, men of high social standing, as well as ordinary men and women served as messengers in the ANE.

The great individual prophets were all males (not that female prophets were unknown in Israel and Mari). As to social position, Jeremiah was a priest, and Amos may have been a gentleman farmer and rancher, or a priest in charge of the royal herds(I opt for the latter). Ezekiel was a priest, and the same may be true for Isaiah of Jerusalem.

6. Authority

The messenger was commissioned and dispatched by and in the name of the person for whom he or she was to serve as an extension. Only in the case of the Egyptian, Wenamon, is there an example of a messenger who claimed to have been sent by a deity. There is no insistence in this claim, however, on the part of Wenamon, neither does he claim to deliver a message from this deity.

The authority of the great individual prophet as a messenger is questionable. Many offer (or it is offered for them) an explanation as to how they became prophets (especially since all purportedly came from other walks of life). These explanations (sometimes called 'call narratives,' but generally located in prophetic autobiographical material) can generally be traced to the question "Since you are not a member of any **professional** prophetic guild, by what authority do **you** prophesy?", and are attempts to authorize their person as well as their utterances in the face of strong opposition from antagonistic spokespersons from both the general populace and from the guildsmen. In many narratives contained in the books of the great individual prophets, these prophets state that Yahweh **sent** them to prophesy or to say such and such to the people of Israel, to groups, or to individuals. One may either reject this claim as fact, accept it as a statement of profound truth, or probe further to ascertain whether these prophets were seizing upon the image of natural folk heros (i.e., the messengers in general) and their legitimizing formulae, in order to make their presence and utterances more acceptable. But if the latter (purely speculation on my part) was indeed the case, it failed to impress their contemporaries, because of the cool-to-violent receptions with which their utterances were greeted.

7. Functions of the Messenger Distributed over the Geographical Range of the ANE Messengers Involved and the GIPs' Functions: A Comparison

a. The Ambassador-at-Large (Mari): The Prophet-at-Large (Bethel) (Amos 7:10)

Among the Mari Letters, Moran makes reference to one Mar-Ishtar, bishop of Esagila, who served as an ambassador-at-large for King Esarhaddon of Assyria.[3] His presence gives me reason to believe that of the messenger-ambassador type there was a special category of persons who were engaged in something on the order of shuttle diplomacy.

It generally appears that the GIPs performed their functions at certain locations. By carefully scrutinizing the language of Hosea, scholars almost unanimously hold that he was a prophet in Isarel (i.e., the northern political entity). In a similar manner, the prophet Isaiah (Isa. 1-24; 28-39), because of his activity, appears to have been limited to Jerusalem. The prophet Amos was from Tekoa in Judah (i.e., the southern political entity Amos 1:1), but unlike Micah who came from Moreshet, or Jeremiah who came from Anathoth (both also in the territory of Judah) and prophesied in Judah, Amos the southerner prophesied in the North (i.e., Israel) at the sanctuary located at Bethel (Amos 7:10). He was not well-received there because of his contrary statements concerning the prevailing theology, and was told to leave Israel and return to Judah and prophesy there. This appears to be the first voluntary cross-boundary venture by a GIP. If this comparison eventuates in demonstrating that the GIPs were messengers, Amos would enjoy the nebulous distinction of being the prophetic messenger/ambassador-at-large. To be sure, Jeremiah is called the prophet to the nations, but the only movement by Jeremiah that has been chronicled is to Egypt after ca. 586 BCE, and then by force! Oracles ascribed to him exist (like those of Amos) against the nations. From where they were delivered, however, is not known.

b. Adjudication and Forensic Functions

The record of legal decision which was rendered in favor of Hala-Bau, the wife of Ur-Bau, concerning a property settlement ends:

> The house of Hala-Bau was confirmed
> Eagadada the **royal messenger** ... [4]

and one other official   served as presidents at the hearing which handed down the decision. A Sumerian messenger functioned here in a legal capacity and adjudicated a property settlement case (Sumer).

In Egypt during the reign of Thutmose III, part of a set of instructions to the vizier Rakhmire advised the vizier that when an official had been charged with some offense, and was summoned before him:

> he is not brought in because of the
> speech of the responsible officer, (but)
> it is known by the speech of his
> messsenger as the one stating it; he is
> by the side of the responsible officer as
> the speaker; . . .[5]

Here the messenger functioned as an advocate who spoke for, or on behalf of, a client official. The messenger-advocate accompanied the charged officer and spoke for him. The messenger-advocates were highly skilled in both verbal and non-verbal communication techniques, for they knew how to ascertain the mood of a given vizier to the advantage of their clients by closely observing the vizier's body movements, especially the unconscious nodding of the head, while he listened to a plea. Therefore, the vizier was warned to be wary of those wily messenger-advocates, for "Lo, they will say (concerning the vizier), the petitioner loves him who nods the head . . ."[6]

Some GIPs engaged in what also appears to be the function of a court officer. Appendices II-IV contain a scheme of how the GIP was to have performed this forensic function as trial advocates in the $r\hat{\imath}b$ or controversy or lawsuit of Yahweh against Israel. Forensic functions were not foreign to the messengers of the ANE, and the GIPs' claim to function as a court officer who convened Yahweh's court and presided over it as the representative of Yahweh the plaintiff (although Yahweh would have also served as judge and witness in this "kangaroo court") is now more understandable. It is **messenger** study which illuminates **prophecy** study.

c. The Delivery of Tidings

Ashurbanipal (668-626 BCE), king of Assyria, stated in one of his annal cylinders that one of the Egyptian vassals of his father Esarhaddon revolted and attacked other vassals whom his father had set up (Assyria). To compound matters, this rebellious vassal (Tirhaka) settled in Memphis, a city which Esarhaddon had added to the territory of Assyria. Ashurbanipal tells that he found out about the rebellion because "A swift **messenger** came to Nineveh and brought me tidings."[7]

On another occasion Gyges of Lydia formed an alliance with Ashurbanipal, but he later took the same action as Tirhaka (Assyria). He was defeated in battle by the Cimmerians, a people whom he had defeated earlier. Ashurbanipal's annal continues: "After him his son took his seat upon his throne. Through his **messenger** he sent me tidings of the disasterous calamity . . ."[8]

A Hittite text shows how one overanxious king reacted to incompetent officers who kept sending him unwelcomed messages about a battle's progress (or better, the lack of progress) (Hatti): "They constantly bring me evil tidings may the weather-god carry you away in a flood!"[9]

Two Ugaritic texts (Text 51:V; 76:III:34) contain accounts of heralds who bring tidings. Text 51 reads: "Receive, Ba'al, the glad tidings which I bring thee."[10] Text 76 contains: "Receive, Ba'al, godly tidings, . . . "[11] In the first instance the tidings are that Ba'al will have a house (i.e., a temple), while the second assures him that he will have a male heir.

In Israelite texts "**He who brought the tidings** answered and said, 'Israel has fled before the Philistines, . . . " (1 Sam. 4:17) concerns the herald. "Let me run, and carry tidings to the king that the Lord has delivered him from the power of his enemies." (2 Sam. 18:19); and ". . . they cut off his head. . . and sent messengers . . . to carry the tidings . . ." (1 Sam. 31:9) show further that the herald-messenger was active in Israel and known among her neighbors.

A Lachish letter-message contains the words: "May Yahweh cause my lord to hear tidings of peace."[12] The author of the letter hoped that this letter would contain some of those tidings.

All of the above examples have in common the fact that the one who announced certain events, or who brought tidings was a messenger in the ANE. Herald-messengers appear to have delivered messages which were in general of a non-verbatim type.

None of the GIPs are said to specifically announce tidings. Concerning the suspected role of messenger ascribed to the prophets, I have already stated, however, that cultically the prophet's main function was to announce what Yahweh was about to do. Although the

Hebrew root *bsr*, 'to announce, bring tidings,' is never used to describe any action by a GIP, it is known to the prophetic books. The prophet Jeremiah exclaimed: "Cursed be the man who brought tidings (*bsr*) to my father, "A son is born to you." (Jer. 20:15). In the book of the prophet Nahum one reads: "Behold on the mountains the feet of him who brings good tidings (*mbsr*)" (Nahum 1:15). Accounts of tidings are also found in Isaiah 40:9; 41:27; 60:6; and 61:1 all of which contain expressions with the root *bsr*.

d. The Delivery of a Verbal Message

Messengers were sent to Tirhaka, king of Ethiopia, by vassal kings of the Assyrians to say: "Let a league be established between us and let us help each other" (Egypt). The Hyksos king, Apepy, sent his messenger to Sequenen-Ra, Prince of Thebes (Egypt), to say: "My messenger has come to thee, concerning the splashing of the hippopotami which are in the pool in the city (of Thebes) . . . they allow me no sleep, day and night the sound of them is in my ear." Joab, David's general, sent messengers to David who said to him: "I have fought against Rabbah; moreover, I have taken the city of waters." (2 Sam. 12:27-28)

The final saying contained in the book of Isaiah of Jerusalem reads:

> . . . the days are coming, when all that
> is in your house, and that which your
> fathers have stored up till this day,
> shall be carried to Babylon; nothing
> shall be left, **says the Lord**. (Isa. 39:6)

This saying, and many more like it, is one reason why the prophets may be said to have been messengers. I continue to maintain that this is not proof of any such claim.

e. Conspiratorial Matters

A conspiracy involving Tirhaka (Egypt), king of Egypt and Ethiopia, and one-time vassals of Ashurbanipal against him was kept alive by the vassals through their sending to Tirhaka saying:

> Let a league be established between us
> and let us be a help to each other. If we
> divide the country among ourselves,
> then there shall not be another lord
> between us.[13]

As the reign of Pharaoh Ramses III drew near to its close, the wives of his harem plotted to have the eldest son of the favorite among them succeed him. Numerous court officials were made privy to the machinations involved in bringing this plot to fruition. It was necessary to bribe these officials "so that messages freely passed out and in between the two sets of conspirators."[14] One of the messages sent out urged the stirring up of discontent and rebelliousness among the subjects: "Excite the people, goad on the enemies to begin hostilities against their lord."[15]

Hoshea, king of Israel, was a vassal to Shalmaneser, king of Assyria:

> But the king of Assyria found treachery
> in Hoshea; for he had sent messengers
> to So, king of Egypt, and offered no
> tribute to the king of Assyria, as he had
> done year by year; . . .(2 Kg. 17:4)

This conspiracy, in that it was unsuccessful, heralded the eventual conquest and decimation of Israel in 722/1 BCE. One sees how in each case messengers played an important role.

As to the GIPs being involved in conspiratorial matters, I would have to say that most (if not all) at one time or another would, by the very utterances ascribed to them, have been suspected of conspiring to overthrow the government by means of seditious talk and by demoralizing the populace. A case in point involves the prophet Jeremiah who states:

> Then I spoke to the priests and to all this people, saying, "Thus says the Lord: Do not listen to the words of your prophets who are prophesying to you saying, "Behold, the vessels of the Lord's house will now shortly be brought back from Babylon, " for it is a lie which they are prophesying to you. Do not listen to them; serve the king of Babylon and live. (Jer. 27:16-17)

In the ears of those present, and especially since the professional salvation prophets were more popular, it is not too far fetched to suppose that Jeremiah was suspected of being a political agent of the Babylonians; an agent openly engaging in a conspiracy to overthrow Jerusalem. Sociologists of religion who deal with marginal group activity which attempts to influence the major cult group would have a field day with Jeremiah and the group he represented.

f. Courting Functions

When the Canaanite king, Kirtu, wished to woo a bride, the wooing took the form of a military expedition with the purpose of laying siege to the bastion of the desired bride's father or guardian (Canaan). The wooing was accomplished in two phases. In the first the suitor employed a **messenger** to carry messages of suit to his beloved as well as to her father or guardian. Secondly, it was customary for the first offer to be refused, at which time the suitor pursued his suit in person. A portion of Kirtu's suit delivered by a messenger reads: "Give me the damsel *Hry*, the fair, thy first begotten, . . ."[16]

An Egyptian papyrus shows that messengers kept two lovers in communication although circumstances kept them from one another (Egypt). The heart-sick male moaned:

> It has been seven days yesterday since I saw the sister, And sickness encroaches upon me, . . . The coming and going of her messengers is that which revives my heart . . . [17]

In Palestine "David sent and wooed Abigail, to make her his wife" shortly after the death of her husband, Nabal. (1 Sam. 25:39).

> And when the servants (*'bdy*) of David came to Abigail at Carmel, and they said to her, "David has sent us to you to take you to him as his wife." And Abigail . . . went after the messengers of David and became his wife. (1 Sam. 25:39d-42)

All of these messengers performed a courting function by carrying messages of suit.

Of the GIPs, only the actions and words of Hosea are relevant here. In Hosea 1:2-3 one reads that Hosea was instructed to: "Go, take to yourself a wife of harlotry, . . . So he went and took Gomer the daughter of Dibliam, ..." Hosea is also instructed to: "Go again, love a woman who is beloved of a paramour and is an adultress; . . . (Hos. 3:1). Although these actions are considered by many scholars to come under the rubric of symbolic actions of the prophets, it is now known that they can be viewed legitimately as courting functions. In fact, the whole of Chapters 1-3 of Hosea is replete with the language of wooing. Chapter 2:14 reads: "Therefore, behold, I will allure her, and bring her into the wilderness and speak tenderly to her," while 2:16 sums: "And in that day, says the Lord, you will call me, 'My husband,' and no longer will you call me, 'My Ba'al.' I make no case here, however, for a view of Hosea as an alleged messenger, for **he** is the one to be married here.

g. Military Matters

Due to the sociological makeup of the ANE, there were always military conflicts abroad in the lands. Where these conflicts raged, messengers of all types were employed on a large scale to maintain the necessary communications links between king and commander, commander and officers, officers and lower rank and filers. In discussion of the ANE and HS messengers in PART I, Chapters I and III, I examined numerous texts where messengers were involved in military matters. There was no ANE country surveyed which did not produce examples of military messengers. For socio-religious reasons the GIPs in their alleged role as messengers performed a similar function. Amos 1-2 contains announcements of Yahweh's war against the nations. Jeremiah 46:25 announces Yahweh's war against Amon and Thebes, Pharaoh and Egypt. This theme may also be found in Jeremiah 48; 49; 50; 51; Isaiah 15; 16; 17; 18; 19; and elsewhere in prophetic literature.

h. Engage in Dialogue

The majority of the time the messenger, when commissioned to deliver a verbatim message, delivered that message and waited for a reply. That usually marked the beginning and the end of the first phase of his/her messenger activity. The return trip and delivery marked the second. There is evidence, however, of messengers going beyond the mere verbatim delivery of a message, for sometimes extenuating and mitigating circumstances made it necessary for more to be said.

The supposedly ailing Babylonian king, Burnaburi-iash, was annoyed with the contemporaneous Egyptian king for not having condoled with him (Egypt). The Egyptian messenger who had been sent to the Babylonian attempted to explain to him that due to the considerable distance which separated their two countries, the king had no possible way of knowing immediately of his illness. The messenger suggested further that the king inquire of his own messenger whether this was not so.

The messengers(s) of Sumeria and Egypt (Sumer; Egypt), in that they adjudicated property disputes and performed as defense counsel for charged officials respectively, most certaily engaged in dialogue with those with whom they dealt. The same would quite naturally accompany the activity of the emissary, the envoy, and the ambassador type messengers at all times.[18]

In Israel, the messenger sent to summon the prophet Michaiah ben Imlah before the kings of Israel and Judah went beyond the mere delivery of his message to suggest to the prophet that since the guild prophets had all prophesied success for the kings' proposed joint venture (to recapture Ramot-gilead in Transjordan), he was urged strongly to follow suit. This, I maintain--on the basis of the later dialogue between Michaiah and Ahab--was not a part of the original message which had been sent by the king (1 Kg. 22:13).

On Palestinian soil, the messenger of King Sennacherib, the Rabshakeh, delivered his lord's message to the representatives of King Hezekiah of Judah. Once he had done so, however, he began to dialogue with these representatives, and to suggest to them that having Egypt as an ally against Assyria was the height of folly (2 Kg. 18: 23-24).

Turning to the GIPs, I point to the whole issue of their dialogue with the professional prophets (or at least with their leaders) over the issue of accurate versus inaccurate revelations, as well as point to their dialogues (usually distasteful) with the priests, professional prophets, kings, people in general, who were unnerved by what these prophets had to say. Amos engaged in dialogue with the Bethel priest, Amaziah, after he (Amos) had made unpopular statements concerning the expected Day of Yahweh, the fate of King Jeroboam II, and the exile of Israel (Amos 7:10-15). Micah of Moresheth tells that after having been told "Do not preach . . . one should not preach of such things; . . ." (Micah 2:6) Micah's "And I said:

. . .", which is followed by the statement in Micah 3:1-4, is a response to either priestly or professional prophetic objections to his utterances. Jeremiah 26:12-15 contains an account of Jeremiah dialoguing with priests, prophets, and people after his Temple sermon, while Isaiah 7:13-17 contains a dialogue between Isaiah of Jerusalem and King Ahaz. In it is found the famous (and still often misunderstood) Immanuel sign.

i. Political Matters

In Egyptian political affairs the replacement of a pharaoh by one of his sons was a matter taken seriously by the members of his harem (Egypt; see e. above). Attempts were made to bribe as many court officials, functionaries, and palace guards as possible into accepting one of the sons of one of the favorites among the mothers of the harem as the next heir. Messengers went out from the harem to the subjects of the pharaoh and delivered messages which urged the stirring up of disaffection toward the eldest son of the royal wife.

During the united monarchy period (ca. 1000-922 BCE) messengers were sent by David to Hanun, king of Ammon, to open diplomatic relations (2 Sam. 10:1-5). Both David and Solomon received messengers from Hiram, king of Tyre (2 Sam. 5:11); 1 Kg. 5:1 [MT 5:15]), while Hezekiah also received the envoys of Merodach-bala-dan (i.e., Marduk-apal-iddina [2 Kg. 20:12]). 2 Kings 10:1-7 contains the letter-message which Jehu sent by messenger to the guardians of the sons of Ahab as part of his plan to liquidate the Omride Dynasty.

The prophetic movement which began in the eighth century was one of several movements within Yahwism which had fought change from without and syncretistic tendencies from within; the Rechabites were another. The prophetic movement, then, of which the GIPs were a major part, was a resistance movement against Canaanite and other outside influences. In that it was a socio-religious resistance movement, it was also a political resistance movement, for there is no neat division of prophetic activity into things religious and things political.

j. Spy Activity

The only evidence I found of messengers being involved in spying was discussed in Chapter III under "Spies and Spy Activity." The only instance where spying could not be proved, but was suspected involved the advisors of Hanun, king of Ammon, telling him that David's envoys were sent to spy out his land (2 Sam. 10:1-5).

Among the GIPs, Jeremiah could possibly have been suspected of spying (for the Babylonians), and Amos might have incurred the suspicions of Amaziah at Bethel about spying for the Jerusalemites. No such open charge, however, was brought against either prophet.

k. Other

Healing functions (Israel), involvement in business and commerce (Assyria, Egypt, Israel), and the task as errand-persons (Sumer, Babylonia, Assyria, Hatti, Egypt, Israel) were some of the functions also recorded concerning the ANE and HS messengers.

None of the GIPs performed any healing functions (cf. Elisha in 2 Kings 5:10; 2 Kings 4:32-35). Jeremiah does purchase a field in Anathoth (Jer. 32:6-15). Symbolic actions that involved the prophet going from one place to another--such as Jeremiah 13:1-7--are the closest that the GIPs come to resembling errand-persons.

8. Maltreatment of the Messenger

Oftentimes the ANE messenger was identified with the contents of the message which he or she delivered. The result was often maltreatment of the messenger.[19] The Egyptian, Wenamon, was maltreated both in Sidon and Byblos. His mission was to bring back enough cedar wood to build a special barge which was to be used in a great religious festival. Egypt, which had once ruled Sidon and Byblos, was no longer in a position of power. Wenamon was treated with contempt because Egypt was at that time (11th century BCE) politically contemptible in the eyes of its former vassals. The barge which Egypt built was to the princes of Sidon and Byblos a reminder of the days when Egypt enjoyed military hegemony over them. A request for cedar for such a purpose in the mouth of Wenamon was tantamount to Egypt requesting it. The former vassals had the opportunity to redress an old grievance.

David sent messengers to Hanun, king of Ammon, to console him after the death of his father (2 Sam. 10:1). These messengers were suspected of having been sent as spies, "So Hanun took David's servants, and shaved off half the beard of each, and cut off their garments in the middle, at their hips, and sent them away" (2 Sam. 10:3-4). Unlike Wenamon, David's maltreated messengers were avenged. David declared war on Ammon and defeated it.

Maltreatment of messengers, however, was David's specialty. A herald came to commander David while he was in Ziklag to report that he had escaped from Saul's camp. David inquired of the progress of Saul's battle against the Philistine coalition. It had gone very badly for Israel. Saul was dead and this herald claimed to have struck the final blow which had killed him.

> And David said to the young man who told him, . . . "How is it that you were not afraid to put forth your hand to destroy the Lord's anointed?" Then David called one of the young men and said, "Go, fall upon him." And he smote him so that he died. (2 Sam. 1:13-15)

A remaining son of the slain Saul, Ishbosheth (Esh- or Ishba'al), was made *nagid* over Israel at Mahanaim (2 Sam. 2:8-9). Two captains of raiding bands, Banaan and Rechab, stole into the house of Ishba'al who was taking a nap, and assassinated him. They cut off his head and brought it to David at Hebron, thinking to please him, and to receive a reward from him.

> But David answered . . . "As the Lord
> lives, . . . when one told me, 'Behold,
> Saul is dead,' and thought he was
> bringing me good news, I seized him and
> slew him at Ziklag, which was the reward
> I gave him for his news . . . And David
> commanded his young men, and they
> killed them, and cut off their hands and
> feet, and hanged them beside the pool at
> Hebron. (2 Sam. 4:9-12)

When Ahimaaz the son of Zadok asked Joab to "Let me run, and carry tidings to the king, . . . " which involved telling David that Absalom was dead, Joab feared what David had done to previous messengers who had brought bad news, and refused to let the young man go to David (2 Sam. 18:19-20). He sent a black soldier instead, but the young Ahimaaz went anyway.

Amos was forbidden to prophesy at Bethel because his prophecies were unwelcome. There is no literary evidence to argue that Amos was physically abused like Michaiah ben Imlah (1 Kg. 22 ff.), or like Uriah ben Shemaiah (Jer. 26:20-23) who was killed for prophesying unpleasantries, but the idea is not far fetched. After a sermon by Jeremiah, the audience was in an indignant uproar. The mob seized him and the priests called for his death (Jer. 26:7-11). Jeremiah was also beaten by the priest, Pashhur (Jer. 20:2) and put in the stocks because of another prophecy. He was beaten again for the same reason in the account recorded in Jeremiah 26:7-9. Jeremiah was shut up in the court of the guard for delivering an unwelcome prophecy (Jer. 32:2-3). King Jehoiakim gave orders that Baruch and Jeremiah be seized on another occasion. Those sent to take them prisoner were unable to find them, however (Jer. 36:26). Jeremiah 37:13-15 records how his life was called for by the irate princes of Judah. He was not killed, but he was thrown into a muddy cistern (38:6).

These GIPs received the same or similar treatment as did messengers of the ANE. The common element was their being identified with the contents of their respective words. As communicators, they shared a common fate.

9. Geographical Distance

Some distance, however minimal, always separated the sender of a message from its intended recipient. Once the sender commissioned the messenger and gave the message, it was necessary for the messenger to travel a certain geographical distance to deliver the intended message. This traveling of distance is one of the major characteristics of the messenger. The distance was bridged by all means of travel possible.

The most striking difference between the messengers of the ANE and the GIPs as alleged messengers is what appears to be the absence of travel from one place (the place of receipt of a 'message') to another (the place of the delivery) on the part of the prophet.[20] It is also not yet clear just where this place of "receipt" would have been. Beginning with Michaiah ben Imlah (1 Kg. 22:1-38) who recounted a vision in which activity took place in Yahweh's heavenly council, Isaiah of Jerusalem (Isa. 6:1-13); Amos (7:1-3, 4-6, 7-9; 8:1-3; 9:1); Jeremiah (26:1) and Deutero-Isaiah (40:1-2) all are said to have had an encounter with the council of Yahweh. Jeremiah 23:18 tells that the prophets who had experienced this encounter **stood** in this heavenly council. Was the 'message' given to the prophet then? One is uncertain, for most scholars would not interpret this "standing" literally. Many 'messages' are attributed to the GIPs, but according to Kingsbury, this encounter with the council occurred only once a year (on whatever level of the mind), and then under specific cultic-ritualistic circumstances.[21] Thus, one of the key problems within the greater problem of whether the prophet can be a messenger, and what such a claim entails, is the **method** of receiving the so-called message. **The circumstances of receipt, and traveling of distance are two of the weakest links in the chain of claims for a messenger status for the GIPs. When this is coupled with the inability of the form-critical claims to buttress the view, one must admit to a total collapse of any kind of argument which has as its aim to demonstrate that the GIPs--or any prophet delivering oracles for** that matter--thought of themselves, were thought of by their contemporaries, or were indeed messengers in any form that would have been acceptable to, or make sense to any person of the ANE between the years ca. 3000 to ca. 30 BCE.

Summary and Critical Evaluation

The question of whether the HS, GIPs should be called messengers had to be approached with two sets of complementary concerns: (1) the types, forms, and characteristics of construction of representative prophetical sayings, as compared with the types, forms and characteristics of construction of representative "oral" and written messages of the ANE messengers, and (2) the activities of the prophets when performing their alleged messenger role as compared with the **demonstrated** activities and roles of messengers of the ANE. Both **saying** and **person** had to be considered (not one to the exclusion of the other) if an accurate assessment was to be made. Chapter VI concentrated on the **saying**, Chapter VII has concentrated on the **person**. Let us assess the results.

With reference to the **person**, a comparison and contrast of the GIP with the ANE messenger at nine major points and eleven functions exposed more than was generally known about the prophet, for both prophet and messenger shared many characteristics and activities in common. Yet contrasts abounded.

The **purpose** of the messenger was to extend temporally and geographically the existing power and deed of another by delivering that person's oral or written message, or by performing a function for that person. The messenger, then, was a prosthesis of the sender. Indications were that the job was both full-time and part-time. By contrast, the prophet (henceforth the GIP is intended unless otherwise indicated) as a religious personality was believed to be a mediator who spoke to the people in the name of their deity, and "inquired" of this deity on behalf of the people. Since the prophet was also a private (in a corporate society!) citizen and a person who oftentimes had another profession, or professions (cf. Amos) without and within the religious sphere, the alleged role as a messenger is, theoretically, one of several activities, *ergo* part-time, if at all.

As to **status** as messengers, there was no question of the ANE personages and figures who were commissioned to carry messages, or those who performed errands, or even those who announced tidings. In the face of Haggai 1:13 calling a prophet a messenger (leading one to strongly suspect, but not at this point to argue for a post-exilic community interpretation of a pre-exilic prophetic role) the status of the prophet as teacher, preacher, oracle-giver, and/or general religious-political figure was not in question; the status as a messenger remained doubtful, however. Up to this point that status still depended mainly on form-critical designations and theological certainty.

The **geographical theater of operation** for both parties was limited to the area defined in the PREFACE of this work as the ANE, with the prophets being limited to the two pre-exilic kingdoms, Egypt and Babylonia. The **temporal period of operation** was seen to have been similar in magnitude and extent to the geographical in that the temporal limits of the ANE messenger far exceeded (and included) those of the prophetic period in the history of Israel. Moreover, my purpose was to show that the ANE understanding of both a **messenger** and a **message** remained consistent long before, during, and long after the demise of the period of the alleged prophetic messenger; from ca. 3000 to ca. 30 BCE.

Men and women of all **types** (i.e., walks of life) served as messengers in the ANE. The GIPs were all men who, as alleged messengers, were of the religious-political type.

The **authority** of the messengers rested solely in the fact that they were dispatched in the name of the person or persons who had commissioned them. Only one messenger, Wenamon, who claimed to have been sent by a deity, was not sent to deliver any message. The authority of the GIPs was questioned even by many of their contemporaries. In fact, many of the GIPs attempted to authenticate their persons and presence, as well as their sayings, in the face of extremely strong antagonism and opposition of various types. Oftentimes in prophetic literature the prophets' attempts to prove their authority (or that of their biographers) is located in their autobiographical accounts of how they came to be *nebi'im*. Sometimes this account is contained within the 'call narrative.' Form-critically, the *Sitz-im-Leben* of this call narrative might have been the ceremony in which the messengers presented their credentials (especially the envoy and the ambassador). Genesis 24:32-48 may contain an example of the presentation of such credentials by a messenger. My study of the ANE messengers provided no such example. With respect to prophets, however, Buss maintained:

> Prophetic autobiographies focus on the prophetic message or, in part, on the divine origin of that message. What matters fundamentally is not the situation of the prophet, but rather the relation of Yahweh to Israel.[22]

The GIPs shared certain identical or similar **functions** with the ANE messengers. This is not to say that **all** of the ANE messengers performed **all** of the following functions, it merely states that **all were** performed by messengers.

Among the many types of messengers I located an **ambassador-at-large** who served King Esahaddon of Assyria. I held him to have been a kind of shuttle diplomat. The only GIP whose actions were remotely similar were those of Amos at Bethel, for he was the only prophet who, it seems, willingly traveled from one sovereign, political entity to another on prophetic business as a kind of **prophet-at-large**. He was unwelcome in Israel, however, and was told to leave, and go back to his own country.

Sumerian and Egyptian messengers performed **adjudicating and forensic functions**. There is likewise cause to associate certain language of the GIPs with legal, or forensic discourses. Many scholars see the prophet as having convened Yahweh's court in which the prophet allegedly served as trial counsel against Israel in a lawsuit or *rîb* (controversy).

The **delivery of tidings**, which appears to have not always required a formal commissioning of the herald, was the chief function of these messengers. Announcements and proclamations by them greatly affected the immediate history whether in Assyria, Hatti, or

Israel. Even in the literature, when a herald announced tidings, significant change followed. In contrast to this, none of the GIPs were held to have specifically delivered tidings (involving the root **bsr**), and the question of whether their sayings affected immediate history must be relegated to the theological domain. It is, however, generally held that the prophets **announced** what Yahweh was about to do, and I noted that the root **bsr** (to announce tidings) was not foreign to prophetic literature.

Messengers **delivered verbal messages** to those for whom they were intended. To maintain that the sayings of the GIPs were also to be identified as messages was, as the previous study (Chapter VI) showed, not possible, for the evidence could not support such a statement.

Often, to foment **conspiratorial matters**, and keep them going, the conspirators relied heavily on the use of trusted messengers. This had been the case in Egypt (against Assyrian overlordship, and to put a desired favorite-son pharaoh on the throne), and in Israel (also against Assyrian overlordship). The suspicion and disdain with which the prophet Jeremiah was viewed by his contemporaries is symptomatic of how most (if not all) of the GIPs were viewed at one time or another. Many of the sayings of these prophets were held to have been seditious and demoralizing at a time when an enemy threatened from without. Many interpreted these sayings as attempts to aid the threatening enemy from within (the city).

Messengers were often the only link between two lovers who, as circumstances dictated, were separated by a certain distance. In this role the messenger performed a **courting function**, and I termed this kind of message the **message of suit**. Only Hosea's language was replete with language designed to woo a loved one. Hosea, however, spoke on his own behalf and not on behalf of another.

During military campaigns the chain of command was maintained by the use of messengers. None of the GIPs were recorded as having been involved in contemporaneous **military matters**; they could be viewed, however, as announcing Yahweh's war against his enemies cultically.

Although one is most familiar with the practice of a messenger delivering a message and awaiting a reply, it was not unheard of for a messenger (other than the ambassador, the emissary or the envoy) to **engage in dialogue** with the recipient of the message. In their role as alleged messengers, the GIPs also frequently dialogued with those to whom their sayings were directed. Usually the prophet was on the defensive when such dialogues were under way.

Those messengers who operated chiefly in the political arena were the ambassadors, the envoys, and the emissaries. The *mazkir* may, with caution, also be assigned here. I have already discussed these messengers in their involvement in conspiratorial matters. Since their involvement in conspiratorial matters was largely a **political matter**, to rehearse them once again would be redundant. It was virtually impossible, therefore, to separate prophetic activity into religious matters and political matters.

Joshua, Absalom and David, among HS figures, employed messengers as spies. Among the GIPs only Jeremiah's activities with respect to Babylonia, could have made him a candidate for such a charge of having been engaged in **spy activity** for Babylon. He was never so charged, however.

The messenger was often maltreated because the contents of the message delivered oftentimes enraged the recipient. **Maltreatment of the messenger** was a specialty for David, but messengers such as Wenamon the Egyptian and David's own envoys to Ammon were also maltreated. Something similar happened to several of the GIPs. Amos was forbidden to prophesy at Bethel by the chief priest of the sanctuary there. Jeremiah was beaten on several occasions, put in the stocks, thrown into a muddy cistern, imprisoned, and threatened with death. He was also kidnapped. Other prophets, such as Uriah ben Shemaiah and Michaiah ben Imlah, were either physically abused and imprisoned, or killed. These prophets, like the ANE messengers, were also identified with the contents of their respective utterances.

One of the axiomatic points of PART I *passim* held that some distance had to separate the sender of a message from its recipient. This distance necessitated movement of the messenger from the point of receipt of a message to the point of its eventual delivery. Thus, some **geographical distance** was traveled. The most striking difference between the messengers and the prophets as alleged messengers was the seeming lack of distance traveled on the part of the GIPs. Exceptions to travel of any kind were Jeremiah 19:14; Ezekiel 11, 15; and Amos at Bethel. But even these examples do not show where the point of receipt of the alleged message would have been. Thus, the problem of ascertaining the point of receipt and documenting the same was connected with the greater problem of how a prophet "received" alleged 'messages.'

It becomes apparent, then, that there is no evidence available to demonstrate or maintain steadfastly on form-critical or any other grounds that the speech of a prophet was the speech of a messenger, or that the prophet was a messenger, and that both he and his audience understood him to have been such. Likewise, an investigation of the HS produced no concrete evidence that the prophets were in general messengers, or were so considered by their contemporaries, especially during the pre-exilic and exilic periods. The investigation produced evidence to demonstrate that only one prophet, the post-exilic prophet Haggai, was referred to as a messenger. At any rate, he was called a messenger, and one of his utterances was called a message. Although it is not an integral part of this investigation, this sole occurrence of an historical prophet being referred to as a messenger appears to point in the direction of a post-exilic understanding and interpretation of this prophet as a messenger. How such a development in post-exilic thought came about, what the factors were in, and what was hoped to be gained by creating such a view for this one prophet (though it is tempting) must remain the subject of a later investigation. This sole example does not suffice, however, to explain how the other historical, pre- and post-exilic prophets of the Hebrew Scriptures, and especially the great individual prophets, came to be considered messengers, or by whom..

Some language found in the prophetic books, whether attributable directly to the GIPs, or to those who edited or redacted their utterances, is so similar to the language employed in the ANE to commission a messenger, or to legitimize a message, or generally characterize messenger activity, that it can be questioned whether or not someone, or better, some school of interpretation did indeed hold the view that the prophets functioned sometimes as messengers. **I emphasize, however, that with the exception of Haggai, no** historical prophet, especially Haggai's contemporary, Zechariah, was ever called or referred to himself, as a messenger in the Hebrew Scriptures.

The purpose and worth of the comparative and contrastive study of the GIPs with the messengers of the ANE by characteristics and functions now takes on its full significance. It is on a comparative socio-functional level, not on a hypothetical form-critical, theological, or ambiguous linguistic level, that the issue of the historical prophet as messenger may be fairly and fruitfully approached. Many of the actions and much language attributed to the GIPs are either clarified, or only become intelligible when seen against the backdrop of the characteristics and functions of the ANE messengers. The emphasis, therefore, should be directed toward the worth of the ANE messengers in helping to clarify the words and actions attributed to the GIPs, and to allow them to stand out in bolder relief as they have been preserved by tradition, and not toward maintaining needlessly and apodictically, in the face of overwhelming evidence to the contrary, that the GIPs were really messsengers--even from Yahweh! In this way the issues such as where and how the alleged messenger moved from the place of receipt to the place of intended delivery--which one would have to demonstrate---are shown to be unimportant and useless, in addition to being totally impossible to answer. In fact, the words of two scholars adequately deliver the death knell to such needless considerations. Johannes Lindblom stated that:

> . . . an analysis of the contact of a religious man with his God cannot be carried through by scientific methods. The supernatural mystery of the religious experiences of the prophets is concealed from us and is inaccessible to scientific inquiry.[23]

And James Sanders adds correctly:

Fortunately, or unfortunately, the prophet's credentials were never verifiable or falsifiable: they were personal experiences, and archaeological evidence will never verify or falsify their claim.[24]

CONCLUSION

A survey of scholarship on the prophets of the Hebrew Scriptures demonstrates that there is a commonly-held and long-standing belief that the Hebrew Scriptural, historical, great, individual prophet was a messenger. There is, however, no clear indication of just where, when, and by whom this belief originated. Whether such a view was indeed tenable was an important attending question. The overall purpose of the present work was therefore manifold.

I started with the awareness of the assumption that the prophet was a messenger in various literatures which dealt with them. I reasoned that the first thing needed was a solid understanding of just what the ancient Near East would have understood a **messenger** to have been, including the sub specialties of messenger in general such as the ambassador, or envoy. Likewise, **message** had to be defined. Both were accomplished in the first three chapters of PART I, the first two chapters providing evidence for the messenger and the message in the Fertile Crescent in general, and the third chapter providing both as well as a taxonomy for types of messages in ancient Israel. With this data base in place, I turned to the question of the prophet as an alleged messenger.

First, I critiqued the use of the word 'message' by certain modern scholars in an effort to determine whether this use--which implied that the prophet was a messenger--was connected with the origin of the belief that the HS, historical prophet was a messenger. The critique yielded an imprecise and/or nebulous use of the word 'message,' but was unable to provide evidence that the genesis of the problem of viewing the prophet as a messenger had its origins in modern scholarship on the prophets. These scholars, too, had been misled by anonymous predecessors. They had functioned more as *epigoni* than as original thinkers.

Second, I investigated whether the origin of the belief that the prophet was a messsenger was to be found in the Hebrew Scriptures themselves. This was accomplished by examining inductively what would have had to have been the origin, development, and decline of such a hypothesized belief within the Hebrew Scriptures, and, by extension, in ancient Israel.

Third, I examined the form-critical categories of 'commissioning formula,' 'messenger formula,' and 'messenger speech' and their relation to HS prophetic speech forms to determine whether the belief that the HS, historical prophet was a messenger had its origins and demonstration in the works of this school of thought.

All three investigations were carried out with the evidence of PART I providing a watchful backdrop. Afterwards, the results of these three investigations were employed in comparative and contrastive studies which first examined the prophetical saying of the GIP in light of the ANE message, and which second examined the historical prophet (i.e., the GIP) as an alleged messenger in the light of the known characteristics of the ANE messenger. I will now summarize and critically evaluate these investigations.

Preliminary investigation revealed that such a view of the GIPs was derived from three possible sources: (1) modern, scholarship on the HS in general, (2) the HS themselves, and (3) form-critical evaluation of the HS with specific attention to the prophetic books. Each of these three possible sources relied heavily on comparisons of the sayings or activities of the prophets, or what was said about them, with the activities of, and the messages delivered by, the messengers of the ANE. It had been taken for granted by scholars that enough information about the nature, purpose, and significance of the ANE messengers, and the messages they delivered, on which many scholars relied, was already in existence and available in a definite work. When preliminary research pointed to a lack of concrete information concerning any of the above points, I decided to investigate the matter thoroughly. Throughout, one of the major problems confronting me was the absence of clarity of speech by scholars when they referred to the prophet as a "messenger," for no clear definition of either **messenger** or **message** as these terms would have been understood in the ANE had been articulated. Without such definitions, any statements made by scholars concerning how and why the HS prophets were messengers by comparing them with ANE messengers--as yet sketchily studied and poorly defined--remained at best tenuous.

Several scholars recognized that many of their statements were inconclusive, and that numerous *lacunae* existed in studies directed toward discussing the HS prophets as "messengers." They called for a more thorough study of the problem. This work responded to that call.

The study of the evidence for the messenger and message of the ANE (i.e., PART I) allowed one to speak clearly and in an informed manner about **only** ANE messengers and messages. One immediate application of that study was to allow me to critique the comparative use of these messengers and messages by modern scholars in their attempts to show that the HS prophets were messengers. I was confronted immediately with the realization that aside from the HS prophets who were alleged to have been messengers, the HS contained many accounts of unquestionable messengers. Some were angels, others were natural elements such as the wind, and birds often served as messengers as well. But these messengers were extra-human, and I reasoned that a study of them at this juncture would be of little or no significance for this study. Since the prophet was a human, and the ANE messengers with whom they could be compared eventually were also human (although there were extra-humans in that literature also), I reasoned that my study at this point was best served by restricting my investigation to the historical narratives of the HS which contained accounts of human-originated messages which they had delivered.

The necessary, preliminary study of the ANE and HS messengers and messages in PART I provided the grid onto which I could plot and assess the various views of the prophet as an alleged messenger. The least problematical of these views was that of general, modern biblical scholarship. The liberal, though imprecise use of 'message' by selected modern scholars was seen to be symptomatic of the use of this term by most modern scholars on the HS and allied works. Although it was very easy for the unskilled reader to conclude from a discussion which constantly spoke of the prophet's 'message' that the prophet must logically have been a messenger, no such conclusion was supportable. The prophet appeared to have been a messenger by force of suggestion. By the elementary process of transformational grammar, 'message' occurring at that point in a sentence employed by modern scholars could be replaced by the words

thought, **sermon**, **utterance**, or even **philosophy**, and the sense of the sentence would not have been altered.

The HS yielded only one statement which held that a specific prophet, the post-exilic prophet, Haggai, was a messenger. A thorough investigation produced no further evidence to support a claim that all HS prophets were viewed as messengers. The one statement, moreover, did not supply any reason why even that prophet had been referred to as messenger. I concluded that no sweeping statements concerning the alleged messengership of the HS prophets could be supported by the evidence produced by the investigation. There was a HS **statement** that Haggai was a messenger: there was no HS view that all prophets were messengers.

The most categorical statements holding that the HS prophets were messengers were made by form critics after they had investigated and categorized the various forms of prophetic speech. This view had begun (i.e., in a published work) with Ludwig Köhler and J. Lindblom, was advanced by, among others, H. Wildberger, and found its supreme articulation in the study of Claus Westermann discussed and critiqued herein. I studied the form-critical categories of 'commissioning formula,' and 'messenger speech,' and 'messenger formula,' for these were the categories most central to maintenance of the view that the prophets had been messengers. These formulae, aside from being similar in construction to certain ANE formulae associated with messenger activity, proved inconclusive when pressed. In fact, closer scrutiny rendered them relatively useless for maintaining this view. The 'commissioning formula,' for instance, was associated with what was understood as private oracles or information which was not intended to be passed on. One would have expected what followed the occurrence of the 'commissioning formula' to reflect the delivery of communication to another. Likewise, 'messenger formula,' highly overworked because of its similarity to the legitimizing formula employed by ANE messengers, also fell into disrepute through my critique. Other formulae occurring in the prophetic books such as "Hear the word of Yahweh," or "Says Yahweh" either functioned in the same capacity as, or replaced altogether, the expected "Thus said (or says) Yahweh." It was also demonstrated that what often followed this formula could not by any stretch of the imagination be considered as an intended message. The 'messenger formula' was used with no apparent consistency in the HS prophetic books, was discussed with equal inconsistency by form-critics, and proved to be most unreliable as an indicator of 'messenger speech.' This inconsistent use of the 'messenger formula' raised my suspicions that its origin lay elsewhere, perhaps during the post-exilic period, and then as a part of the redacting and editing phase of the pre-exilic prophetic *corpus*. Proof of this suspicion, however, remains the task of future research. This suspicion was strengthened, however, by the statement contained in the pre-exilic prophetical work, Jeremiah 23:31. "Says the Lord," or "Says Yahweh" (Hebrew *n'm yhwh*) appears to be the legitimizing formula here, **not** *kh 'mr yhwh*! The only definitive statement I could make about the 'messenger formula' was that its occurrence in a given text signalled that what followed was held to have been important: by whom, information was too inconclusive to say. The appearance of *kh 'mr yhwh* in the biblical, prophetical material did not necessarily imply the presence of a prophet as messenger, nor did it guarantee that it had been an original part of the prophetic utterance before which it might have been located as it stood in the received text(s).

The form-critical category 'messenger speech' was imbedded within a sea of various types of prophetic speech. It became necessary first to separate the prophetical saying from the remaining types, then examine the prophetical sayings to isolate the *dbr yhwh* which might qualify as 'messenger speech.' This form-critical designation was characterized by its two-part structure. 'Messenger speech' contained a **report** written in the **perfect**, and a **summons** written in the imperative. Several prophetical sayings reflected this same structure, and were even preceded by the *kh 'mr yhwh* 'messenger formula.' When form critics continued to search for more such 'messenger speeches,' they found that this designation applied to a relatively small number of literary examples within and without the prophetic books but always within the HS *corpus*. Many sayings and examples existed which contained only one of the two components of 'messenger speech.' Form-critical investigators were forced to recognize the limitations of their approach to this problem: they called for (but did not appear to be willing to conduct it themselves) broader comparative work.

A portion of that comparative work is contained in this study which examined the form-critical category 'messenger speech,' in light of the "oral" and written messages of the ANE. Formally, 'messenger speech' **never** corresponded with any of the ANE messages. As to **the components** of 'messenger speech,' when compared with the **components** of the "oral" messages, only one of the ANE examples surveyed contained both the **report** in the perfect, and the **summons** in the imperative (1 Sam. 6:21); the **components** of the messages were different (with this one exception) from the **components** of 'messenger speech.' Only one **written** example of 'messenger speech' corresponded in form with the **written** messages of the ANE, and mainly because it **was** also a letter which had been written by Jeremiah to the captives in Babylonia (Jer. 29:4-23). Otherwise, a comparison of the sustained prophetical saying with the written messages of the ANE did not help the plight of 'messenger speech.' Moreover, 'messenger speech,' which was allegedly the judgment word of Yahweh to Israel, or to others, by its nature, would have had to have been a **'message' to one of unequal status** and rank than its source, whereas messages were sent **from** persons of all statuses and ranks **to** persons of all ranks and statuses.

Without going outside the 'messenger speech' *genre* to compare it with messages of the ANE (which proved in essence that no comparison of 'messenger speech' with messages from the ANE could verify that the speech of a prophet was the speech of a messenger) it was demonstrated that if one continued to examine prophetic speech alone, holding tenaciously to the idea of 'messenger speech,' one would eventually encounter almost insoluble form-critical problems. The greatest of these proved to be the **mixed saying**.

There were few "perfect" examples of 'messenger speech.' All of them had to be gleaned from the HS, prophetic books. The "perfect" examples with which they had been compared before the present study was undertaken had also come from the HS, this time from the historical narratives. Both types of literature, however, had been subjected to extensive editing processes. When a broader and more necessary base for comparison was employed, i.e., PART I, the comparison broke down, and with it the view that comparing 'messenger speech' with messages of the ANE would support a claim that the saying of the GIPs were messages.

Three views, the general, modern, HS, scholarly view, the view which held that the HS supported a contention that all prophets were messengers, and the form-critical view were all shown to be unable to support a claim that the GIPs were messengers, or that their sayings were messages. With there still being numerous similarities between what the prophets are reported to have said and done, as well as with the language used in the prophetic books to describe some of the characteristics and functions of the GIPs, some of which readily make no sense, it became obvious that the information gleaned from the study of the ANE messengers and messages was still of great comparative value for studying the HS prophets. The information gleaned from the messenger study in PART I raised this value even more. Instead of a **literary** comparative and form-critical approach, I conducted a function-comparative study of the GIPs and the ANE messengers according to the characteristics and functions performed by both in society. This approach proved to be more fruitful to my overall investigation and netted the best results. By comparing and contrasting the GIPs with the ANE messengers I demonstrated that a part of the actions of the GIPs as depicted in the Hebrew Scriptures was enabled to stand in bolder relief, thus making the prophet(s) more intelligible at numerous points of comparison. Rather than attempting to use the messenger and message in the ANE to explain how and why the prophet was a messenger, an attempt which would have been doomed from the start to failure, it was realized that the best use of this material was its assistance in explaining, clarifying, and making more intelligible the language used by, associated with, and used in the HS when referring to the GIPs, and to certain of their depicted activities. This study also contrasted the two (GIPs and ANE messengers) and demonstrated how different the two types were in terms of their purposes, authority, and function in ANE society. The negative side of the equation mentioned in the preface of this book was indeed reduced. It is now known how the great individual prophets were **not** understood and viewed by their contemporaries, as well as how they did **not** function in their various societies. Thus, the *via negativa* netted us the best results. Some questions concerning how the prophets **did** function and how they **were** viewed in their societies, i.e., the positive side of the equation, are raised and discussed in **The Bible And Liberation: Political And Social Hermeneutics**, ed. Norman K. Gottwald, (Maryknoll, NY: Orbis Books, 1983). I especially suggest the reading of Robert R. Wilson's work therein entitled "Prophecy and Society in Old Testament Research" pp. 202-234, which in turn leads the reader to his full-length book on the subject. Pages 202-203 of that work also called for the study just undertaken.

NOTES TO THE CHAPTERS

PART I: INTRODUCTORY

[1] Norman K. Gottwald, **A Light to the Nations: An Introduction to the Old Testament**, (New York: Harper & Row, Publishers, 1959), p. 57.

CHAPTER I

[1] Alexander Heidel, **The Babylonian Genesis: The Story of the Creation**, (Chicago: The University of Chicago Press, 1963 c. 1951), p. 37.

[2] H.W. Johns, **Babylonian and Assyrian Laws, Contracts and Letters**, (New York: Charles Scribner's Sons, 1904), p.9: "The early Babylonian letters usually open with the formula, "To A say: Thus saith B, "which he believes to be a carry over from the days when such a formula preceded the actual verbal delivery. Without taking Johns to task here, it should be stated that one finds this opening for numerous written messages throughout the ANE, and most notably in the Tel El-Amarna correspondence. Its presence may represent a phase wherein both the oral and written messages existed side by side, and not a phase which assumes the exclusion of one or the other.

[3] Kenneth A. Kitchen, **Ancient Orient and Old Testament**, (Chicago: Inter-Varsity Press, 1966), p. 124.

[4] Ibid., p. 124.

[5] Ibid., p. 144.

6 C.J. Gadd, **A Sumerian Reading-Book**, (Oxford: Clarendon Press, 1924), pp. 177-194.

7 Ibid., p. 73.

8 Ibid., pp. 98-99.

9 Ibid., p. 99.

10 Ibid., p. 147.

11 Ibid., p. 149.

12 Ibid., p. 175.

13 S.N. Kramer, :Sumerian Sacred Marriage Texts," in **The Ancient Near East: Supplementary Texts and Pictures Relating to the Old Testament**, ed. J.B. Pritchard (Princeton: Princeton University Press, 1969), p. 638.

14 Ibid., p. 638.

15 Ibid., p. 638.

16 Howard La Fay, "Ebla: Splendor of an Unknown Empire," **National Geographic**, Vol. 154, No. 6 (December 1978), p. 741.

17 I.J. Gelb, "The Early History of the West Semitic Peoples," **JCS**, XV (1961):35.

18 James B. Pritchard, ed., **The Ancient Near East: An Anthology of Texts and Pictures**, (Princeton: Princeton University Press, 1958), pp. 42 ff., and Alexander Heidel, **The Gilgamesh Epic and Old Testament Parallels**, 2d. ed., (Chicago: University of Chicago Press, 1949).

[19] Stephen Langdon, **Lectures on Babylonia and Palestine,** (New York: G.E. Stechert & Co., 1906), p. 93.

[20] Ibid., p. 93.

[21] Ibid., p. 94.

[22] Ibid., p. 94.

[23] Ibid., p. 94.

[24] See Pritchard, **ANET,** p. 288.

[25] Ibid., p. 288.

[26] Robert Francis Harper, **Assyrian and Babylonian Literature: Selected Translations,** (New York: D. Appleton and Company, 1904), p. 57.

[27] Ibid., p. 64.

[28] Ibid., p. 64.

[29] Ibid., p. 96.

[30] Ibid., p. 96.

[31] Ibid., p. 102.

[32] Ibid., p. 102.

[33] Ibid., p. 102.

[34] Ibid., p. 103.

[35] O.R. Gurney, **The Hittites,** (Melbourne, London, Baltimore: Penguin Books, 1966 c. 1952), p. 170.

36 Ibid., p. 170.

37 Ibid., p. 175.

38 Ibid., p. 176.

39 At any rate, one should bear the foregoing in mind when discussion of the messenger formula begins.

40 Gurney, **Hittites**, p. 179.

41 Ibid., p. 178.

42 Ibid., pp. 183-184.

43 Ibid., pp. 184-185.

44 So much so that the word *lak* is found in Punic as a *nomen masculinum* in the form *ba'almal'ak*, a name in all likelihood found earlier among the Phoenicians. See F.L. Benz, **Personal Names in Phoenician and Punic Inscriptions**, (Rome: 1972), p. 344.

45 John Gray, **The Canaanites, Ancient Peoples and Places,** Vol. 38, gen. ed. Dr. Glyn Daniel (New York: Frederick A. Praeger, Publisher, 1964), p. 113.

46 Ibid., p. 149.

47 Ibid., p. 149.

48 Ibid., p. 150.

49 Ibid., p. 132.

50 There are several Canaanite deities who either serve other deities, or who have only a local significance. Most of these deities

have two names and are not themselves objects of worship. *Koshar (Kothar) wa-Hassis*, 'skillful and shrewd,' who builds Ba'al's house (temple) and Aqhat the Hero's composite bow, and the god(s) *Qadesh wa-Amrar*, 'holy and blessed,' who save(s) Ashera, and *Gepen wa-Ugar*, 'vineyard and field' are among such deities. Since double names may refer to single or double figures, one cannot be certain whether Ba'al sent one or two messengers. See Georg Fohrer, **History of Israelite Religion**, (New York: Abingdon Press, 1972), pp. 51-52.; U. Cassuto, "Baal and Mot in Ugaritic Texts," **IEJ**, XII (1962):77-86; and V. Jacobs and I. Rosensohn, "The Myth of Mot and Al'eyan Ba'al," **HTR**, XXXVIII (1945):77-109.

[51] Georg Fohrer, **History of Israelite Religion,** p. 55 and John Gray, **The Canaanites**, p. 133.

[52] Gray, **Canaanites**, p. 154. More is said of this legend later, when it will be shown to be similar to the account of Absalom's death which is reported to King David his father.

[53] James Baikie, **Egyptian Papyri and Papyrus-Hunting**, (London: The Religious Tract Society, 1925), p. 78.

[54] Ibid., p. 82.

[55] Ibid., p. 83.

[56] Ibid., p. 119.

[57] Ibid., p. 128.

[58] Ibid., p. 132.

[59] Ibid., p. 133.

[60] Ibid., p. 134.

[61] Ibid., pp. 134-135.

62 Ibid., p. 137.

63 Jack Finegan, **Light From the Ancient Past: The Archaeological Background of Judaism and Christianity**, (Princeton: Princeton University Press, 1959 c. 1946), pp. 91-92.

64 Thomas E. Peet, **A Comparative Study of the Literatures of Egypt, Palestine, and Mesopotamia: Egypt's Contribution to the Literature of the Ancient World**, (London: Oxford University Press, 1931), p. 75.

65 Ibid., p. 75.

66 John A. Wilson, trans., "The Expulsion of the Hyksos," **ANET**, ed. James B. Pritchard, (Princeton: Princeton University Press, 1931), p. 174.

67 Ibid., p. 177.

68 James H. Breasted, ed., **Ancient Records of Egypt: Historical Documents from the Earliest Times to the Persian Conquests**, 5 Vols., (Chicago: The University of Chicago Press, 1906-7), Vol. I, p. 209.

69 Breasted observed that the phrase "caused that something be entrusted to me," is literally "put on my neck." In reference to the message, it "evidently furnishes the formula to be used by the messenger in reporting the replies of the official to whom he has been sent." Breasted, **Egypt**, II, pp. 275-276.

70 Ibid., p. 276.

71 Whether this is a hearing presided over by the vizier, or a local hearing over which the vizier's messenger presides is not clear from the context. Ibid., p. 277.

[72] Ibid., p. 275.

[73] This means that if the petitioner sees no one in front of him, he may say so, and then be conducted to the vizier by his messenger. Ibid., p. 273.

[74] Ibid., p. 274.

[75] Ibid., pp. 280-281.

[76] Ibid., p. 107.

[77] Ibid., p. 108.

[78] Ibid., p. 108.

[79] Ibid., p. 141.

[80] Ibid., p. 260.

[81] Ibid., p. 48.

[82] Ibid., p. 49. Only in light of the foregoing discussion of the King's-Messenger does the phrase "arm of his messenger" become intelligible. It refers to the might of a military commander in battle.

[83] Ibid., p. III, p. 330.

[84] James Baikie, **Egyptian Papyri**, p. 62.

[85] Ibid., p. 62.

[86] Ibid., p. 63.

[87] Ibid., p. 63.

[88] Ibid., p. 173.

[89] T.E. Peet, **A Comparative Study of the Literatures of Egypt, Palestine and Mesopotamia**, p. 102.

[90] Ibid., p. 118.

[91] Ibid., p. 95.

[92] Ibid., p. 95.

[93] Ibid., p. 61, and Baikie, **Papyri**, pp. 194-195.

[94] Breasted, **Egypt**, II, p. 379. The above refers specifically to the vizier, overseer of the treasury, chief overseer of the estate, superintendent of the granary, high priests, divine fathers, and priest of Amon.

[95] Ibid., p. 269.

[96] Ibid., p. 268.

[97] Ibid., p. 269.

[98] Baikie, **Papyri**, p. 22.

[99] Ibid., p. 22.

[100] Ibid., p. 22.

[101] Ibid., p. 22.

CHAPTER II

[1] See S. Gandz, "The Dawn of Literature," **Osiris** 7 (1939):261-522, and R. Culley, "An Approach to the Problem of Oral Tradition," **VT**, 13 (1963):113-125.

[2] Dennis Pardee, "An Overview of Ancient Hebrew Epistolography," **JBL**, 97/3 (1978):321-346.

[3] Pritchard, **ANET**, p. 482.

[4] Ibid., p. 482.

[5] Georg Fohrer, **History of Israelite Religion**, p. 228. The "answerer" mentioned above was a prophet-like member of the *homines religiosi.*

[6] William L. Moran, "Akkadian Letters," **ANET Supplementary Texts**, pp. 626-632.

[7] Moran, **"Letters,"** p. 625.

[8] Ibid., p. 627. According to Moran, letters to gods are also known from Sumerian sources and are attested in Akkadian as late as the seventh century BCE.

[9] Claude H.W. Johns, **Babylonian and Assyrian Laws, Contracts and Letters, Library of Ancient Inscriptions**, (New York: Charles Scribner's Sons, 1902), p. xi.

[10] Ibid., p. 320.

[11] Ibid., p. 320.

12 E.A. Wallis Budge and L.W. King, eds., **Annals of the Kings of Assyria in the British Museum**, Vol. 1 (London: Harrison and Sons, 1902), p. xi.

13 Ibid., p. xxii.

14 L. Waterman, ed. and trans., **Royal Correspondence of the Assyrian Empire**, (Ann Arbor: University of Michigan Press, 1930-36), pp. 140-143; R.H. Pfeiffer, **State Letters of Assyria, American Oriental Series**, Vol. 6 (New Haven: American Oriental Society, 1935), pp. 173 ff.; and R.H. Pfeiffer, **ANET**, 2d. Ed., p. 450.

15 Waterman, **Royal Correspondence**, p. 354. Another such message is found on page 356.

16 Ibid., p. 359. The "sealed dispatch" refers to the fact that cuneiform letters were sometimes enclosed in an outer envelope which served to protect the letter from damage and forgery, and to identify the enclosure. The outer envelope usually contained only an excerpt from the enclosed document.

17 Jack Finegan, **Light From the Ancient Past: The Archaeological Background of Judaism and Christianity**, (Princeton: Princeton University Press, 1946, 2d. ed., 1959), p. 201.

18 Budge and King, **Annals**, p. 279.

19 Ibid., pp. 279-280.

20 Ibid., pp. 289-290.

21 Ibid., pp. 302-303.

22 Ibid., p. 311.

23 Ibid., p. 353.

[24] Chapters III and V will raise questions about evidence concerning the commissioning of messengers in specific instances.

[25] O.R. Gurney, **The Hittites**, pp. 113-114.

[26] Ibid., p. 114.

[27] Ibid., p. 114.

[28] Ibid., p. 115.

[29] Ibid., p. 116.

[30] Ibid., p. 31.

[31] Ibid., p. 31. Gurney also adds that the Egyptian queen who sent these messages was most probably Ankhsenamun, daughter of Amenophis IV and widow of Tutankamun.

[32] Jack Finegan, **Light From the Ancient Past**, p. 199.

[33] John Gray, **The Canaanites**, p. 39. The recipient of this message was the king of Egypt.

[34] James Ross, "The Prophet as Yahweh's Messenger," p. 101.

[35] G.R. Driver, **Canaanite Myths and Legends**, Old Testament Studies, No. III, (Edinburgh: Y. & T. Clark, 1956), p. 81.

[36] Ibid., p. 81.

[37] Pritchard, ed., **ANET**, p. 144.

38   Cyrus H. Gordon, **Ugaritic Literature: A Comprehensive Translation of the Poetic and Prose Texts,** (*Roma: Pontificium Institutum Biblicum*, 1949), pp. 116-117. The remaining letter-messages are found in Cyrus H. Gordon, **The Loves and Wars of Baal and Anat and Other Poems From Ugarit,** (Princeton: Princeton University Press, 1943), p. 45 ff.

39 Pritchard, **ANET**, p. 569.

40 Ibid., p. 569.

41 Ibid., p. 569.

42 Ibid., p. 569.

43 Ibid., p. 569.

44 E. Würthwein, **The Text of the Bible**, (New York: The Macmillan Company, 1957), p. 88.

45 James B. Pritchard, ed., **The Ancient Near East: An Anthology of Texts and Pictures**, (Princeton: Princeton University Press, 1958), p. 213.

46 This is an extremely well-studied letter. Among those who have researched it are J.D. Amusin and M.L. Heltzer, "The Inscription from Mesad Hashavyahu," **IEJ**, Vol. 14 (1964):148-157; J. Naveh, "Some Notes on the Reading of the Mesad Hashavyahu Letter," **IEJ**, Vol. 14 (1964):158-159; and F.M. Cross, Jr., "Epigraphic Notes on Hebrew Documents of the Eighth-Sixth Centuries B.C.: The Murabba'at Papyrus and the Letter found Near Yabneh-Yam," **BASOR**, No. 165 (1962):34-46.

47 J. Naveh, "A Hebrew Letter from the Seventh Century BC," **IEJ**, Vol. 10 (1960):129-139.

48 Pritchard, **ANET**, p. 211.

[49] Ibid., p. 262.

[50] Ibid., p. 274.

[51] Budge and King, **Annals**, p. xxiii.

[52] Ibid., p. xxiii.

[53] W.F. Albright, "The Amarna Letters," **ANET**, p. 263.

[54] John Bright, **A History of Israel**, p. 362.

[55] Ibid., p. 372.

[56] H.L. Ginsberg, "Aramaic Letters," **ANET**, 3rd. with Supplement, p. 633. For further study of these documents see **ANET**, pp. 278-282; G.R. Driver, **Aramaic Documents of the Fifth Century BC;** and E.G. Kraeling, ed., **The Brooklyn Museum Aramaic Papyri**.

[57] James Baikie, **Egyptian Papyri**, p. 68.

[58] Ibid., p. 69.

[59] Ibid., p. 277.

[60] James Breasted, **Egypt**, IV, pp. 288-289.

[61] Ibid., II, p. 49.

[62] Ibid., p. 380.

[63] Ibid., p. 380.

[64] Ibid., IV, p. 420.

[65] Ibid., p. 420.

[66] Ibid., p. 421.

[67] Ibid., pp. 441-442.

CHAPTER III

[1] Robert Young, **Analytical Concordance to the Bible**, (New York: Funk and Wagnalls, 1955).

[2] John W. Ellison, superv. ed., **Nelson's Complete Concordance to the Revised Standard Version Bible**, (New York: Thomas Nelson & Sons, 1957).

[3] Solomon Mandelkern, *Veteris Testamenti Concordantiae: Hebraicae Atque Chaldaicae*, 2 Vols. (Gräz: Akademische Druck-u. Verlagsanstalt, 1955).

[4] These imperatives must not be understood as having full weight, for Balak is not communicating with an underling, but with one from whom he is attempting to purchase what he considers to be an urgently-needed service.

[5] Klaus Koch, **The Growth of the Biblical Tradition: The Form-Critical Method**, p. 190.

[6] Ibid., p. 189.

[7] Ibid., p. 189.

[8] Other examples are found at 1 Kings 18:5,40 and 2 Kings 7:14.

[9] Koch, **The Growth of the Biblical Tradition**, p. 190.

[10] Ibid., p. 190.

[11] 2 Samuel 17:15-22 tells how this network operated.

[12] But not all scholars agree with this expression. See Gwilym Jones, "Holy War of Yahweh War?" **VT**, Vol. XXV (1975):642.

[13] A possible meaning for messenger here is 'architect' if one considers that this word is located among a list of names of objects and persons who are involved in the building trades.

[14] John Bright, **A History of Israel**, p. 283.

[15] The Hebrew text of this passage is fraught with difficulties due to omissions.

[16] See Isaiah 36-39 for a duplicate of this account.

[17] The underlined words call attention to the construction of the message and the manner in which the messenger was commissioned. The commissioning portion contains two imperatives and the message contains two imperatives. These are characteristics of a message which is sent to a subordinate, and the speech of a superior to an underling. For a full discussion see Chapter III, 4).

[18] This type of imperative message in discussed in Ch. III, 4).

[19] Mitchell Dahood, "Textual Problems in Isaiah," **Catholic Biblical Quarterly**, 22 (1960):403-404.

[20] Ibid., p. 403.

[21] Ibid., p. 404.

[22] James Barr, **Comparative Philology**, p. 23. See, however, Ernest R. Martinez, comp., **Hebrew-Ugaritic Index to the Writings of Mitchell Dahood: A Bibliography with Indices of Scriptural Passages, Hebrew and Ugaritic Words, and Grammatical Observations**, (Rome: Pontifical Biblical Institute, 1967), p. 49 where reference is made to five places where Dahood has discussed Qoheleth 10:20. In **Ugaritic-Hebrew Philology: Marginal Notes on Recent Publications**, (Rome: Pontifical Biblical Institute, 1965), p. 61, Dahood suggests that *madda'* in Qoheleth 10:20 = Ugaritic *md'* = friend. The discussion thus remains an open one.

[23] Barr, **Philology**, p. 20. *md'* has also been used as 'bedroom-bedchamber' in parallelism with *mskb*, 'bedroom.'

[24] Ibid., p. 27.

[25] John Bright, **A History of Israel**, p. 201.

[26] J. Begrich, *Sofer* und *Mazkîr*," **ZAW**, 17 (1940/1):3.

[27] Ibid., p. 4.

[28] Ibid., p. 6.

[29] Ibid., p. 12.

[30] Nelson's **Complete Concordance to the RSV**, p. 538.

[31] Rudolf Kittel, ed., *Biblia Hebraica*, (Stuttgart: Privileg. Württ. Bibelanstalt, 1949), p. 597.

[32] Ibid., p. 661.

PART II: INTRODUCTORY

[1] Claus Westermann, **Basic Forms of Prophetic Speech,** (Philadelphia: The Westminster Press, 1967), p. 13.

[2] Ibid., p. 13.

[3] Georg Fohrer, **History of Israelite Religion,** (New York: Abingdon Press, 1972), p. 268.

[4] Ibid., p. 171. Examples are multiplied at pp. 230-238.

[5] Ibid., p. 317.

[6] Ibid., pp. 253, 258, 260, 262, and 266.

[7] John Bright, **A History of Israel,** 2d. Ed. (Philadelphia: The Westminster Press, 1976).

[8] Ibid., p. 286.

[9] Ibid., p. 288.

[10] Ibid., p. 291.

[11] Ibid., p. 288.

[12] Ibid., p. 289.

[13] Ibid., p. 290.

[14] Fohrer, **Israelite Religion,** pp. 355 and 371 contain other examples.

[15] Norman Snaith, **The Distinctive Ideas of the Old Testament,** (London: The Epworth Press, 1960 c. 1944), p. 59.

[16] Ibid., p. 59.

[17] Fohrer, **Religion**, p. 247.

[18] Ibid., p. 248.

[19] Ibid., pp. 239-240.

[20] See, however, Malachi 2:7 where a priest is called a messenger.

CHAPTER IV

[1] James F. Ross, "The Prophet as Yahweh's Messenger," **Israel's Prophetic Heritage**, Eds. B.W. Anderson and W. Harrelson (New York: Harper, 1962), p. 99.

[2] See Chapter I (Assyria) where messengers from an Assyrian king also instruct.

[3] Martin J. Buss, **The Prophetic Word of Hosea: A Morphological Study,** (Berlin: Verlag Alfred Töpelmann, 1969), p. 18.

[4] Ibid., p. 18.

[5] The Mari material is quite well documented. See for example A. Malamat, "Prophetic Revelations in New Documents from Mari and the Bible, " **VT Supplement**, Vol. XV (1966):207-227; A. Malamat, "History and Prophetic Vision in a Mari Letter," *Eretz-Israel*, V (1958):67-73; A. Malamat, "Prophecy in the Mari Documents," *Eretz-Israel*, IV (1956):74-84; W.L. Moran, "New Evidence from Mari on the History of Prophecy," *Biblica*, 50 (1969):15-25; A. Lods, *"Une tablette inédite de Mari interessante pour l'histoire*

ancienne du prophétisme sémitique," **Studies in Old Testament Prophecy, Studies in Honor of T.H. Robinson,** 1950, pp. 103-110; H.B. Huffmon, "Prophecy in the Mari Letters," **BA**, XXI (1969):112-138; F. Ellermeier, *Prophetie in Mari und in Israel,* (Hertzberg am Harz: Verlag Erwin Jungfer, 1968); J.F. Ross, "Prophecy in Hamath, Israel, and Mari," **HTR**, LXIII (1970):1-28; H. Schult, "Vier weitere Mari-Briefe 'prophetischen' Inhalts," *ZDPV*, LXXXII (11966):228-232; C. Westermann, "Die Mari-Briefe und die Prophetie in Israel," *FAT*, (1964):171-188.

[6] James A. Sanders, **Torah and Canon**, (Philadelphia: Fortress Press, 1974 c. 1972), p. 57.

[7] Ibid., p. 57.

[8] A. Malamat, "History and Prophetic Vision in a Mari Letter," *Eretz-Israel*, pp. 67-73, and Georg Fohrer, **History of Israelite Religion**, p. 226. On *muhhum* and *muhhutum* see V. Christian, "*Sum. lu-an-na-ba-tu = akk. mahhu 'Ekstatiker*," *Wiener Zeitschrift für die Kunde des Morgenlandes* LIV (1957):9-10 where the Sumerian word *lu-an-na-ba-tu* is believed to mean "the man who enters heaven."

[9] Georg Fohrer, **Israelite Religion**, pp. 226-227. Note also that the word 'message' which might be expected here is conspicuously absent.

[10] **ANET Supplement**, p. 623.

[11] Fohrer, **Israelite Religion**, p. 227.

[12] Ibid., p. 227.

[13] Ibid., p. 227.

[14] James Sanders, **Torah and Canon**, p. 58.

[15] Ibid., p. 62.

[16] Ibid., p. 68.

[17] Ibid., p. 68.

[18] Fohrer, **Religion**, p. 228.

[19] T.J. Meek, **Hebrew Origins,** (New York: Harper & Row, Publishers, c. 1960), p. 133 believes "the Hebrew word for "law" *torah*, carries this same import, because "message" or "oracle" is clearly its root meaning." In an accompanying note Meek continued:

> It used to be derived from a root meaning "to cast (lots)," but W.F. Albright, **JBL** XLVI (1927), 178 ff. challenges this derivation, although he does not deny the connection with Akkadian *tertu*, the meaning of which is "oracle," a message sent from deity (p. 133).

[20] J. Lindblom, **Prophecy in Ancient Israel**, (Oxford: Basil Blackwell, 1963), p. 149.

[21] Ibid., p. 149. Lindblom goes on to state that "the prophetic oracles and messages can in general be called visions irrespective of whether they really are, or have simply been given the literary form of visions." (p. 148). This seems, however, like a statement of convenience made by Lindblom to support a rather weak claim.

[22] Ibid., p. 149.

[23] Additional instances of the practice of "inquiring of the Lord" include Judges 1:1's "After the death of Joshua the people of Israel inquired of the Lord, 'Who shall go up for us against the Canaanites, to fight against them?'" Amos 5:4 contains the admonition: "Seek me and live;" wherein Yahweh "speaks" to Israel. This admonition may mean to inquire of the priests and prophets for proper instruction. Here one notices the herald/messenger formula, but it is not in response to any inquiry made to Yahweh; *au contraire*! Hilkia the priest delivered a scroll found in the Jerusalem Temple to King Josiah, who became penitent and rent his clothes upon hearing its contents, because the ordinances of the law book had not been obeyed or kept. He commanded that inquiry be made of the Lord. The prediction of the prophetess, Hulda, followed (2 Kings 22: 11-20). 2 Chronicles 20:3's "Then Jehoshaphat feared, and set himself to seek the Lord, and proclaimed a fast throughout all Judah," shows the king's reactions after hearing that his enemies were encamped as close as Engedi. He, it will be remembered, suggested the same practice to Ahab earlier, before their joint campaign against the Syrians. Jahaziel, a Levite cult priest, gave him a favorable reply. Finally, in addition to the telltale clue that the tent of meeting and the ark of the *berit* traditions are two separate traditions (since the ark tradition is explained parenthetically), 2 Chronicles 1:2-5 contains another example of "inquiring of the Lord." Verse 5c states: "And Solomon and the assembly sought the Lord." This account is similar to the account of Jehoshaphat and all of the people of Judah and Jerusalem seeking or inquiring of the Lord. In verse 7 of the Solomon account, however, a theophany occurs, thus blotting out the historical sequel of events. I hold, therefore, that something similar to what occurred in the Josiah account took place, and is also what is expected when it was "inquired of the Lord." Each response is favorable, thus bespeaking a cultic, oracular response on the part of a priest or cult prophet(ess). Hulda's response is a borderline case since the predicted disaster was deferred. The individual prophet's (Amos) response was that Yahweh was no longer being sought, i.e., being inquired of.

24 "God is the ruling Lord:" writes Ludwig Koehler, "that is the one fundamental statement in the theology of the Old Testament." in **Old Testament Theology**, A.S. Todd, trans., (London: Lutterworth Press, 1957 c. 1935), p. 30. The question of the "Kingship" of Yahweh, or Yahweh as "king" presents many problems for scholars. One such scholar, A. Alt, "interprets this kingship as the notion of Yahweh enthroned in the midst of a host of subordinate divine beings, a concept dating from the pre-monarchical period in Palestine"(Georg Fohrer, **History of Israelite Religion**, p. 166). The issue of the divine heavenly council is thus also at the center of the debate over what is meant by the title "king" when referring to Yahweh. The scope of the present work precludes addressing this problem further. However, Fohrer provides a synopsis on page 166 of his **History**. See also O. Eissfeldt, "*Jahwe als König*," *ZAW*, XLVI (1928):81-105; J. Gray, "The Hebrew Conception of the Kingship of God," *VT*, VI (1956):268-285.

25 Snaith, **Ideas**, p. 53.

26 Fohrer, **Religion**, p. 104.

27 Ibid., p. 104.

28 See also Psalms 29:1; 82:1; 6-7; 89:5-7 (MT 6-8), and W. Hermann, "*Die Göttersöhne*," *ZRGG, XII (1960):242-251; O. Eissfeldt, "Gott und Götzen im Alten Testament,*" **ThStKr**, CIII (1931):151-160. See the excellent summary of the heavenly beings and demons among which are found some 'messengers' by virtue of their function, in Fohrer, **History**, pp. 173-174.

29 Edwin C. Kingsbury, "The Prophets and the Council of Yahweh," **JBL LXXX III/3** (1964), p. 279. "The reason," says Kingsbury, "for the omissions is clear; the contemporary readers understood the allusions clearly, but later generations of readers and editors either misunderstood the allusions or removed them." (p. 279).

30 Ibid., p. 280.

³¹ Ibid., p. 282.

³² Ibid., p. 282. Chapters 1 and 10 are believed to retail the same vision or experience.

³³ Ibid., p. 283.

³⁴ Ibid., p. 283. He notices that "one of Jeremiah's complaints was that those false prophets who, during the course of Israel's history, spoke favorably, had never stood in the heavenly council" (Jeremiah 23:18). He therefore argued: "If we take this preachment to imply that Jeremiah had stood in the council of Yahweh, then a third of the common elements is added." (p. 283).

³⁵ Ibid., pp. 283-284.

³⁶ Ibid., p. 284.

³⁷ Ibid., pp. 284-285.

³⁸ Ibid., p. 286. Like most other HS institutions and ideas, the idea of a heavenly council goes through periods of development. In the post-exilic period one finds concerns directed toward Yahweh's transcendence and the angels. Fohrer, **History**, p. 3764, states:

> The realm between Yahweh and man was far from empty. Because God's transcendence was perceived as distance, this realm was filled with the intermediary world of angels, who constituted a link between the distant God and man. Thus, the earlier conception of Yahweh's heavenly court was gradually transformed into an

angelology whose beginnings can
already be made out in the Old
Testament.

[39] For further works concerning the council see H. Wheeler Robinson, **Inspiration and Revelation in the Old Testament**, (Oxford: Clarendon Press, 1946), pp. 161-172; "The Council of Yahweh," **JTS**, XLV (1945):151-157; and Frank M. Cross, Jr., "The Council of Yahweh in Second Isaiah," **JNES**, XII (1953):274-277.

[40] Fohrer, **History**, p. 267.

[41] James Sanders, "Hermeneutics," **IDBSV**, p. 405.

[42] Gerhard von Rad, "*Die Falschen Propheten*," *ZAW*, (1933):109.

[43] Ibid., p. 116.

[44] Ibid., p. 112.

[45] Ibid., p. 118.

[46] J. Lindblom, **Prophecy in Ancient Israel**, p. 52.

[47] However, see Georg Fohrer, **History**, p. 240 for a partial listing. The list omits perjoratively the symbolic action of the prophet Zedekiah in 1 Kings 22:11 and follows immediately upon a rather misleading and uninformed conclusion as to how false prophets came into being. He included Hananiah's symbolic action by showing that he destroyed a prop of the symbolic action of his adversary, Jeremiah.

[48] See Richard V. Bergen, **The Prophet and the Law**, (Cincinnati: Hebrew Union College-Jewish Institute of Religion, 1974); M.O.R. Boyle, "The Covenant Lawsuit of the Prophet Amos: III I-IV 13," *VT*, 21 (1971):338-362; B. Gemser, "The *rîb* or Controversy-

Pattern in Hebrew Mentality," in **Wisdom in Israel and the Ancient
Near East,** eds. M. Noth and D.W. Thomas, pp. 120-137; J. Harvey,
*"Le 'Rîb-Pattern' requistoire prophetic sur la rupture de
l'alliance,"* **Biblica** 43 (1962):172-196; Franz Hesse, *"Wurzelt
die prophetische Gerichtsrede im Israelitischen Kult?"*
ZAW, 65 (1953):45-53; Herbert B. Huffmon, "The Covenant Lawsuit
in the Prophets," **JBL,** 78 (1959):285-295; George Mendenhall, **Law
and Covenant in Israel and in the Ancient Near East,** (Pittsburgh:
The Biblical Colloquium, 1955); L.A. Sinclair, "The Courtroom Motif
in the Book of Amos," **JBL,** 85 (1966):351-353; G.E. Wright "The
Lawsuit of God: A Form-Critical Study of Deuteronomy 32," in
Israel's Prophetic Heritage,eds, B.W. Anderson and W. Harrelson,
pp. 26-37; and E. Würthwein, *"Der Ursprung der prophetischen
Gerichtsrede,"* **ZTHK** 49 (1952):1-16.

[49] James Sanders, **Torah and Canon,** p. 73.

[50] Ibid., p. 73.

[51] Sanders holds that studying the prophets in light of the
metaphor of the covenant lawsuit is fruitful if one looks for seven
kinds of statements in the prophetic literature. "These seven
statements," he cautions, "are all intermingled both within the record
as we have it and within the oracles and pronouncements of the
prophets." (p. 74). These seven basic categories are reproduced in
Appendix I of the present work.

[52] Fohrer, **History,** p. 316.

[53] Charles Laymon, ed. **The Interpreter's One-Volume
Commentary on the Bible,** (Nashville: Abingdon Press, 1971), p. 364.

[54] Martin Buss, **The Prophetic Word of Hosea,** pp. 34-35.

[55] E. Würthwein, **The Text of the Bible,** (New York: The
Macmillan Company, 1957), p. 5.

[56] Ibid., p. 6.

[57] Otto Eissfeldt, **The Old Testament: An Introduction**, trans. P.R. Ackroyd (New York: Harper & Row, Publishers, 1965), p. 560.

[58] Ibid., p. 410.

[59] John Bright, **A History of Israel**, p. 312. Here one must also be mindful that if Josiah was such a good king, and the superscription of the book of Zephaniah says that he prophesied during Josiah's reign, (3:2) might be an earlier prophecy belonging to the latter days of Manasseh.

[60] Fohrer, **History**, p. 359.

[61] Bright, **History**, p. 322.

[62] Eissfeldt, **Introduction**, pp. 561-562.

CHAPTER V

[1] Edmond Jacob, **Theology of the Old Testament**, trans., A.W. Heathcote and P.J. Allcock (New York: Harper & Row, Publishers, 1958), pp. 130-131.

[2] Ibid., p. 131.

[3] Ibid., pp. 130-131.

[4] Klaus Koch, **The Growth of the Biblical Tradition: The Form-Critical Method**, trans., S.M. Cupitt (New York: Scribner, 1969), p. 191.

[5] Ibid., p. 191.

[6] Ibid., p. 191.

[7] Martin Buss, **Prophetic Word**, p. 28. Also see below for a discussion of examples.

[8] See Chapter I, Note 2, *infra*.

[9] The proclamation formula is discussed below.

[10] The formula *kh 'mr yhwh* is discussed below.

[11] Buss, **Hosea**, p. 5.

[12] As demonstrated above.

[13] Lindblom, **Prophecy in Israel**, p. 109.

[14] Koch, **Biblical Tradition**, p. 191.

[15] Friedrich Baumgartel, "*Zu den Gottesnamen in den Büchern Jeremia und Ezechiel*," in *Verbannung und Heimkehr, Festschrift W. Rudolph*, (Tübingen: JCB Mohr, 1961), pp. 20-23.

[16] Koch, **The Growth of the Biblical Tradition**, p. 161.

[17] Hans W. Wolff, **Hosea: A Commentary on the Book of the Prophet Hosea**, trans. Gary Stansell, ed. Paul D. Hanson (Philadelphia: Fortress Press, 1974).

[18] Ibid., p. 66.

[19] Ibid., p. 66.

[20] Ibid., p. 66.

[21] Ibid., p. 66. Note, too, the formula in Joel 1:2.

[22] J. Lindblom, **Prophecy**, p. 109.

[23] Buss, **Hosea**, p. 59. But see Micah 3:1 for a notable exception.

[24] L. Koehler, "*Deuterojesaja (Jesaja 40-55) stilkritisch untersucht,*" *BZAW* 37 (1923):102-109.

[25] J. Lindblom, "*Die prophetische Orakelformel,*" in *Die literarische Gattung der prophetischen Literatur*, reviewed in C. Westermann, **Basic Forms of Prophetic Speech**, pp. 34-36.

[26] H. Wildberger, "*Jahwehwort und prophetische Rede bei Jeremiah,*" in Westermann, **Basic Forms**, pp. 48-52.

[27] G. von Rad, **Old Testament Theology**, Vol. II trans. D.M.G. Stalker (New York: Harper & Row, 1962), pp. 70 ff.

[28] Hans W. Wolff, "*Die Begründungen der prophetischen Heils-und Unheilssprüche,*" *ZAW*, 52 (1931):6.

[29] Koch, **Biblical Tradition**, p. 192.

[30] Ibid., p. 192.

[31] Ibid., p. 192.

[32] Richard Elliott Friedman, **Who Wrote the Bible?**, (Englewood Cliffs, NJ: Prentice Hall, 1987).

[33] G. von Rad, **Studies in Deuteronomy, Studies in Biblical Theology**, No. 9 trans. D.M.G. Stalker (London: SCM Press, Ltd., 1953), pp. 78-81.

[34] See Lindblom's comment below, Note 36.

[35] Von Rad, **Deuteronomy**, p. 82.

[36] But see J. Lindblom, **Prophecy in Ancient Israel**, p. 60 where he states that *ish elohim* which corresponds to *amel-ili* in Mesopotamian does not always imply an oracle-giver of the so-called messenger style.

[37] See also Jeremiah 22:29.

[38] Lindblom, **Prophecy**, p. 49. Cf. also Jeremiah 29:60.

[39] But see John Bright, **A History of Israel**, pp. 284-285 where he writes of the possibility of another date.

[40] Fohrer, **History**, p. 135.

[41] Lindblom, **Prophecy**, p. 223.

[42] Ibid., p. 112.

[43] Lindblom's statement raises the question of the existence of the formula *kh 'mr yhwh*, which, one would expect, should have been uttered to legitimize what followed. As such, the presence of the formula would have been the distinguishing characteristic even in the days of the pre-exilic prophets, and their hearers would not have had any difficulty telling the difference. It may be doubted, however, whether this legitimizing formula was indeed *kh 'mr yhwh*. Jeremiah 23:31 contains the curious complaint "Behold, I am against the prophets, says the Lord, who use their tongues and say, "Says the Lord." It criticizes the use by the professional, guild prophets of what was most likely the legitimizing formula to preface their contradictory utterances. They are accused of daring to utter *n'm (yhwh)* and not

kh 'mr yhwh. In fact, the MT at this point fails to include the word *yhwh*! which would normally be expected. Its inclusion would not diminish the fact that the formula *kh 'mr yhwh* is highly suspect.

44 Lindblom, **Prophecy**, p. 112.

45 Fohrer, **History**, p. 242. The effectual power of the *dbr* of Yahweh is discussed in Fohrer, pp. 233-234.

46 Ibid., p. 249.

47 Buss, **Prophetic Word**, p. 64.

48 This summary is designed to show the major categories, and does not attempt to be exhaustive.

49 See Westermann, **Basic Forms**, p. 90 ff., and Fohrer, **History**, p. 248 for additional variations.

50 Lindblom, **Prophecy**, p. 124.

51 Buss, **Prophetic Word,** p. 124.

52 Fohrer, History, pp. 224-225.

53 Ibid., p. 225.

54 Lindblom, **Prophecy**, p. 224.

55 Ibid., p. 224.

56 Ibid., p. 224.

57 Ibid., p. 224.

[58] Georg Fohrer, **History**, pp. 238-239. See also J. Hempel, *"Prophetische Offenbarung," ZSTH* IV (1926):91-112; F. Horst, *"Die Visionsschilderungen der alttestamentlichen Propheten,"* EvTh. XX (1960):193-205; S. Mowinckel, "Ecstatic Experience and National Elaboration in the Old Testament Prophecy," **AcOr** X (1935):264-291.

[59] Westermann, **Basic Forms**, p. 111.

[60] Ibid., p. 111.

[61] Ibid., p. 111.

[62] Lindblom, **Prophecy**, pp. 108-109.

[63] Westermann, **Forms**, pp. 111-112.

[64] Ibid., p. 106. Westermann observes this same two-part construction in Numbers 22 and in 2 Chronicles 36:23.

[65] Ibid., p. 130.

[66] See James Ross, "The Prophet as Yahweh's Messenger," in **Israel's Prophetic Hertitage**.

[67] Fohrer, **Israelite Religion**, pp. 262-263. Such breakup of biblical material is not unusual. See e.g., R.N. Whybray, **The Succession Narrative: A Study of II Samuel 9-20; I Kings 1 and 2, Studies in Biblical Theology,** (Napierville, Ill.: Alec R. Allenson, Inc., 1968).

[68] Fohrer, **History**, p. 269.

[69] Ibid., p. 269.

[70] Westermann, **Forms**, pp. 114-115.

[71] Ibid., p. 111, and Micah 3:5.

[72] See for example Fohrer, **Israelite Religion**, pp. 224-225.

[73] See Lindblom, **Prophecy**, p. 224.

[74] Westermann, **Forms**, p. 106.

[75] Ibid., p. 130.

[76] Ross, "The Prophet as Yahweh's Messenger," p. 99.

[77] Westermann, **Basic Forms**, pp. 114-115.

CHAPTER VI

[1] Westermann, **Basic Forms**.

[2] Ibid., p. 111.

[3] R.F. Harper, **Assyrian and Babylonian Literature: Selected Translations,** (New York: D. Appleton and Company, 1904), p. 98.

[4] James Baikie, **Egyptian Papyri and Papyrus-Hunting,** (London: The Religious Tract Society, 1925), p. 83.

[5] James B. Pritchard, ed., **The Ancient Near East: An Anthology of Texts and Pictures**, (Princeton: Princeton University Press, 1958), p. 133.

[6] Baikie, **Papyri**, p. 83.

[7] E.A. Wallis Budge and L.W. King, eds., **Annals of the Kings of Assyria in the British Museum**, Vol. 1 (London: Harrison and Sons, 1902), p. 279.

[8] Baikie, **Papyri**, p. 63.

[9] Budge and King, **Annals**, pp. 302-303.

[10] G.R. Driver, **Canaanite Myths**, p. 81.

[11] Leroy Watermann, ed. and trans., **Royal Correspondence of the Assyrian Empire**, (Ann Arbor: University of Michigan Press, 1967), p. 354.

[12] Pritchard, **ANET**, p. 213.

[13] Baikie, **Papyri**, p. 277.

[14] Fohrer, **Israelite Religion**, pp. 239-240.

[15] Ibid., pp. 224-225.

[16] Other short, poetic sayings are found at Isa. 28:16-17; 29:22-24; 30:15; Jer. 4:3-4; 4:27-28; 6:6-8; and Amos 5:16.

[17] Examples of other sustained, poetic, prophetical sayings are found at Isa. 19:2-4; 14:29-31; Jer. 5:14-17, Micah 6:9-16; Zeph. 1:2-6.

[18] See above discussion.

[19] See also Isa. 37:33-35 and Zeph. 1:2-6.

[20] Westermann, **Prophetic Speech**, p. 111.

[21] Buss, **Hosea**, p. 64.

[22] Ibid., p. 64.

[23] Ibid., p. 65.

CHAPTER VII

[1] Georg Fohrer, **History of Israelite Religion**, p. 318.

[2] Bright, **History of Israel**, p. 362.

[3] W.L. Moran, "Akkadian Letters," **ANETST**, p. 625.

[4] C.J. Gadd, **A Sumerian Reading-Book**, (Oxford: Clarendon Press, 1924), p. 175.

[5] James H. Breasted, ed. **Ancient Records of Egypt: Historical Documents from the Earliest Times to the Persian Conquest**. Vol. II (Chicago: University of Chicago Press, 1906-7), p. 269.

[6] Ibid., p. 269.

[7] Harper, **Selected Translations**, p. 96.

[8] Ibid., p. 103.

[9] O.R. Gurney, **The Hittites,** (Baltimore: Penguin Books, 1952), p. 179.

[10] Pritchard, **ANET**, p. 133.

[11] Ibid., p. 142.

[12] Pritchard, **ANE**, p. 213.

[13] Harper, **Translations**, p. 98.

[14] Baikie, **Papyri**, p. 82.

[15] Ibid., p. 82.

[16] J. Gray, **The Canaanites**, (New York: Frederick A. Praeger, Publisher, 1964), p. 150.

[17] Thomas E. Peet, **A Comparative Study of the Literature of Egypt, Palestine, and Mesopotamia**, (London: Oxford University Press, 1931), p. 95.

[18] See 7b of the present chapter.

[19] But for a completely different angle on the reaction to bad or unpleasant news see Delbert Hillers' work "A Convention in Hebrew Literature: The Reaction to Bad News," **ZAW**, **Band** 77, **Heft** 1 (1965):86-90.

[20] But see Jeremiah 19:14 and Ezekiel 3:11,15.

[21] Kingsbury, "Council of Yahweh," p. 286.

[22] Buss, **The Prophetic Word of Hosea**, p. 51.

[23] Lindblom, **Prophecy in Ancient Israel**, p. 219.

[24] Sanders, **Torah and Canon**, p. 58.

APPENDICES

APPENDIX I

The seven principal categories of prophetic literature in the covenant lawsuit tradition reproduced from James A. Sanders, **Torah and Canon**, (Philadelphia: Fortress Press, 1974 c. 1972), p. 75.

The Prophet's Story: The Court Officer

1a Autobiographical material   The prophet's call   References

1b Biographic material   and credentials   authority

Israel's Story: The Accused

2a Epic traditions   Israel's call and
2b Other history   credentials

Hope in Reformation:The Prophet as Mediator   The mercy of
3a Pleas to people to repent   the court
3b Pleas to God to relent

Judgment: The Prophet as **Messenger** (Emphasis mine)

4 Indictments   Reasons for judgment
5 Sentences   Judgment

Hope in Transformation: The Prophet as Evangel   Judgment
and
6 Transformation   Purpose for judgment   Salvation
7 Restoration   Israel's new call
and credentials

APPENDIX II

Amos 3: 1-15
Lawsuit against the children of Israel

I.   **A description of the scene of judgment**

"Proclaim it upon the palaces at Ashdod, and upon
the palaces in the land of Egypt, And say: "Assemble
yourselves upon the mountains of Samaria," (Amos
3:9).

II.   **The speech of the plaintiff** (represented by the
prophet)

A. **Heaven and earth are appointed judges**

There is no mention of heaven and earth being
appointed judges. Ashdod and Egypt, however, are
to assemble themselves as witnesses on the
mountains of Samaria (Amos 3:9).

B. **Summons to the defendant or judges**

"Hear this word that the Lord has spoken.
(Amos 1a).

C. Address in the second person to the defendant

"Against you, O children of Israel, against the
whole family which I brought up out of the land
of Egypt . . ." (Amos 3:1b).

1. Accusation in question form to the defendant

"Will two walk together . . . Will a lion
roar in the forest . . . will a bird fall in
a snare . . . Shall a horn be blown in a
city . . .?" (Amos 3:3-6).

2. Refutation of the defendant's possible arguments

"You have I known of all the families of the
earth." (Amos 3:2a).

3. Specific indictment

"For they know not to do right, saith the
Lord, who store up robbery and violence in
their places." (Amos 3:10).

D. Pronouncement of guilt

"Behold the great confusion therein, and the
oppressions in the midst thereof." (Amos 3:9)

E. Sentence (in the second or third person)

"Therefore I will visit upon you all your
iniquities." (Amos 3:2b); "I shall visit the
transgressions of Israel upon him, I will
punish the altars of Beth-el . . . and I will

smite the winter house . . . and the houses of
ivory . . .And the great houses shall have an
end, saith the Lord." (Amos 3:14-15).

APPENDIX III

Amos 4:1-13

Lawsuit against the women of Samaria and those who transgress at Gilgal and Beth-el

I.   **A description of the scene of judgment** (or punishment)

Bethel and Gilgal may possibly serve as both places of Yahweh's judgment and punishment. (Amos 4:4a)

II.   **The speech of the plaintiff**

A. **Heaven and earth are appointed judges**

"For, lo, He that formeth the mountains, and
createth the wind, . . . that maketh the
morning darkness, and treadeth upon the high
places of the earth; . . ." (Amos 4:13)

B. **Summons to the defendant or judges**

"Hear this word, ye kine of Bashan, . . ."
(Amos 4:1a)

C. Address in the second person to the defendant

" . . . For so ye love to do, O ye children of
Israel," (Amos 4:5)

1. Accusation in question form to the defendant

There are no specific questions, but all of
the statements from Amos 4:6 to Amos 4:11
would make more sense as questions, and
might have been at one time.

2. Refutation of the defendant's possible arguments

"Yet you have not returned to me," after
vss. 4:6,8,9,10 and 11.

3. Specific indictment

"That oppress the poor, and oppress the
needy, and say unto their lords: Bring that
we may feast." (Amos 1:1b)

D. Pronouncement of guilt

"Come to Bethel, and transgress, to Gilgal, and
multiply transgression." (Amos 4:4a)

E. Sentence (in the second or third person)

"Lo, surely the days shall come upon you, That
you shall be taken away with hooks . . . ye
shall be cast into Harmon." (Amos 4:2-3) and
"Therefore thus will I do to thee, O Israel;"
(Amos 4:12) following immediately upon Amos
4:6 to 4:11 also serves as the sentence.

APPENDIX IV

Hosea 4:1-19

Lawsuit against the children of Israel

I. A description of the scene of judgment

"Therefore doth the land mourn," (Hosea 4:3a)

II.   The speech of the plaintiff

A. Heaven and earth are appointed judges

The field, the earth and the sea of Hosea
4:3, because they have suffered abuse, may,
here, serve as witnesses.

B. Summons to the defendant

"Hear the word of the Lord, ye children of
Israel." (Hosea 4:1a)

C. Address in the second person to the defendant

"Though you, Israel, play the harlot . . .
And come not ye to Gilgal, neither go ye up
to Beth-aven, nor swear: 'As the Lord liveth.'"
(Hosea 4:15)

1. Accusation in question form to the defendant

There is no questioning technique present

2. Refutation of the defendant's possible arguments

"The more they were increased, the more they sinned against me." (Hosea 4:7a)

3. Specific indictment

"Because there is no truth, nor mercy, nor knowledge of God in the land." (Hosea 4:1b)
"Israel is like a stubborn heiffer;"
(Hosea 4:16a)

D. Pronouncement of guilt

"Ephraim is joined to idols;" (Hosea 4:17);
"They take to harlotry; her rulers deeply love dishonor." (Hosea 4:18a)
"They feed on the sin of my people, and set their hearts on their iniquity." (Hosea 4:8)

E. Sentence (in the second or third person)

"Therefore shalt thou stumble in the day . . ."
(Hosea 4:5); "I will change their glory into shame." (Hosea 4:7); And I will punish him for his ways," (Hosea 4:9); "And they shall eat, and not have enough," (Hosea 4:10); "And they shall be ashamed of their sacrifices."
(Hosea 4:19)

SELECTED BIBLIOGRAPHY

Amusin, J.D. and Heltzer, M.L. "The Inscription from *Mesad Hashavyahu.*" **Israel Exploration Journal** Vol. 14 (1964):148-157.

Avishur, Y. "**KRKR** in Biblical Hebrew and in Ugaritic." **Vetus Testamentum.** Vol. XXVI (July 1976) no. 3:257-261.

Baikie, James. **Egyptian Papyri and Papyrus-Hunting.** London: The Religious Tract Society, 1925.

Balla, Emil. **Die Botschaft der Propheten.** Tübingen: JCB Mohr, 1958.

Barr, James. **Comparative Philology and the Text of the Old Testament.** Oxford: The Clarendon Press, 1968.

Batten, Loring W. "Hosea"s Message and Marriage." **Journal of Biblical Literature.** XLVIII (1929):257-273.

Bauer, Hans and Leander, Pontus. *Historische Grammatik der Hebräischen Sprache des Alten Testaments.* Halle A.S.: Niemeyer, 1922.

Begrich, J. *"Sofer und Mazkîr."* **Zeitschrift für die Alttestamentliche Wissenschaft.** 58 (1940):1-29.

Bentzen, A. **Introduction to the Old Testament.** 2 Vols. Copenhagen: GEC Gad, 1948-49.

Bergen, Richard V. **The Prophets and the Law.** Cincinnati: Hebrew Union College-Jewish Institute of Religion, 1974.

Boyle, M. O'R. "The Covenant Lawsuit of the Prophet Amos: III I-IV 13" *Vetus Testamentum*. 21 (1971):338-362.

Breasted, James Henry, ed. **Ancient Records of Egypt: Historical Documents from the Earliest Times to the Persian Conquest**. 5 Vols. Chicago: University of Chicago Press, 1906-7.

Bright, John. **A History of Israel**. 2d ed. Philadelphia: The Westminster Press. 1976.

Brueggeman, Walter. **In Man We Trust: The Negative Side of Biblical Faith**. Richmond, Virginia: John Knox Press, 1973 c. 1972.

Budge, E.A. Wallis and King, L.W., eds. **Annals of the Kings of Assyria in the British Museum**. Vol. 1 London: Harrison and Sons, 1902.

Cassuto, Umberto. "Baal and Mot in the Ugaritic Texts." **Israel Exploration Journal** XII (1962):77-86.

Chiera, Edward. **They Wrote On Clay: The Babylonian Tablets Speak Today**. Edited by George W. Cameron. Chicago: The University of Chicago Press, 1938.

Christian, V. "Sum. *lu-an-na-ba-tu* = akkad. *mahhu* 'Ekstatiker.'" *Wiener Zeitschrift für die Kunde des Morgenlandes*. LIV (1957):9-10.

Clifford, Richard J. **The Cosmic Mountain in Canaan and the Old Testament**. Harvard Semitic Monographs Vol. 4 Cambridge, Massachusetts: Harvard University Press, 1972.

Conn, Robert L. **The Sacred Mountain in Ancient Israel**. Unpublished Ph.D. Dissertation. Stanford University, 1974.

Cowley, A. **Aramaic Papyri of the Fifth Century, BC**. Oxford: Clarendon Press. 1923.

Crenshaw, J.L. **Prophetic Conflict: Its Effect Upon Israelite Religion**. Berlin, New York: De Gruyter, 1971.

Cross, Frank Moore, Jr. "Epigraphic Notes on Hebrew Documents of the Eighth-Sixth Centuries BC: II. The *Murabba'at* Papyrus and the Letter Found *Near Yabneh-Yam*." **Bulletin American Schools of Oriental Research**. No. 165 (1962):34-46.

_____."Ugaritic *DB'T* and Hebrew Cognates." *Vetus Testamentum*. 2 (1952):162-164.

_____."The Council of Yahweh in Second Isaiah." **Journal of Near Eastern Studies**. XII (1953): 274-279.

Crown, A.D. "An Alternative Meaning for *'ish* in the Old Testament." **Vetus Testamentum**. Vol. XXIV (1974):110.

Culley, R. "An Approach to the Problem of Oral Tradition." **Vetus Testamentum**. 13 (1963):113-125.

Dahood, Mitchell, S.J. "Textual Problems in Isaiah." **Catholic Biblical Quarterly**. 22 (1960):400-409.

_____.**Canaanite Myths and Legends from Ugarit**. Old Testament Studies. Number III. Edinburgh: T and T Clark, 1956.

_____.**Semitic Writing from Pictograph to Alphabet**. The Sweich Lectures of the British Academy. London: Published for the British Academy by Geoffrey Cumberledge, Oxford University Press, 1948.

Eissfeldt, Otto. **The Old Testament: An Introduction**. Translated by P.R. Ackroyd. New York: Harper & Row Publishers, 1965.

_____. "*Yahweh als König.*" **ZAW**. XLVI (1928):81-105.

_____. "*Gott und Götzen im Alten Testament.*" **ThStKr**. CIII (1931):151-160.

Eliade, Mircea. **Cosmos and History**. New York: Harper & Row, 1954.

Ellermeier, F. *Prophetie in Mari und Israel*. Herzberg am Harz: Verlag Erwin Jungfer, 1968.

Ellison, H.L. **Men Spake From God**. Studies in Hebrew Prophets. Exeter: Paternoster Press, 1966.

Fay, Howard La. "Ebla: Splendor of an Unknown Empire." **National Geographic**. Vol. 154 No. 6 (December 1978): 730-759.

Finegan, Jack. **Light From the Ancient Past: The Archaeological Background of Judaism and Christianity**. Princeton, NJ: Princeton University Press, 1959 c. 1946.

Finkelstein, J.J. "Hebrew *HBR* and Semitic *HBR*." **Journal of Biblical Literature**. 75. (1956):328-331.

Fischer, Loren R., ed. **Ras Shamra Parallels: The Texts from Ugarit and the Hebrew Bible**. 2 Vols. Rome: Pontifical Biblical Institute, 1972.

_____. **The Claremont Ras Shamra Tablets**. *Analecta Orientalia* 48. Rome: Pontifical Biblical Institute, 1971.

Fohrer, Georg. **History of Israelite Religion**. Translated by David E. Green. New York: Abingdon Press. Originally published as *Geschichte der Israelitischen Religion.* Berlin: Walter de Gruyter & Co., 1968, 1972.

_____. "Remarks on Modern Interpretation of the Prophets." **Journal of Biblical Literature**. LXXX (1961):309-319.

Freer, Kenneth O. **A Study of Vision Reports in Biblical Literature**. Unpublished Ph.D. Dissertation. Yale University, 1975.

Gadd, J.C. **A Sumerian Reading-Book**. Oxford: Clarendon Press, 1924.

Gandz, S. "The Dawn of Literature." **Osiris**. 7 (1939):261-522.

Gelb, I.J. "The Early History of the West Semitic Peoples." **Journal of Cuneiform Studies**. XV (1961):27-47.

_____. **A Study of Writing**. Rev. 2d. ed. Chicago: University of Chicago Press, 1963 c. 1953.

Gordis, Robert. "Hosea's Marriage and Message: A New Approach." **Hebrew Union College Annual**. XXV (1954):9-35.

Gordon, Cyrus H. **The Loves and Wars of Baal and Anat and Other Poems from Ugarit**. Princeton: Princeton University Press, 1943.

_____. **Ugaritic Literature: A Comprehensive Translation of the Poetic and Prose Texts**. *Roma: Pontificium Institutum Biblicum*, 1949.

Gottwald, Norman. **All the Kingdoms of the Earth: Israelite Prophecy and International Relations in the Ancient Near East**. New York: Harper & Row, 1964.

_____, ed. **The Bible and Liberation: Political and Social Hermeneutics**. Maryknoll, NY: Orbis Books, 1983.

Graham, William C. "Some Suggestions Toward the Interpretation of Micah 1:10-16." **The American Journal of Semitic Languages and Literature**. Vol. XLVII No. 4 (July 1931):241-245.

Gray, J. "The Kingship of God in the Prophets and Psalms." *Vetus Testamentum*. XI (1961):1-29.

_____. "The Hebrew Conception of the Kingdom of God." *Vetus Testamentum*. VI (1956):268-285.

_____. **The Canaanites.Ancient Peoples and Places**. Vol. 38 Gen. Ed. Dr. Glyn Daniel. New York: Frederick A. Praeger, Publisher, 1964.

Gurney, O.R. **The Hittites**. Melbourne, London, Baltimore: Penguin Books, 1952.

Harvey, J. "*Le 'Rîb-Pattern' requistoire prophetic sur la rupture de l'alliance*." *Biblica*. 43 (1962): 172-196.

Harper, Robert F. **Assyrian and Babylonian Literature: Selected Translations**. New York: D. Appelton and Company, 1904.

Healy, John F. "Syriac *NSR*, Ugaritic *NSR*, Hebrew *NSR* II, Akkadian *NSR* II." Vol. XXVI No.4 (October 1976): 429-437.

Hehn, J. "*Zum Problem des Geistes im Alten Orient und im Alten Testament*." *ZAW*. XLIII (1925):210-225.

Heidel, Alexander. **The Babylonian Genesis: The Story of the Creation**. Chicago: The University of Chicago Press, 1963 c. 1957.

_____. **The Gilgamesh Epic and Old Testament Parallels.** 2d. Ed. Chicago: The University of Chicago Press, 1949.

Heintz, J.G. "*Oracles prophetiques et 'Guerre sainte' selon les archives royales de Mari et l'Ancient Testament.*" *Vetus Testamentum Supplement.* Vol. XVII (1969):112-138.

Hempel, J. "*Prophetische Offenbarung.*" *ZsTh.* IV (1926): 91-112.

Hermann, W. "*Die Göttersöhne.*" *ZRRG.* XII (1960):242-251.

Hertzberg, H.W. "*Der Prediger.*" *Kommentar zum Alten Testament.* XVII No. 4 (1963):120-125.

Hesse, Franz. "*Wurzelt die prophetische Gerichtsrede im Israelitischen Kult.?*" *ZAW.* 65. (1953): 45-53.

Horst, F. "*Die Visionsschilderungen der alttestamentlichen Propheten.*" *Ev.Th.* XX (1960):193-205.

Huffmon, H.B. "Prophecy in the Mari Letters." **Biblical Archaeologist.** XXXL (1968):101-124.

_____. "The Covenant Lawsuit in the Prophets." **JBL.** 78 (1959):285-295.

Jacob, Edmond. **Theology of the Old Testament.** Translated by A.W. Heathcote and P.J. Allcock. New York and Evanston: Harper & Row, Publishers, 1958.

Jacobs, V. and Robinson, I. "The Myth of Mot and "Aleyan Ba'al." **Harvard Theological Review.** XXXVIII (1945): 77-109.

Johns, Claude H.W. **Babylonian and Assyrian Laws, Contracts, and Letters**. New York: Charles Scribners Sons, 1904.

Jones, Gwilym H. "Holy-war" or "Yahweh war?" *Vetus Testamentum*. Vol. XXV (1975):642-650.

Kapelrud, Arvid S. **Baal in the Ras Shamra Texts**. Copenhagen: GEC Gad. 1952.

Kingsbury, Edwin C. "The Prophets and the Council of Yahweh." **Journal of Biblical Literature**. LXXXVIII No. 3 (1964):279-286.

Knight, Harold. **The Hebrew Prophetic Consciousness**. London: Lutterworth Press, 1947.

Koch, Klaus. **The Growth of the Biblical Tradition: The Form-Critical Method**. Translated by S.M. Cupitt. New York: Scribner, 1969.

Koehler, L. and Baumgartner, W. *Hebräisches und Aramäisches Lexikon zum Alten Testament*. Leiden: EJ Brill, 1974.

_____. **Old Testament Theology**. Translated by A.S. Todd London: Lutterworth Press, 1953. Originally published as *Theologie des Alten Testaments*. Tübingen: JCB Mohr (Paul Siebeck), 1935.

_____. *"Deuterojesaja (Jesaja 40-55) stilkritisch untersucht." Beihefte zur Zeitschrift für die Alttestamentliche Wissenschaft*. 37 (1923):102-109.

Kraeling, Emil G. ed. **The Brooklyn Museum Aramaic Papyri**. New Haven:American Oriental Society, 1954.

_____. "New Light on the Elephantine Colony." **Biblical Archaeologist.** XV (1952):50-67.

Kramer, Samuel N. **From the Tablets of Sumer.** Indian Hills, Colorado: The Falcon's Wing Press, 1956.

Kuschke, Arnulf, ed. *Verbannung und Heimkehr: Beiträge zur Geschichte und Theologie Israels im 6. und 5. Jahrhundert v. Christus. Wilhelm Rudolph zum 70. Geburtstage, dargebracht von Kollegen, Freunden und Schülern.* Tübingen: JCB Mohr, 1961.

Labuschagne, C.J. "Ugaritic *blt* and *bilti* in Isaiah X:4." *Vetus Testamentum.* Vol. XIV (1964):97-100.

Lindblom, Johannes. **Prophecy in Ancient Israel.** Philadelphia: Fortress Press, 1972.

_____. **Prophecy in Ancient Israel.** Oxford: Basil Blackwell, 1963.

Lods, A. "*Une tablette inédite de Mari, intéressante pour l'histoire ancienne du prophétisme sémitique.*" pp. 103-110. In **Studies in Old Testament Prophecy.** New York: Scribner, 1950.

Long, B.O. "Prophetic Call Traditions and the Reports of Visions." *ZAW.* 84 (1972):494-500.

Luckenbill, Daniel D. **Ancient Records of Assyria and Babylonia.** 2 Vols. Chicago: The University of Chicago Press, 1926-27.

Malamat, A. "Prophetic Revelation in New Documents from Mari and the Bible." *Vetus Testamentum Supplement.* Vol. XV (1966):207-227.

_____. "Prophecy in the Mari Documents." *Eretz-Israel*. (1958):74-84.

_____. "History and Prophetic Vision in a Mari Letter." *Eretz-Israel*. V (1958):67-73.

Meek, Theophile J. **Hebrew Origins**. New York: Harper & Row, Publishers, 1963 c. 1960.

Mendenhall, George. **Law and Covenant in Israel and the Ancient Near East**. Pittsburgh: The Biblical Colloquium, 1955.

Miller, P.D. "The Divine and the Prophetic Call to War." *Vetus Testamentum*. XIV (1964):371-372.

Moran, W.L. "New Evidence from Mari on the History of Prophecy." *Biblica*. 50 (1969):15-56.

Mowinckel, Sigmund. "'The Spirit' and 'The Word' in the Pre-exilic Reforming Prophets." **Journal of Biblical Literature**. 53 (1934):199-227.

_____. "Ecstatic Experience and Rational Elaboration in the Old Testament Prophecy." *Acta Orientalia*. (Leiden) X (1935):264-291.

Naveh, J. "A Hebrew Letter from the Seventh Century BC." **Israel Exploration Journal**. Vol. 10 (1960):129-139.

_____. "Some Notes on the Reading of the *Mesad Hashavyahu* Letter." **Israel Exploration Journal**. Vol. 14 (1964):158-159.

Noth, Martin. *Geschichte und Gotteswort im Alten Testament, 1949 = Gesammelte Studien zum Alten Testament*. 2d. ed. München: Kaiser, 1960 c. 1957.

Obermann, Julian. **Ugaritic Mythology: A Study of its Leading Motifs.** New Haven: Yale University Press, 1948.

Orlinsky, Harry M. "The Hebrew Root *SKB*." **Journal of Biblical Literature.** 63 (1944):19-44.

Peet, Thomas E. **A Comparative Study of the Literature of Egypt, Palestine, and Mesopotamia: Egypt's Contribution to the Literature of the Ancient World.** London: Oxford University Press, 1931.

Pfeiffer, Robert H. **State Letters of Assyria: A Transliteration and Translation of 355 Official Assyrian Letters Dating from the Sargonis Period (722-625 BC).** American Oriental Series. Vol. 6 New Haven, Connecticut: American Oriental Society, 1935.

Pope, Marvin H. **El in the Ugaritic Texts.** Leiden: EJ Brill, 1955.

Porter, Bertha and Moss, Rosalind L.B. **Topographical Bibliography of Ancient Egyptian Hieroglyphic Texts, Reliefs, and Paintings.** 7 Vols. Oxford: The Clarendon Press, 1969.

Pritchard, James B. ed. **The Ancient Near East: Supplementary Texts and Pictures Relating to the Old Testament.** Princeton: Princeton University Press, 1969.

_____. **The Ancient Near East: An Anthology of Texts and Pictures.** Princeton: Princeton University Press, 1958.

_____. **The Ancient Near East in Pictures: Relating to the Old Testament.** Princeton: Princeton University Press, 1954.

Puuko, A.F. *"Ekstatische Propheten mit besonderer Berücksichtigung der finnisch-ugrischen Parallelen."* *Zeitschrift für die Alttestamentliche Wissenschaft.* LIII (1935):23-35.

Rabin, Chaim. ed. *Scripta Hierosolymitana.* **Studies in the Bible.** Vol. VIII Jerusalem: Magnes Press, The Hebrew University, 1961.

Rad, Gerhard von. **The Message of the Prophets.** Translated by D.M.G. Stalker. London: ACM Press, Ltd. 1968.

_____. **Old Testament Theology: The Theology of Israel's Prophetic Traditions.** Translated by D.M.G. Stalker. 2 Vols. New York: Harper & Row, Publishers, 1965.

_____. **Studies in Deuteronomy. Studies in Biblical Theology.** No. 9 Translated by D.M.G. Stalker. London: SCM Press, Ltd., 1953.

_____. *"Die Falschen Propheten."* *Zeitschrift für die Alttestamentlische Wissenschaft.* LI (1953): 109-120.

Rast, Walter. **Tradition History of the Old Testament. Old Testament Series.** Philadelphia: Fortress Press, 1972 c. 1971.

Roberts, B.J. **The Old Testament Texts and Versions: The Hebrew Text in Transmission and the History of the Ancient Versions.** Cardiff: University of Wales Press, 1951.

Robinson, H. Wheeler. "The Council of Yahweh." **Journal of Theological Studies.** XLV (1945):151-157. **Inspiration and Revelation in the Old Testament.** Oxford: Oxford University Press, 1946.

Ross, J.F. "Prophecy in Hamath, Israel, and Mari." **Harvard Theological Review**. LXIII (1970):1-28.

_____. "The Prophet as Yahweh's Messenger." In **Israel's Prophetic Heritage**, pp. 98-107. Edited by Bernhard W. Anderson and Walter Harrelson. New York: Harper, 1962.

Rowley, Harold H. **From Joseph to Joshua: Biblical Traditions in the Light of Archaeology**. London:Oxford University Press, 1951 c. 1950.

_____. **Prophecy and Religion in Ancient China and Israel**. New York: Harper and Brothers Publishers, 1956.

_____. *et al*. **Studies in Old Testament Prophecy: Presented to Prof. T.H. Robinson by the Society for Old Testament Study**. New York: Charles Scribners Sons, 1950.

_____. **The Servant of the Lord, and Other Essays on the Old Testament**. London: Lutterworth Press, 1952.

Saggs, H.W.F. **The Greatness That Was Babylon: A Sketch of the Ancient Civilization of the Tigris-Euphrates Valley**. New York: Hawthorn Books, 1962.

Sanders, James A. **Torah and Canon**. Philadelphia: Fortress Press, 1974, c. 1972.

Schaeffer, Claude F.A. **The Cuneiform Texts of Ras Shamra-Ugarit**. London: Oxford University Press, 1939.

Schult, H. *"Vier weitere Mari-Briefe 'prophetischen' Inhalts." Zeitschrift des Deutschen Palästina-Vereins*. LXXXII (1966):228-232.

Sinclair, L.A. "The Courtroom Motif in the Book of Amos." **Journal of Biblical Literature**. 85 (1966):351-353.

Smith, Morton. "The Common Theology of the ANE." **Journal of Biblical Literature**. LXXI (September 1952) Part III:135-148.

Snaith, Norman H. **The Distinctive Ideas of the Old Testament**. London: The Epworth Press, 1960 c. 1944.

Soden, W. von. *"Verkündigung des Gotteswillens durch prophetisches Wort in den altbabylonischen Briefen aus Mari."* **Die Welt des Orients**. I 5 (1950):397-403.

Sperber, A. "Hebrew Based Upon Greek and Latin Transliterations." **Hebrew Union College Annual**. 12/13 (1937/38):103-274.

Stier, Rudolf E. **The Words of the Lord Jesus, the Risen Saviour and the Angels**. Translated by J. Strong and H.B. Smith. 4th American Edition. New York: N. Tibbals, 1864.

_____. *Die Reden der Engel in Heiliger Schrift*. Barmen: W. Langweische, 1860.

_____. **The Words of the Angels, or: Their Visits to the Earth, and the Messages They Delivered**. London: Alexander Strahan, 1863.

Tucker, Gene M. **Form Criticism of the Old Testament. Old Testament Series. Guides to Biblical Scholarship**. Edited by J. Coert Rylaarsdam. Philadelphia: Fortress Press, 1971.

Ungnad, Arthur. *Babylonische Briefe aus der Zeit der Hammurapi-Dynastie*. Leipzig: JC Hinrich, 1914.

Vaux, Roland de. *"Titres et fonctionnaires égyptiens à la cour de David et de Solomon."* 1939. Reprinted in *Bible et Orient*. pp. 186-201. Paris: Les Editions du Cerf, 1967.

Ward, James M. **Amos and Isaiah: Prophets of the Word of God.** Nashville: Abingdon Press, 1969.

Waterman, Leroy ed. and trans. **Royal Correspondence of the Assyrian Empire.** Ann Arbor: University of Michigan Press, 1967.

Westermann, Claus. **Basic Forms of Prophetic Speech.** Translated by Hugh C. White. Philadelphia: The Westminster Press, 1967.

_____. "*Die Mari-Briefe und die Prophetie in Israel.*" **Forschung am Alten Testament.** (1964): 171-188.

Whybray, R.N. **The Succession Narrative: A Study of II Samuel 9-20; I Kings 1 and 2. Studies in Biblical Theology.** Napierville, Ill.: Alec R. Allenson, Inc., 1968.

Widengren, G. **Literary and Psychological Aspects of Hebrew Prophets.** Uppsala: Universitets Asskrift, 1948.

Wieder, Arnold. "Ugaritic-Hebrew Lexicographical Notes." **Journal of Biblical Literature.** 84 (1965):160-164.

Wolff, Hans W. Hosea: **A Commentary on the Book of the Prophet Hosea.** Translated by Gary Stansell. Edited by Paul D. Hanson. Philadelphia: Fortress Press, 1974.

Woude, A.S. van Der. "*mal'ak Jahweh: een Godsbode.*" **Nieuwe Theologische Tijdschrift.** XVIII (1963/64):1-13.

Wright, G. Ernest. "The Lawsuit of God: A Form-Critical Study of Deuteronomy 32." **Israel's Prophetic Heritage.** Edited by Bernhard W. Anderson and Walter Harrelson. New York: Harper, 1962.

Würthwein, E. **The Text of the Bible**. New York: The Macmillan Company, 1957.

_____. *"Der Ursprung der prophetischen Gerichtsrede." Zeitschrift für Theologie und Kirche*. 49 (1952):1-16.

GRAMMARS AND LEXICOGRAPHICAL WORKS CONSULTED

A Hebrew and Chaldee Lexicon to the Old Testament. Translated by S. Davidson, New York: Leypoldt and Holt, 1867.

Ellison, John W. sup. ed. **Nelson's Complete Concordance of the Revised Standard Version Bible**. New York: Thomas Nelson & Sons, 1957.

Gesenius' Hebrew and Chaldee Lexicon. Translated by S. Tregelles. Grand Rapids, Michigan: Wm. B. Eerdmans Publishing Company, 1969.

Gordon, Cyrus H. **Ugaritic Textbook**. Rome: Pontifical Biblical Institute, 1965.

Holladay, William L. **A Concise Hebrew and Aramaic Lexicon of the Old Testament**. Grand Rapids, MI: Wm. B. Eerdmans, 1971.

Jastrow, Marcus. **A Dictionary of the Talmud**. 2 Vols. in 1. Brooklyn, New York: Traditional Press, 1950.

Mandelkern, Solomon. *Veteris Testamenti Concordantiae: Hebraicae Atque Chaldaicae*. Lipsiae: Veit et Comp., 1896.

Richardson, H. Neil. **A Practical Handbook for the Study of Biblical Aramaic: with Notes on the Language of the Genesis Apocryphon**. Boston: Boston Univertsity Bookstore, 1971. 2d. Rev. Ed. 1978 (Unpublished).

Whitaker, Richard. **A Concordance of the Ugaritic Literature**. Cambridge, Mass.: Harvard University Press, 1972.

Young, G. Douglas. **Concordance of Ugaritic**. *Analecta Orientalia Commentationes Scientificae de Rebus Orientis Antiqui* 36 Roma: Pontificium Institutum Biblicum, 1956.

Young, Robert. **Analytical Concordance to the Bible**. Grand Rapids, MI: Wm. B. Eerdmans Publishing Company, 1975.

INDEX OF AUTHORS

ANCIENT NEAR EASTERN
TERMINOLOGY INDEX

INDEX OF BIBLICAL
AND POST-BIBLICAL
REFERENCES